Secretarial Duties

John Harrison
M.Inst.A.M., F.S.C.T., A.F.C.S.
Head of Department of Business Studies,
Eastleigh Technical College

Fifth Edition

PITMAN

PITMAN PUBLISHING LIMITED
39 Parker Street, London WC2B 5PB

Associated Companies
Copp Clark Ltd, Toronto
Fearon–Pitman Publishers Inc, Belmont, California
Pitman Publishing New Zealand Ltd, Wellington
Pitman Publishing Pty Ltd, Melbourne

© John Harrison 1960, 1964, 1967, 1970, 1975

Fifth edition 1975
Reprinted 1976
Revised 1977

Reproduced and printed by photolithography and bound in
Great Britain at The Pitman Press, Bath

ISBN 0 273 00371 2

Preface

Changes in the administration of office work brought about by the introduction of mechanical and electronic aids call for more adaptable office staff, better informed about the latest techniques and with the ability to understand and operate new and more sophisticated systems. Secretarial Duties and the associated subjects of Office Practice and Clerical Duties are becoming increasingly important in the education and training of office staff. It is inevitable, therefore, that greater emphasis will be placed on the acquisition of the office skills outlined in this book both by training officers within commerce and industry and by school and college authorities.

This new edition of *Secretarial Duties*, with the additional information on business documents, provides the student with a comprehensive coverage of the duties of secretarial and clerical staff. Although this book was intended primarily for students preparing for the R.S.A. Secretarial Duties and L.C.C. Private Secretary's Certificate and Diploma examinations, in its new enlarged form it also covers most aspects of Office Practice and Clerical Duties examinations. It also provides a reference source for clerical and secretarial staff and should be a useful addition to the office bookshelf. Past examination questions are given at the end of each chapter for class, homework and examination purposes. The following abbreviations are used throughout the book to make reference to the examination from which a question is taken—

R.S.A. BK.1	R.S.A. Book-keeping Stage I
R.S.A. OM	R.S.A. Use of Office Machinery
R.S.A. OP.1	R.S.A. Office Practice Stage I
R.S.A. OP.2	R.S.A. Office Practice Stage II
R.S.A. SD.2	R.S.A. Secretarial Duties Stage II
R.S.A. COS.	R.S.A. Certificate in Office Studies (Clerical Duties)
L.C.C. P.S.C.	London Chamber of Commerce Private Secretary's Certificate
L.C.C. P.S.D.	London Chamber of Commerce Private Secretary's Diploma

I am grateful to the Royal Society of Arts and the London Chamber of Commerce for permission to reproduce their past examination papers.

Office staff and business studies students must keep abreast of the changing pattern of office services and it is with this object in mind that this fifth edition has been compiled. Secretarial Duties are affected by the introduction of new legislation, equipment and methods and by changes in banking and postal services, and all of those which concern office staff have been incorporated in this new edition.

JH

Contents

Chapter 1
Handling the Post

INCOMING MAIL

The handling of the incoming mail in an office needs to be carried out systematically and efficiently in order to have the correspondence quickly available for distribution. The staff responsible for opening the mail will usually arrive at the office earlier than the normal starting time so that the incoming correspondence is sorted and distributed without delay. The steps normally taken to organize this work include.

1. Business envelopes are separated from those which are marked "Private", "Confidential" or "Personal".

2. The business envelopes are slit open with a paper knife or letter-opening machine.

3. The contents of the envelopes are unfolded and enclosures neatly pinned to the letters which they accompany.

4. Every document received is stamped with a date stamp. Care must be taken not to obliterate important typewritten or printed matter. A rubber stamp or machine (see Fig. 2) indicating the time as well as the date of receipt is very useful.

5. Registered mail must be signed for when the postman calls. Correspondence with remittances, whether registered or not, is generally entered in a remittances book. The remittances are checked with the amounts indicated on the letters or accounts which they accompany, and the amount, method of payment and opener's initials are written on the corner of the document. Any discrepancy must be checked at once by the clerk in charge of mailing. In some firms the remittances book is taken to the chief cashier, who is required to sign for each item in the book.

6. The correspondence is now ready for sorting into departments or sections. After the piles of correspondence have been checked, they are taken into the employer's office, or distributed to the various departments.

7. Private and confidential letters which must not be opened, are delivered to the persons concerned.

8. All envelopes are rechecked to make sure that nothing has been left in them, and it may be considered advisable for them to be kept for a few days, as, occasionally, the postmark or address on the envelope may be used to answer a query in the letter.

9. Occasionally an inwards correspondence book is used and brief details of all correspondence received are entered in it. This procedure, however, is not widely used today.

If an incoming letter contains a number of points which require the attention of several departments, a special arrangement must be made so that each department concerned deals promptly with its particular matter. There are several ways in which this can be done. Three are given here:

1. A list of the various departments concerned could be attached to the letter and, as it is sent round the offices, each departmental head crosses his name off the list after taking the necessary action.

2. The department dealing with the main point of the letter could have the original and be responsible for passing on the minor queries to the other departments concerned.

3. The postal room clerk could have several copies made of the entire letter and send one copy to each of the departments concerned.

The third method is, in the author's opinion, the most satisfactory. The secretary should note that it is unbusinesslike to incorporate in one letter matters involving several departments.

Letter opening Machines

Machines which slit envelopes are of great assistance in opening the mail in any postal department where from fifty to several hundred envelopes are handled daily. There are two main types of letter-opening machine: one is operated by depressing a lever and is similar to the guillotine paper-cutting machine; the other is automatic, operated either by hand or by electricity.

The guillotine type has two blades. Envelopes are fed singly into the machine, the lever is depressed and the top edge of the envelope is cut away. The opened envelope is then removed from the machine for the contents to be taken out.

With the automatic type, the envelopes are placed into the machine and collected by a belt which allows only one envelope at a time to pass through the cutting mechanism. A narrow strip is cut from the top of the envelope, which is then ejected and dropped into a receiving box. Any size of envelope can be accommodated up to a thickness of approximately 12·7 mm ($\frac{1}{2}$ in).

Automatic Time and Date Stamping Machine

This machine, as illustrated in Fig. 2, may be used for automatically stamping the time and date of receipt on incoming correspondence. It is an electrically operated machine which prints the year, month, date and time, in the form given below:

1974 JAN 10 AM 9: 13

Fig. 1 Time and date stamp impression

Printing is performed automatically once the document is inserted in the machine. Additional information such as a company name, department, trade mark, etc. may be incorporated on the printing plate. It is similar to a clocking-in machine and may be used for any documents which require precise timing.

OUTGOING MAIL

The procedure for outgoing mail will depend on the volume of post handled and the equipment available, but after letters have been typed they will generally receive the following treatment:

1. Letters are delivered to the executives for signature.

2. If there are any enclosures, these are checked and attached to the appropriate letters.

3. The letters and enclosures are collected from the departments and delivered to a central mailing office. To ensure that the mail is prepared for the post on time, a deadline will be set after which letters will not be accepted by the mailing office for dispatch that day.

4. The addresses on the envelopes are checked with the addresses on the letters. Window envelopes, which have an opening (or window) in the front, may be used to save typing the name and address twice.

5. The letters are folded and inserted into their envelopes.

6. The flaps of the envelopes are tucked in or sealed.

Fig. 2 Automatic Time and Date Stamping Machine
(Reproduced by permission of Smiths Industries Limited)

7. The packages are weighed and stamped or franked by machine.

8. Details of the mail are recorded in a postage account.

9. Special items of mail, such as registered, recorded delivery, air mail, etc., which require labels or forms or have to be handed over the counter of the post office, will be kept apart from the remainder of the post.

10. The envelopes are tied in bundles with all the addresses facing in one direction.

11. The postal clerk arranges for the mail to be delivered to the post office, completes any necessary forms and collects the receipts for the items referred to in 9.

This procedure is explained in more detail in the following paragraphs:

Typing of Envelopes

1. The modern practice is to use the "block" method of writing the name and address with each line starting at the same point of the typewriter scale in single-line spacing. Spreading the name and address over the envelope does not help the postal officials.

2. To comply with Post Office regulations, every address must be placed parallel with the long side of the cover and a clear space must be left above it for postage stamps and postmarks.

3. The name should be typed half-way down the envelope.

4. Each item of the address should start on a separate line.

5. The post town should be typed in block capitals. If there is any doubt about the correct postal address, reference should be made to a telephone directory, *Postal Addresses*, or to the book *Post Offices in the United Kingdom*, a copy of which may be seen at any Head Post Office.

6. Postcodes, consisting of a group of letters and figures, have been issued to many towns and correspondents are required to write the appropriate code in block capitals below the post town on the envelope. Because machines cannot read handwritten postal addresses, post office staff operating coding machines will translate the code into machine language. This will appear on the envelope as a pattern of phosphorescent dots which sorting machines can read at every stage of the journey, until the envelope reaches the postman who will deliver it.

In towns which formerly had postal district numbers, these may be omitted provided the postcode is included in the address. Where the county name is required in the address this may be written on the same line as the post town when the postcode is used and it is desired to restrict the number of lines used. Postcode directories giving the codes for residents in each town may be referred to at head post offices.

7. "Personal" or "Urgent" or "For the attention of . . ." is usually typed two spaces above the address.

8. "Messrs" should be used when addressing a partnership except when the name of the firm is preceded by the word "The" or a title; for example:

Messrs Johnson & Brown
Messrs Richardson & Company
The Superior Art Printing Company
Sir Alan Jones & Sons

"Messrs" should not be used before the name of a limited company, as:

Laxton Printing Works Ltd
Sir Isaac Pitman and Sons Ltd

If the name of a limited company embraces the names of individuals there is still no necessity to use the courtesy title "Messrs." A limited company is an incorporated body, i.e. *one* legal person and communications are addressed to the company and not to the members referred to in the name.

9. "Mr" or "Esq" may be used for addressing a gentleman, and the typist must follow her employer's preferences. If "Esq" is used no other

title, such as "Dr" "Sir," "Major" or "Mr" must be included, and the "Esq" must be typed immediately after the name, for example:

Mr A W New
P F Andrews Esq BSc
Major M Wood

10. When the abbreviations "Sen" (Senior) or "Jun" (Junior) are used, they should be typed immediately after the name and before "Esq", qualifications, decorations, etc.:

Peter Hutchinson Jun Esq
J Holden Sen Esq MBE

11. University degrees are not used in private correspondence, but a doctor's degree is an exception. The prefix "Dr" is not typed in the address, but the name is followed by the degree, for example:

Norman Parkin Esq LLD

12. A married woman is usually addressed on the envelope by her husband's Christian name or initial, for example:

Mrs Barrie Cotter

13. A widow is addressed by her own Christian name, as:

Mrs Dorothy Norton

14. Two unmarried women should be addressed "The Misses", for example:

The Misses J and M Thomson

Post Office Mechanization

To facilitate the sorting of mail by using electronic machines, the Post Office is asking all its customers to post their mail in evelopes within a preferred range of sizes.

The Post Office has powers to require that, at a future date, only the Post Office Preferred (POP) range of envelopes and cards will be accepted at the lowest postage rates. Letters outside this range weighing up to two ounces will be charged additional postage. To fall within the preferred range envelopes should be at least 90 mm × 140 mm and not larger than 120 mm × 235 mm.

Aperture envelopes (that is those with a cut-out address panel not covered with transparent material) will be classed as outside the POP range, but window envelopes (that is those with address panels covered with transparent material) will be treated as falling within the POP range provided they conform in size, shape and weight of paper.

Addressing Machines

These are used for addressing envelopes for circulars and also for heading invoices, statements and circular letters. Fuller details of the different types available are given on page 161.

Enclosures

These must be checked carefully by the dispatch clerk. Enclosures, i.e. documents which are enclosed with a letter, may be indicated by:

(*a*) "Enc" typed at the bottom of the letter;

(*b*) the solidus (/) typed in the margin in line with the sentence which mentions the document which is enclosed;

(*c*) a label affixed to the letter; labels may be issued in duplicate and numbered—one copy is affixed to the enclosure and one to the letter.

Folding

Letters and enclosures for posting should be folded carefully and neatly. Care should be taken not to fold a document more than is necessary to fit it into its envelope.

Where large quantities of circulars, invoices, statements, price lists, etc., have to be folded for the post, a folding machine may be used. (See Fig. 3.) Folding machines, which are either hand or electrically-operated, are capable of making up to three folds. The papers are automatically fed into the machine, and the position of the folds is changed by adjusting a lever or knob on a setting scale.

Envelope Sealing Machine

An envelope sealing machine is capable of moistening the gum and sealing the flaps on envelopes. The envelopes are fed automatically into the machine and the process enables large quantities of envelopes to be sealed securely.

Stamping of Mail

It is important that the letters all have stamps of the correct values; if they are insufficiently stamped, double the deficiency becomes payable on delivery. A good reliable pair of scales is indispensable in the mailing room.

Fig. 3 Folding Machine
(Reproduced by permission of Nig Banda Ltd.)

Franking Machines

If a franking machine as in Fig. 4 is used, adhesive stamps are dispensed with and printed impressions are made instead on the envelopes. A certain amount of credit is secured at the post office and every time the machine prints an impression the amount of postage used is recorded on the machine's meter. The recordings are given either in units of $\frac{1}{2}$p or 1p. The amount of credit in hand can be calculated by deducting the amount used, as shown in the meter, from the amount purchased. All types of mail can be franked, including ordinary inland letter post, postcards, registered letters, telegrams, parcels and foreign letters.

Franking machines are purchased or hired from certain office equipment manufacturers, and a licence must be obtained from the local head post office.

To operate the machine, a lever or knob is set to the required postal value, and when the envelopes are passed through the machine an imprint is made, showing the date, postal district and value. An advertising slogan, or the user's name and address can also be printed on the package at the same time.

If a package is too thick to pass through the machine a strip of gummed label should be used. Gummed labels can be inserted into the machine to receive the franked impression and then affixed to the package. Some machines contain a special label device which automatically cuts, feeds and delivers franked labels ready for affixing to parcels or other bulky packages.

Fig. 4 Electric Franking Machine
(Reproduced by permission of Roneo-Neopost Ltd.)

The amount of postage which can be printed at one impression depends on the size of the machine, but the most comprehensive models print denominations up to a maximum of £999·99.

Correspondence franked by a machine must be arranged with all the names and addresses facing in the same direction; it must be securely tied in bundles and handed in either at a specified post office or placed in posting boxes if special envelopes are used to contain the franked envelopes. At the end of every working day, whether the franking machine has been used or not, a docket must be completed showing the reading of the meter and the docket must be submitted to the post office at the end of the week. The postal clerk is responsible for changing the date on the machine, cleaning the type and ensuring that the supply of red dye is adequate. A lock is fitted to prevent unauthorized use and the machine should be locked at the end of the day's work and whenever it is not required. A refund can be obtained from the post office for any envelopes franked in error. Such envelopes must be retained and submitted periodically to the post office, who will prepare a postal draft for the value of the impressions less 5 per cent.

Advantages

1. A saving in time compared with choosing, tearing off, moistening and affixing stamps.
2. Greater security by eliminating the use of stamps which may be lost or stolen. Franking impressions do not exist until the machine is operated and then they are non-negotiable.
3. Ease of planning future requirements as there is no need, which there is with stamps, to forecast the varying quantities of different denominations required.
4. Better control of expenditure as the meters show at a glance the amount used and the amount of credit.
5. A saving in printing costs as an advertisement or return address can be printed simultaneously with the franking impression.
6. Assists in speeding up the despatch of mail from the post office as the envelopes are not held up for franking by post office officials.
7. A postage book may be dispensed with when a franking machine is used since the machine meter indicates the amount of postage paid.
8. Eliminates the drudgery of moistening and sticking stamps on to envelopes.

Disadvantages

1. The savings referred to in the advantages must be offset against the cost of the machine and the fact that operators may waste postage by franking wrong amounts or not producing legible impressions.
2. A franking machine is unlikely to be an economic proposition for small firms with fewer than 20–30 letters daily.
3. Because of security a franking machine cannot be made available to a large number of people, which necessitates the use of loose postage stamps for mail which has to be despatched after the franking machine has been locked away.
4. Although a franking machine indicates the amount of postage used, it does not provide a record of letters posted.
5. Franked envelopes cannot be posted as easily as those which are stamped as they must be taken to the post office or posted in a specially prepared envelope.

Postage Book

After the letters have been stamped, particulars of the letters posted may be entered in a postage book which serves as:

(a) a check on the number of stamps used, and
(b) a record of all letters posted.

The postal clerk brings down the balance in the postage book every morning showing the difference between the amount of stamps purchased and the amount used; the value of any remaining stamps must agree with the balance shown in the book.

Stamps bought		Details of Name and Town	Units used		Remarks
£ 1 5	28	13 February 19 — Balance b/F Cash Received	£		
		Underwood London London		09	
		Turner Crewe		09	
		Cartwright & Sons Oxford		50	Registered
		Smith Oxford		07	
		Circular to Area Representatives	1	68	24 @ 7p.
		Peters London		09	
		Gardner London		09	
		Crewe Bros. Oxford		07	
		Pheasant Oxford	1	00	Parcel
			3	68	
		Balance b/F	2	60	
6	28		6	28	
2	60	14 February 19 — Balance b/F			

Fig. 5 Postage Book

A postage book may be dispensed with when a franking machine is used, as the machine meter indicates the amount of postage used, but it does not provide a record of letters posted.

Fig. 5 shows a typical page from a small postage book.

Where postage stamps are still in use and details of correspondents are not required, the postal clerk may simply keep a record of the total number of stamps used each day, as illustrated in Fig. 6.

Collection of Mail by the Post Office

Instead of the postal clerk having to deliver large quantities of mail to the post office, arrangements can be made for a postman to collect it from the office, provided the following quantities are being dispatched:

1. First and second-class letters, when the number amounts to 1 000 or the total postage amounts to £25;

Stamps bought		Stamps used		Total	
£		Number	Denomination	£	
10	81		1st October 19 – Balance b/f		
		30	7p	2	10
		42	9p	3	78
		11	10p	1	10
		6	15p		90
		4	20p		80
			Balance c/f	8	68
				2	13
10	81			10	81
2	13		2nd October 19 – Balance b/f		

Fig. 6 Daily Stamp Record

2. Special collections of ordinary parcels where the number at any one time is fifty or more;

3. The post office will make a regular collection of ordinary parcels if there are at least ten at a time.

These services are provided without charge, but the post office usually requires three hours' notice; application for free collection may be made in person, in writing or by telephone.

Inserting and Mailing Equipment

A number of mailing operations have been mechanized. The machine, which is called an inserting and mailing machine, collates up to eight enclosures, opens the envelope flap, inserts the enclosures into the envelope, moistens the flap, seals the envelope, prints a postal impression on to the envelope and counts and stacks the envelopes.

It is claimed that this machine will produce from four to six thousand finished packets per hour. Besides the usual inserts, such as letters, cards, circulars, etc., the machine will handle photographs, celluloid cards, wall-paper samples, capsules, and other types of merchandise samples.

Collation of Documents

The work of sorting, collating and stapling documents is frequently allocated to the junior clerks in the postal room.

When documents which require stapling are typed, wider margins should be allowed on the side of the paper where the staples are to be fixed. If the sheets are typed on both sides, odd page numbers require a wider margin on the left side and even page numbers a wider margin on the right. This avoids covering any typewritten matter by the portion fixed with the staples.

There are several ways of collating and stapling documents, two of which are described here.

If, for example, one hundred pages of a ten-page document are to be stapled, the copies of each page of the document should be stacked in neat piles along a table, the piles containing pages 1 to 10 consecutively. Each pile should be "fanned" to allow the air to pass between the sheets and facilitate their collection. The clerk, wearing a finger stall, should then walk along the side of the table and collect one sheet from each pile. The document, with page 1 on the top and page 10 at the bottom is handed to another member of staff, who first stacks the papers together to make the edges perfectly square or uses a jogger (see page 14) and then fixes a wire staple at the left-hand corner of the document.

The second method of collating documents, advocated by time and motion study experts, is as follows:

The pages are arranged on a table in this way:

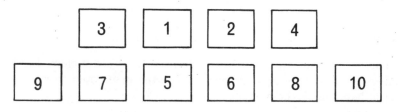

They are collected from the table with both hands; the right hand collecting page 10, the left page 9, and so on in the order indicated above until one page has been collected from each pile with page 10 at the bottom and page 1 at the top. The papers, as they are collected from the piles, are placed on the desk in front of the clerk and as a result there is less movement and both hands are fully employed.

A guillotine is a useful item of equipment for the mailing room. This is a razor-sharp cutting device used for slicing quantities of paper and cardboard to the required size and for straightening tattered or uneven edges of paper.

A stapler is a small machine which is used for fixing wire staples into the pages of a document. The wire staples, which are issued in blocks of fifty to one hundred, are clamped into the machine by means of a spring clip. The document to be stitched is inserted into the stapler and the knob is pressed down with a sharp instant action. If this sharp action is applied the jamming together of several staples in the machine is avoided.

A long arm stapler is one which is approximately one foot in length and used for stapling the centre of folded documents such as magazines, manuals, etc.

A good stapler should be used so that it will be smooth and easy in operation. Time and motion study tests have proved that to fasten papers with pins or clips takes about seven seconds, whereas with a stapler, it takes only three seconds.

Collating Equipment

The considerable table space normally used for spreading out stacks of paper for collation is saved when a collating machine is employed. Most collating machines are electrically operated and foot controlled. The stacks of papers are fitted into individual shelves and the top sheet from each shelf is automatically ejected in readiness for rapid hand collection. The compact arrangement of the shelves eliminates much of the fatigue normally experienced when reaching for papers from stacks spread out over a table.

Fully automatic collating machines which eject sheets from separate sections on to a revolving belt for eventual hand collection are also available. This type of machine enables one operator to collate two thousand sets of papers in an hour.

Mail Room Equipment

In addition to the various items of equipment already referred to in this chapter, the following may also be used in the mail room to assist in the efficient handling of the post:

1. Jogger: a machine which vibrates papers into alignment ready for stapling or binding.

2. Document Destroying Machine: for shredding confidential and secret documents or providing packing material for parcels.

3. Package Tying Machine: for tying string round parcels.

4. Tucking and Folding Machine: for preparing notices which are to be mailed without envelopes.

5. Rolling and Wrapping Machine: for preparing newspapers, magazines and journals for mailing.

6. Trolleys or Baskets: for the collection and distribution of mail.

7. Dispensers: for adhesive tape, glue and sealing wax.

8. Sponge or Roller Moistener: for moistening stamps and envelopes.

9. Rubber Stamps: for various purposes, such as marking the firm's name and address or the name of a postal service on packages, or for stamping a facsimile signature on a document.

QUESTIONS

1. Draw up simple rules for a new employee, who, under your supervision, will deal with the receipt and distribution of incoming mail, including registered postal packets. *R.S.A. SD.2*

2. In addressing correspondence what is the particular significance of
   (*a*) post town
   (*b*) postcode? *R.S.A. SD.2*

3. (*a*) How is a franking machine obtained for the mail room of a business?
   (*b*) Explain how such a machine replaces the use of postage stamps. *R.S.A. SD.2*

4. Draft a report to your employer, suggesting steps which could be taken to deal with a greatly increased volume of incoming and outgoing mail. This is at present handled by one clerk, who keeps the postage book and stamps. *R.S.A. SD.2*

5. You have duplicated 100 copies of a 30-page document. You and one assistant have to collate the pages in order that they may be distributed. Describe the manner in which you would set about this, and what equipment you would find useful. *R.S.A. SD.2*

6. (*a*) What do you consider to be the most effective method of dealing with a company's incoming post totalling some three hundred letters daily?
   (*b*) It has been reported to your employer that the clerk dealing with the outgoing post complains of having to stay late every evening in order to deal with last minute batches of letters. Your employer asks you to investigate and draft recommendations for coping with this problem. *L.C.C. P.S.D.*

7. (i) When should the title "Messrs." be used? Why should it not be used before the name of a limited liability company?

(ii) When they are on the Bench (in court) Justices of the Peace are called "Your Worship". How would you address an envelope to a Mr. John Brown who is a Justice of the Peace? *R.S.A. SD.2*

8. Briefly describe two methods of dealing with incoming mail which requires the attention of more than one department. Your answer should include the advantages and shortcomings, if any, of each method. *L.C.C. P.S.C.*

9. There is some concern in your Company because letters appear to be going astray.

You are asked to devise a system for handling the incoming mail ensuring the maximum of security, especially for remittances.

Set out in detail your plan. *R.S.A. COS.*

10. Give the following information about each of three machines of your choice which you would expect to find in a mail room:

(*a*) its purpose;

(*b*) its advantages;

(*c*) very briefly, how it is operated. *R.S.A. SD.2*

11. (*a*) Machines for franking the post can be purchased or hired from certain office equipment firms, but the user must comply with various Post Office conditions. List any such conditions which you know.

(*b*) It may not be economical to use a franking machine if the number of items posted each day is not very large, and there are also disadvantages in its use, even to a large firm. What are these disadvantages and why do many firms consider that franking machines should nevertheless be used? *R.S.A. SD.2*

12. Some incoming mail needs to be seen by more than one person or department in a firm. Suggest what can be done to make sure that three people see the contents of a letter:

(*a*) when there is no urgency;

(*b*) when the matter is urgent. *R.S.A. OP.1*

13. The Senior Executives of your firm have complained that the morning's mail is late in being delivered from the mail room to their offices with a consequent delay in starting the day's business. The Office Manager has asked you to investigate the present method of handling the incoming mail and to devise a more satisfactory system which will not only ensure that the correspondence is available for distribution before the senior executives arrive in the morning, but will also take into account the need for security in the handling of remittances. Write a memorandum to the Office Manager setting out the procedure you would recommend. *R.S.A. OP.2*

14. If you were responsible for operating a franking machine, state what action you should take for the following:

(i) faint impressions of printed information

(ii) an envelope franked in error

(iii) preparing franked mail for despatch

(iv) the franking machine control card at the end of each day

(v) closing the franking machine at the end of each day. *R.S.A. OM*

15. If you wrote to a friend called Sarah, you might address her as " Dear Sarah". How would you address the following:

(*a*) Mrs Mary Alton, secretary to the managing director of another firm. You often speak to her by telephone.

(*b*) A limited company.

(*c*) Sir John Howarth, with whom your employer has a friendly business relationship. Your employer will sign the letter.

(*d*) A firm of accountants with whom you have had no previous dealings? *R.S.A. SD.2*

16. A salesman for a firm which supplies postal franking machines has called on your employer and explained to him a number of ways in which your firm would benefit by having a franking machine.

Your firm sends out about thirty letters a day and very seldom sends out circulars. At present, the outgoing letters are collected by a clerk from each office between 1630 and 1700 hrs. and posted in the nearest box (unless too large to go through the opening) by about 1730 hrs.

Your employer feels that there must be disadvantages as well as advantages in the use of a franking machine and asks you to write a report for him on the *disadvantages* in relation to your firm.

Write such a report. *R.S.A. SD.2*

17. What is a Postcode Directory? Where would you find one? *R.S.A. SD.2*

Chapter 2
Services of the Post Office

All who are concerned with the dispatch of mail should be conversant with the many services offered by the Post Office, and the following is a summary of the essential details. Current rates of postage, together with full information of all Post Office services, are contained in the *Post Office Guide*, to which reference should be made when in doubt.

LETTERS AND CARDS

Inland

Letters and cards may be sent by two classes of service, known respectively as First Class and Second Class. Second-class letters will normally be delivered up to one working day later than first-class letters except that, over long or difficult journeys, or when posted in large consignments, they may take a little longer. The class of a letter is determined by the amount of postage paid. A first-class letter is a letter or card paid at not less than the first-class rate of postage: a second-class letter is one paid at less than first-class postage. No written indication of service is necessary except where this is separately specified for certain categories of mail. All letters may be sealed, including those previously sent by the printed paper rate.

There is a limit of $1\frac{1}{2}$ lb. weight for second-class letters, but there is no weight limit for first-class letters.

Overseas

Letters and cards may be sent abroad by air mail or surface mail. Air mail letters to destinations outside Europe should have a blue air mail label affixed to the top left-hand corner on the address side or alternatively the words "BY AIR MAIL" may be written boldly in the same place.

Air letters may be sent to any address in the world for a cheaper rate of postage provided they are written on either the stamped air letter form which is obtainable from post offices or on privately manufactured forms for which the postage may be prepaid either by means of a postage stamp or a franked impression. They must not contain enclosures.

18

The "All-up" Service

Letters and cards for European destinations go automatically by air or surface mail, whichever is the quicker. The payment of air mail postage is unnecessary and air mail labels should not be used. This is known as the "All-up" service.

CIRCULARS

Second-class Letters Posted in Bulk

A rebate of postage is allowed on second-class letters posted in bulk when the number exceeds 4 250. The rebate must be applied for in advance of posting on a special form obtainable at any head post office. The packets must be identical in shape and size. The letters must be available for posting at the same time or in batches as the local Head Postmaster requires. Rebate items are liable to be held back in favour of the fully paid mail and are generally dealt with in off-peak periods. They should be arranged in bundles of fifty in geographical divisions with their addresses all arranged in the same direction.

Prepayment of Postage

Prepayment of postage in money on large quantities of circulars or other items may be arranged at head post offices. The conditions under which packets may be prepaid are that:

1. The number of postal packets, other than parcels, is not less than 120; and the number of parcels is not less than 20.

2. The packets, with the addresses arranged in the same direction, are securely tied in bundles of 50 (or, for bulky packets, in bundles of 10), the articles in each bundle being chargeable with the same rate of postage, which must be shown on the outside of the bundle. The appropriate class of posting (first or second) must also be shown.

3. Parcels are handed in separately from other postal packets.

Overseas Printed Papers

Printed papers may be sent abroad by air mail or surface mail at reduced rates of postage. These may include catalogues, greetings cards, printed notices, photographs, books and circulars printed in imitation of typewriting reproduced from duplicators and copiers. Copies obtained by means of a typewriter including top or carbon copies are, however, not admissible. The packets, which should be clearly marked "Printed Papers" in the upper left-hand corner of the address side, should be unsealed so that they can be easily examined. Certain items such as books, maps, newspapers and pamphlets may be eligible for despatch at reduced rates of postage.

Overseas Bulk Postings

Firms who have large numbers of Printed Paper items for despatch abroad to a single addressee in another country may make arrangements for their postings to be accepted in bulk under the Direct Agents Bag Service. This service is available for both Ordinary-rate and Reduced-rate Printed Papers. Items sent by this service may not be registered or insured. To qualify for acceptance under these arrangements, postings must be made at regular intervals and must be presented to the Post Office in mail bags made ready for despatch abroad in conformity with international requirements.

Overseas Small Packets

This service provides for the transmission of goods, whether dutiable or not, in the same mails as printed papers which, as a rule, travel more quickly than parcels. The sender must write his name and address on the outside of the packet and must write the words "Small Packet" in the top left-hand corner on the address side of the packet. The packets must be wrapped in such a way that they may be easily examined without any seal being broken. Letters, notes or documents having the character of current and personal correspondence may not be sent in a small packet.

Customs Declarations

All packets posted for abroad at the letter rate of postage and containing goods, whether or not dutiable in the country of destination, must be declared to customs. If the value of the goods does not exceed £40 a green label form of declaration is sufficient, but for goods in excess of £40 or if the goods are sent by the insured box service a non-adhesive declaration form should be used.

PARCELS
Inland

Parcels posted to an address in the local parcel delivery area, i.e. those places which have in their postal address the same post town name as that of the office of posting, have a small reduction of postage. The maximum weight is 22 lb. The address should be written on the parcel itself, and not merely on the label, which may become detached.

In case the wrapping becomes damaged, or the parcel cannot be delivered, the sender's address should appear both inside the parcel and on the cover. On the cover it should be kept distinct from the address to which the parcel is sent, and should preferably be to the left of and at right angles to the name and address of the adressee.

Compensation Fee Parcels

This service, which has replaced registered parcels, provides for compensation up to £100 for loss or damage to parcels. The amount of compensation paid cannot exceed the market value of the contents if lost or the depreciation in value if damaged or, in either case, the limit appropriate to the compensation fee paid. The registered letter service has to be used if compensation cover is required in excess of £100 and up to a maximum of £500.

The sender of a compensation fee parcel must complete a certificate of posting with the addressee's name and address and the amount of compensation required and hand it to the post office counter clerk together with the parcel, compensation fee and postage. The clerk initials and date stamps the top portion of the certificate of posting and returns it to the sender. Posting lists may be used, instead of separate certificates of posting, when posting a large number of parcels. No special marking is required except for parcels containing fragile or perishable items.

Overseas

Parcels may be sent abroad by air mail or surface mail.

Customs Declarations

All parcels and other packages for places abroad are liable to be opened for examination in the country of destination, and the contents are subject to the customs and other requirements of that country. The sender is required to make an accurate declaration of the nature and value of the contents. Customs declaration forms for this purpose can be obtained beforehand from any post office which accepts parcels for abroad. Forms should be completed with a pen or typewritten. If the contents are not fully described, or are under-valued, the parcel is liable to seizure and penalties may be incurred. Two main kinds of customs declaration form are in use, namely an adhesive form, to be affixed to the parcel, and a non-adhesive form, of which two or more copies may be required. A dispatch note is required with non-adhesive forms.

The types of form required for each country are specified in the *Post*

Office Guide, for example a parcel despatched to Nicaragua requires one non-adhesive form and a despatch note.

SERVICES FOR URGENT DELIVERY OF POSTAL PACKETS
(arranged in the order of speed of delivery)

1. Express All the Way

An "express all the way" service is available for which a charge is made per mile and in this service a red "express" label is used and the package is conveyed all the way to the addressee's address by messenger.

2. Airway Letters

On certain air routes operated by BAC first-class letters are conveyed by the next available direct air service from the air terminal or town terminal of the airlines where they are handed in, and either left at the airport or town terminal to be called for, or transferred from the town terminal to the ordinary post by the airlines. The maximum weight accepted is 1 lb. This service is not available to the Irish Republic, or to any country overseas.

3. Railex

Any post office which is an express delivery office will accept an unregistered packet, convey it to the appropriate railway station or port and dispatch it for transmission to the station or port of destination. A messenger will collect the packet and deliver it to its address provided that it arrives during the hours when the messengers are on duty. The sending post office must write out, pre-pay and dispatch a telegram requesting the delivery post office to arrange to collect the packet on arrival.

Railway Letters

First-class letters are conveyed by the first available train from the railway station where they are handed in, and—

1. transferred on arrival to the nearest post office letter-box, or

2. left at the station of destination to be called for. The sender may arrange for a post office messenger to meet the train at the station of destination and deliver the letter.

Railway Parcels

Railway parcels may be left at any express delivery post office for conveyance by a post office messenger to a railway station for dispatch by train. The sender may arrange for a post office messenger to call at the station of destination, collect the parcel and deliver it at its address, or it may be left at the station of destination.

4. Special Delivery

If a letter is urgent it can be sent by the "Special Delivery" service for a special fee in addition to first-class postage. The letter receives priority and is delivered from the addressee's post office to the addressee's address by special messenger or, if it arrives during the hours when messengers are not on duty, it is delivered by the first post in the morning. The words "Special Delivery" must be boldly and legibly marked above the address on the left-hand side of the cover of the letter or parcel. A broad blue or black perpendicular line must also be drawn from top to bottom on both the front and back of a letter and completely round a packet or parcel.

5. First Class Letters and Packets
(see page 18)

REGISTERED POST AND RECORDED DELIVERY SERVICES

A comparison

	Registered Post	*Recorded Delivery*
Labels used for displaying the serial numbers	R LONDON, E.C.420 No 3008	R 225055 Recorded Delivery
Uses	For sending articles of value for which some security handling is required and to have entitlement to compensation for loss. (Compensation for parcels is covered by the Compensation Fee Parcel Service—see page 21.)	For the correspondent who requires not only proof of posting but, if necessary, proof of delivery and is not so concerned in receiving compensation for loss. It is specially suitable for dispatching documents of little or no monetary value in which proof of delivery may be required in a court of law.
Preparation and posting	Coins must be packed in such a way that they cannot move about inside the envelope. Ordinary envelopes must be marked with a vertical and a horizontal blue line on the back and front of the envelope. Any knots	The package must be handed in at a post office and not posted in a posting box. The sender completes a recorded delivery form, detaches the the numbered gummed label and sticks it on the packet above and to the left of the

**Registered Post and Recorded Delivery Services—
A comparison** (*cont.*)

	Registered Post	*Recorded Delivery*
Preparation and posting (*cont.*)	must be covered with sealing wax or with a metal seal crushed by a press. If the package is fastened by means of strips of adhesive paper or tape, each strip must bear a stamped impression of the sender's name or business or the sender's signature. Packets should be marked in the bottom left-hand corner with the word "registered". If it is necessary for a higher fee than the basic one to be paid it must be marked on the packet according to the amount for which the packet is to be covered. The package must be handed in at a post office and not posted in a posting box. The sender must hand the packet to the post office counter clerk together with the cost of postage at the first-class rate, plus the fee for registration, making sure that an adequate fee is paid to cover the level of compensation required. In return the counter clerk will give the sender a certificate of posting which has been initialled and date-stamped.	address. He must stamp the packet for the normal postage at the first or second-class rate, plus the fee for recorded delivery. The sender hands the packet and the certificate to the post office counter clerk who initials and date stamps the certificate and returns it to the sender.
The services which may be used	All kinds of inland first-class postal packets except airway letters, railway letters or parcels and railex.	All kinds of inland postal packets except parcels, airway letters, railex and railway letters or parcels and Cash on Delivery packets.

	Registered Post	*Recorded Delivery*
Record of Posting received at the time of posting		
Record of Delivery	The packet is signed for by the recipient on delivery.	The packet is signed for by the recipient on delivery and a record kept by the Post Office.
Certificate of Delivery	Obtained by paying an additional fee and completing an advice of delivery form either at the time of posting or later: if requested at the time of posting it contains the recipient's signature, otherwise the certificate will be signed by a Post Office official.	Obtained by paying an additional fee and completing an advice of delivery form either at the time of posting or later: it is signed by a Post Office official—not by the recipient
Compensation	Up to a maximum of £500.	Up to a maximum of £2.
Restrictions	Compensation will not be paid in respect of money unless it is enclosed in one of the special registered envelopes (made in linen) sold by the Post Office.	This service may not be used for money such as coins, banknotes, cheques and jewellery.
Security	Registered mail receives special security treatment.	Mail is carried with the ordinary unregistered post and receives no special security treatment.

Note:

If several registered packets are sent by the same person they should be accompanied by a list, in duplicate, of the addresses; one list is retained at the post office and the other, when completed and signed, is returned to the sender. These are usually kept in book form and are issued by the Post Office.

REPLY-PAID POSTAL SERVICES

Business Reply Service

This service enables a person or firm to receive cards or letters from clients without prepayment of postage. The postage at the first or second-class rate, with a fee on each item, is paid by the addressee. A licence to use the service must be obtained from the Post Office.

Freepost

A person who wishes to obtain a reply from a client or a member of the public without putting him to the expense of paying postage may include in his communication or advertisement a special address. The reply bearing this address can then be posted in the ordinary way but without a stamp and the addressee will pay postage on all the replies that he receives. (The replies may only be sent as second-class mail). The Freepost service can be used by anyone who obtains a licence, though it is chiefly designed to meet the needs of business firms and advertisers.

This service can be used to attract a response not only through the press, but through television and direct mail. The postage at the second-class rate, plus a small fee on each item, is paid by the addressee.

Postage Forward Parcel Service

The Postage Forward Parcel Service enables a person or firm to receive parcels from clients without prepayment of postage; the postage, with a small fee on each parcel, being paid by the addressee. A licence to use this service must be obtained from the Post Office. This service is designed primarily to meet the needs of business firms and advertisers who wish to obtain a parcel from a client without putting him to the expense or trouble of paying postage.

Reply Coupons—Overseas

Reply coupons, obtainable from the larger post offices in this country, enable anyone sending a letter to a place abroad to prepay a reply, i.e. instead of the sender enclosing a stamped addressed envelope he encloses a reply coupon which is exchangeable for postage stamps at post offices abroad. There are two categories: Commonwealth reply coupons, which are valid only within the British Commonwealth (except Australia, Canada, Ceylon, Lesotho, Pakistan, Singapore, Trindad and Tobago) and the

Irish Republic, and International reply coupons which are valid in any foreign country of the Universal Postal Union.

Other post office services and devices which a trader can use to encourage prospective customers to communicate with him include:

Freefone telephone service (page 44)
Telephone-answering machine (page 40)
Prepaid Reply Telegrams (page 54)
Use of Telegraphic address (page 53)
Telex service (page 55)

OTHER SERVICES

Datapost

This service provides for the overnight delivery of packages containing computer data. It is a door-to-door service for firms who use computers which are remote from their own premises. Packages are collected at individually agreed times and delivered to the computer at a pre-arranged time next morning. Any item requiring vital overnight delivery is acceptable as long as it falls within the normal letter post regulations. To take advantage of Datapost, there has to be a need by the firm for a regular, repetitive service, either daily, weekly or monthly. Charges are negotiated on the basis of a contract, taking into account weight, destination and timing of collection and delivery.

Newspapers

Publications registered at the Post Office as newspapers will be given first-class service at the second-class rate, but only if specially posted by publishers or their agents and prominently marked Newspaper Post. All other newspapers are transmitted as first or second-class letters.

Cash on Delivery

A trade charge up to a maximum of £50 specified by the sender for collection on delivery of a parcel or registered letter can, under certain conditions, be collected by the Post Office and remitted to the sender by means of a special order.

Late Posted Packets

Posting boxes for the receipt of first-class letters prepaid with extra postage in addition to the ordinary postage are provided on all Travelling Post Offices, that is, mail trains to which sorting carriages are attached.

Registered letters and recorded delivery packets are accepted in Travelling Post Offices at railway stations up to five minutes before the departure times on payment of a fee in addition to the registration or recorded delivery fee and first-class postage. The fees must be affixed in stamps before a letter is presented at the station.

Redirection of Postal Packets

Letters, registered packets, postcards and newspapers are retransmitted by post without additional charge, provided the packet is unopened and re-posted not later than the day after delivery, Sundays and public holidays not being counted. If an adhesive label is used to indicate the new address, the name of the original addressee must not be obscured, otherwise the packet will be liable to surcharge as unpaid.

Registered and Recorded Delivery packets must not be dropped into a letter-box but must be handed over the counter of a post office.

Parcels may be redirected free of charge if the redirected address is in the same delivery area as the original address; otherwise redirected parcels are liable to additional postage at the prepaid rate.

Redirection of Mail by the Post Office

If a person or business moves from one address to another, redirection of letters, parcels and other postal packets is undertaken by the Post Office at various rates depending on the period of redirection required. A form entitled "Request for Redirection of Postal Packets" should be completed and sent to the local delivery office serving the old address.

Certificate of Posting

If proof is desired that an unregistered letter or other postal packet has been posted to a particular person, it must be handed in at a post office and a certificate of posting requested. A small charge is payable by means of a postage stamp, which must be affixed by the sender to the certificate. A single certificate for several postal packets of the same kind posted at the same time can be obtained if a list of the names and addresses is presented with them. It must be clearly understood that packets for which these certificates are issued are not registered and that they will be treated as if they had been posted in a letter-box; that in the event of loss, damage, or delay, the certificates will confer no title to compensation; and that they furnish no proof of the nature of the contents.

Private Boxes

A private box may be rented at a normal delivery office for the reception of postal packets "to be called for", except on Sundays, by the renter or his agent as an alternative to delivery by postmen at the place of address. The service makes it possible to obtain correspondence in advance of the normal time of delivery.

Private Bags

A private bag may be used for the posting and receipt of correspondence. The bag, which must be conveyed by the user or his agent, is locked at the post office before it is handed over.

Poste Restante

Poste Restante means post remaining. To assist travellers with no fixed address, correspondence and parcels may be addressed to them at all post offices, except town sub-offices. The words "Poste Restante" or "To be Called For" must be included in the address. At the expiry of two weeks (one month for a packet originating at a place abroad) postal packets are treated as undeliverable.

To ensure delivery to the right person, addressees must, when calling for mail, produce evidence of their identity.

Other services offered by the Post Office include the issuing of broadcast receiving, dog, game and gun licences; stamp duties; national savings certificates and stamps, premium bonds and post office savings; national insurance stamps; and the payment of various pensions and allowances.

SOURCES OF REFERENCE ON POSTAL SERVICES

Post Office Guide

This guide, which is published by the Post Office annually, contains information on all of the services referred to in this chapter together with details of remittance, telephone and telegraphic services and detailed letter and parcel services for countries abroad. Monthly supplements are also issued giving particulars of amendments to the *Post Office Guide* due to alterations in charges and services.

Air Mail Leaflet

Full particulars of the services available by air and the current postage rates are given in the *Air Mail Leaflet*, which may be obtained at any post office. A standing order may be placed with the local head postmaster for new editions of the leaflet to be supplied by post, free of charge as and when published.

QUESTIONS

1. Your firm receives many inquiries from overseas customers. What types of postal services are available for the dispatch overseas of letters, literature and samples? *R.S.A. SD.2*

2. Explain the "two-tier postal system" and its importance to the office. *R.S.A. OP.1*

3. (*a*) What are the main points to follow when packing and labelling a parcel?
   (*b*) What steps have to be taken when sending a parcel overseas?
   (*c*) What steps should you take before signing for a parcel in the office? *R.S.A. OP.1*

4. Your employer, Mr X, has left by the 1000 hrs. train for a conference about 100 miles away. The conference begins on the evening of the same day. During the morning you find that he has left behind him important papers which he will wish to use at the conference. What will you do? *R.S.A. SD.2*

5. (*a*) Explain the postal regulations regarding the redirection, by the public, of letters and parcels. Are redirected parcels subject to additional postage charges?
   (*b*) If your firm is removing to new premises, what arrangements can be made with the Post Office for the redirection of letters and parcels? Is any charge made for this service? *R.S.A. SD.2*

6. What is the difference between recorded delivery and registered post? *R.S.A. OP.1*

7. Describe the Post Office services which can be used to ensure that written or verbal communications are received:
   (*a*) speedily;
   (*b*) safely. *R.S.A. OP.2*

8. Explain the various services of the Post Office which a trader can use to encourage prospective customers to communicate with him. *R.S.A. OP.2*

9. (*a*) What are "window" or "aperture" envelopes and when are they used? Mention their advantages and disadvantages.

(*b*) What happens if:

(i) a letter weighing under 1 oz. contains a 2p stamp;

(ii) a letter contains no stamp;

(iii) there is no reply when a postman brings a registered letter? *R.S.A. OP.1*

10. It is 1430 hrs. and you have to get in touch with an applicant for an important post in your organization to ask him to attend for interview the following morning at 1030 hrs.

State what Post Office services are available to you and whether you could make sure of getting a reply from the applicant if he lives about 40 miles away. *R.S.A. COS.*

11. Which Post Office services would you use to send the following:

(*a*) jewellery;

(*b*) a summons to appear in Court;

(*c*) some proofs which you wish to reach the printer on the day on which you send them;

(*d*) money wanted very urgently by a member of your staff who is working temporarily in another town? *R.S.A. SD.2*

12. If a member of your staff, who is visiting another town, telephones and leaves a message for you that he urgently requires the following:

(*a*) certain documents;

(*b*) the address of a client;

(*c*) £10;

which Post Office services would you use? *R.S.A. SD.2*

13. If you were sending the following articles by post, which service would you use? Give reasons briefly.

(*a*) Legal documents which are valuable (not in terms of money) and for which you wish to have proof of delivery.

(*b*) A gold and diamond ring, value £80.

(*c*) An envelope (6½ in. × 9½ in.—165 mm. × 242 mm.) containing a letter with enclosures (not valuable) and weighing about 6 oz. *R.S.A. OP.1*

14. Describe briefly the post office services you would use in each of the following instances:

(*a*) to enable customers in this country to reply to you without having to pay postage;

(*b*) to enable customers abroad to reply to you without having to pay postage;

(*c*) to collect money from customers in mail order transactions;

(*d*) to convey an urgent parcel required the same day in a town about 200 miles away;

(*e*) to send a legal document in which proof of delivery may be required in a court of law;

(*f*) to despatch an urgent letter after the last post has been collected from the post office;

(*g*) to obtain correspondence in advance of the normal time of delivery;

(*h*) to send £15 required the same day in another part of the country.

Give reasons for your answers. *R.S.A. OP.2*

Chapter 3
Using the Telephone

The telephonist is judged by the caller to be representative of the organization by which she is employed, and if a telephone inquirer does not receive a clear and courteous greeting he immediately tends to form a bad opinion of the organization as a whole. What she says and the tone in which she says it can influence the response she receives from the caller. Time is money in business, especially when it is spent on the telephone, and it is important to guard against conducting unnecessarily long conversations.

When speaking on the telephone the operator should always try to sound friendly and helpful. She should listen to, and show an interest in, what the caller has to say and speak clearly, unhurriedly and, unless she is talking above a noisy background, not loudly. A medium to low-pitched voice is desirable and consonants should be clearly emphasized. Words with the same vowel-sound, e.g. "five" and "nine" can sound alike on the telephone and special care is therefore necessary when quoting figures, names and unfamiliar words. The telephone alphabet (see page 46) should be used to spell out words which the caller may have difficulty in recognizing. Avoid the use of slang expressions such as "Hang on", "Right oh!", "Okay", etc. which do not give a good impression in business. Matters overheard on the telephone must be treated in the same strict confidence as the contents of any correspondence dealt with by the secretary. Above all the telephone operator must have a good speaking voice. She should learn to recognize all who use the telephone in the organization by sight, name and voice. Familiarity with the organization's work is desirable, and also a knowledge of the part played in the organization by each executive, section and department. The telephonist is then able to handle calls efficiently and connect callers instantly to the right sections. The private secretary responsible for handling her employer's telephone calls must also have the qualities of a good telephonist. Tact is necessary to avoid putting undesired calls through to high-level executives of the organization. The private secretary is responsible for shielding her employer from unnecessary calls which will waste his time. It is her duty to recognize those callers to whom her employer will wish to speak, and to know how to handle the others tactfully.

A GUIDE FOR TELEPHONE USERS

When Answering the Telephone . . .

1. Always answer promptly when it rings and announce your identity.

(*a*) If the call is received via your private exchange switchboard give your name and department (if necessary);

(*b*) If you are receiving an incoming call direct state the name of the establishment, for example, "Brown and Company". A greeting such as "Good morning, Brown and Company" has a pleasing effect.

(*c*) If an internal call is being received, state your own name and position, if necessary; for example, "Miss Brown, Production Manager's Secretary".

2. Avoid saying "Hello" as this wastes time and does not help the caller.

3. Try not to keep a caller waiting. If there is likely to be a long delay in connecting the caller it may be better to ring him back and save his time on the telephone. This is particularly important if the call is made from a call-box telephone where the caller may not be in possession of additional coins.

4. Have a message pad and pencil at hand so that you can write down a message. Pick up the receiver with your left hand so that your right hand is free for writing (vice versa, of course, if you are left-handed).

5. You may have to leave the telephone for a while in order to make an enquiry or collect some information. If so, let the caller know how long you expect to be and ask if he would prefer you to call him back. In these circumstances, arrange for your calls to be answered in your absence.

6. When an incoming call has to be transferred from one extension to another, convey the caller's name and request to the new extension so that he does not have to repeat his message.

7. If a delay occurs before a caller can be connected, keep him informed of the action you are taking.

8. If an incoming call is disconnected, replace the telephone receiver as the person making the call will re-establish the connexion as soon as possible.

9. If you receive a call which is a wrong number remember that the intrusion is not intentional and that it is probably just as irritating to the caller as it is to you. No apology is required of you, but one made by the caller should be accepted politely.

10. Always try to make a conscious effort to greet people cheerfully, even at the end of the day, and if you know a caller's name, do not hesitate to use it when addressing him.

The telephonist is responsible for seeing that each caller is connected to someone who can deal with his business. A caller who wishes to speak to an executive absent from his office should not be kept waiting but asked whether he would like to:

    (*a*) speak to someone else;
    (*b*) be rung back by the executive;
    (*c*) ring again later; or
    (*d*) leave a message.

Whatever the answer, the caller's name, business address and telephone number should be noted.

Taking Messages

Calls and messages should never be entrusted solely to memory, which may well prove unreliable and the important facts should be written down while they are being received.

The following important points should be noted:

1. Date and time of the call.
2. The name of the person for whom the telephone call was made.
3. Caller's name, address and telephone number.
4. Precise details of the message received.

The message should be repeated back to the caller to make sure that it has been taken down correctly.

Figure 7 is an example of a typical message sheet. The sheet should either be typed or written with a pen. As soon as the message has been recorded it should be placed on the executive's desk so that it can be seen by him immediately on his return.

When Making a Telephone Call . . .

(1) Check the correct code and number before dialling. If you are in doubt, look it up in the Dialling Instructions Booklet (Code) and the Telephone Directory (number) and make a note of it.

(2) Dial your number carefully, taking the dial right round to the finger stop and allowing it to run back freely each time you dial a figure. After dialling the number, allow sufficient time for the call to connect.

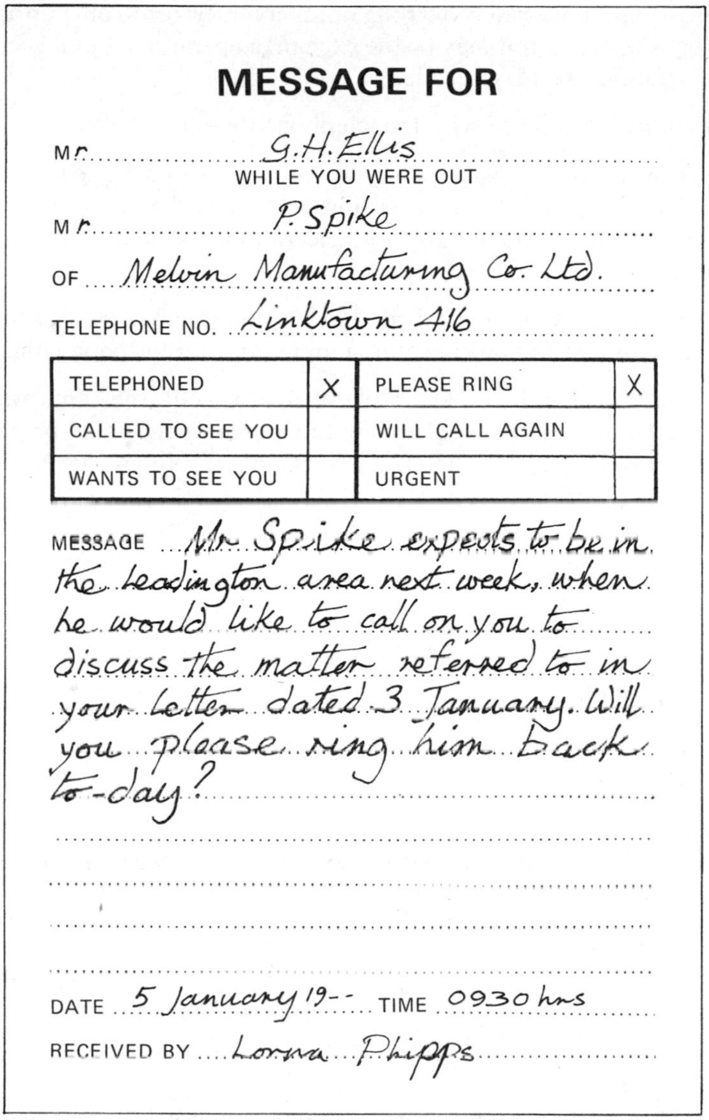

MESSAGE FOR

M r. .... *G.H.Ellis* ....
WHILE YOU WERE OUT
M r. .... *P. Spike* ....

OF .... *Melvin Manufacturing Co. Ltd.* ....

TELEPHONE NO. .... *Linktown 416* ....

TELEPHONED	X	PLEASE RING	X
CALLED TO SEE YOU		WILL CALL AGAIN	
WANTS TO SEE YOU		URGENT	

MESSAGE *Mr Spike expects to be in the Leadington area next week, when he would like to call on you to discuss the matter referred to in your letter dated 3 January. Will you please ring him back to-day?*

DATE *5 January 19--* TIME *0930 hrs*

RECEIVED BY .... *Lorna Phipps* ....

Fig. 7 Message Sheet

(3) If you make a mistake while dialling, replace the receiver for a short while and then start dialling again from the beginning of the number.

(4) When the person called answers say who you are and to whom you wish to speak.

(5) If you are connected to a wrong number remember to offer an apology. It may be your fault, or it may be the exchange operator's, but it is certainly never the fault of the person called.

(6) Familiarize yourself with the telephone tones (see below).

(7) When the call is answered say to whom you wish to speak and then give your name. Also state the extension number of the person you require, if you know it. If you do not know it, ascertain it and make a note of it for future use.

(8) If a number cannot be dialled, dial 100 and ask the operator to obtain it for you, stating the number required and your own telephone number.

(9) A telephone call should be planned in exactly the same way as a business letter and before even dialling the number you should be prepared with any necessary papers at hand. It is also advisable to prepare beforehand a short list of points to be discussed.

Private External Calls

The use of the business line for private calls is inadmissible, except in special cases of urgency. The rules governing this matter should be known to all members of the staff and should be strictly kept.

Telephone Tones

(*a*) *Dialling Tone*
A low pitched burr indicates that the exchange equipment is ready for you to start dialling.

(*b*) *Ringing Tone*
A repeated double beat tells you that the number is being rung. Allow two minutes for the number to answer; if there is no reply by then replace the telephone, wait a little while and try again.

(*c*) *Engaged Tone*
A single high-pitched note repeated at regular intervals usually means the number being called is in use, but it can also mean that the exchange equipment is engaged. In either case, you should replace the telephone and try again in about five minutes.

(*d*) *Number Unobtainable Tone*
A continuous high-pitched note indicates that the number is either out of service or spare. If you hear this tone, check that you have the correct

number (and dialling code) and then dial again. If you hear the tone again dial "100" and tell the Post Office operator what has happened.

(*e*) *Pay Tone*
High-pitched rapid pips tell you that you are being called from a "Pay-on-answer" coin box. Allow the caller sufficient time to put his money in the box.

(*f*) *"Lines Engaged" Announcement*
On some STD calls you may hear a pre-recorded voice saying: "Lines from . . . are engaged, please try later". This means that there is overload on the trunk lines from the district mentioned and you should replace the handset and wait a few minutes before dialling again.

(*g*) *Continental Tones*
It should be noted that the above descriptions apply only to Inland telephone calls. Some of the tones you may hear if you dial your own calls to the continent are different.

Subscriber Trunk Dialling (STD)

A system which allows for trunk calls to be obtained by callers themselves by dialling is operative to most parts of the country. Group routing and charging equipment—"GRACE" for short—takes the place of the telephone operator. This equipment interprets the instructions given by the caller when he dials, directs the trunk call to its destination and, when the call is answered, controls the recording of the charge on the caller's meter. A unit method of charging is used for STD calls in which the amount of time bought for each unit depends upon the distance of the call, the day of the week and the time of the day when the calls are made.

To make a call by Subscriber Trunk Dialling the caller dials a code before dialling the telephone number. The time bought for 3p units is as follows:

Distance	*Mon.–Fri.* *0900–1300 hrs.*	*Mon.–Fri.* *0800–0900 hrs.* *1300–1800 hrs.*	*Cheap rate* *at all other* *times*
Local	2 mins.	3 mins.	8 mins.
Up to 56 kilometres	30 secs.	45 secs.	3 mins.
Over 56 kilometres	10 secs.	15 secs.	1 min.

Coin boxes in public call boxes take 2p and 10p coins. 2p pays for 2 minutes on a local call at all times. The time bought for a 2p unit on a trunk call is based on the distance, day and the time of the call. Telephone charges are subject to VAT.

With the introduction of local and trunk timed calls it is essential for staff to be trained to use the telephone sparingly and not to waste time with unnecessary conversation. When answering an incoming call the telephonist must be ready to deal with it promptly, since charging starts as soon as she answers.

Trunk Calls

A trunk call is an expensive means of communication and is not normally made if a letter will serve the purpose equally well. To make a trunk call the operator should be given the appropriate number or, where subscriber trunk dialling is in operation, the number should be dialled. If the operator says that a call cannot be put through immediately and that she will ring again later, the secretary must remain near the telephone until the call has been received. If she must leave the office, she should tell the operator to cancel the call, or pass the duty of dealing with the matter to an assistant.

Telephone Numbers

The operator should maintain a complete and up-to-date list of all extension numbers with the name of the section or executive using each extension. An example of a page of a telephone number index, supplied by the Post Office for students, is given in Fig. 8. The index should be placed where she can refer to it while she is seated at the switchboard. One of the excellent systems of strip indexing may be used for this purpose; details are given on page 104. An index of telephone exchanges is a useful aid, and copies may be purchased from any Telephone Manager.

Tape Callmaker

A tape callmaker is a new device for recording and storing up to four hundred telephone numbers (up to 18 digits each) on magnetic tape and dialling them automatically.

To locate a number, a touch of a two-way drive switch spins the tape through the alphabet in seconds and the exact position is located by a thumbwheel. The call is made by lifting the handset of the telephone, and after waiting for the dialling tone, pressing the call button.

This machine saves time in looking up and dialling calls and eliminates human errors in dialling.

		Telephone numbers		
Name and address of company	Department and contact	Dialling Code	Exchange and number	Extension
Huffman Inc Schwanenplatz Lucerne Switzerland	T. Bleuler Sales Manager	041	21 48 86	5
Hutton & Sons 14 Palace Gardens Guildford	R. Hutton Director	0483	216 418	1

Fig. 8 Telephone Number Index

Switchboard

A switchboard is used in a large office where there are several extensions and all incoming calls are taken and transferred to the various executives or departments by means of intercommunicating switches and signals. The private secretary may have a small switchboard in her office in order to receive all of her employer's calls and handle them according to his wishes.

There are three main kinds of telephone exchanges which may be installed in an organization:

PBX is the abbreviation for a private branch exchange which may be manual or automatic. It is used for the purpose of connecting calls from extension telephones to other extensions (internally) and to or from other exchanges (public or private). This can be either a Private Manual Branch Exchange or a Private Automatic Branch Exchange as described below.

PMBX is the abbreviation for a private manual branch exchange in which the telephonist makes all the connections between the extensions within the organization and the incoming and outgoing calls.

PABX is the abbreviation for a private automatic branch exchange and in this system it is possible for external calls to be dialled from the extensions without using the services of the switchboard operator. Extensions can also dial one another and a separate telephone is not required for internal calls.

The switchboard operator must, however, be used for receiving and routing incoming calls.

Telephone Answering Machines

Telephone-answering machines may be employed when the office staff are not available to receive telephone calls. When the office staff leave at night or at lunch time the machine can be fitted to the telephone to provide a continuous telephone answering and recording service. Each caller hears a pre-recorded announcement inviting him to record a message. The calls received are then transcribed from the recording machine and message sheets prepared for the staff concerned. These machines are suitable for businesses in which urgent messages are delivered at all hours of the day and night, such as with television servicing, motor vehicle repairs and servicing, import and export, as well as manning the telephone at lunch times and on Saturday mornings.

A new development of the telephone answering machine is the Interrogator which enables a business executive to extract information from a recording machine by remote control. The Interrogator is fitted to a telephone and when callers ring in a pre-recorded announcement is given and messages are recorded. By using a special code number the executive can telephone in to his office and listen to the messages which have been received on the machine. He can also record a message himself and programme the machine to erase the messages and reset itself to continue recording more messages. Alternatively, he can leave the messages intact for future reference and the interrogator will continue recording. Both sides of a telephone call can be recorded on this machine which is especially useful when an accurate, verbatim record of the conversation is required later for transcription.

The Interrogator is a useful device for people who travel a great deal and who are required to keep in touch with information at their base of operations.

Telephone Writers

Electrowriter systems transmit handwritten messages and sketches to any number of receiving stations over any distance. The machine is in the form of an electronic jotting pad which may be connected to an ordinary telephone. After dialling the appropriate number the caller presses a switch and writes on the pad with a special pen. What he writes is instantly reproduced on an electrowriter at the other end. A permanent written record is retained at both the transmitting and receiving ends which is important when sending business documents. As written confirmation is usually required before an action can be carried out, the electrowriter speeds up this operation and eliminates intermediate typing. Automatic answering equipment enables data to be transmitted in the evenings and at other times when the office is unmanned. Another advantage of this system is that verbal misunderstandings are eliminated as it transmits the most complex data and diagrams. Electro-writers are being used for transmitting quality control data between laboratories and processing departments; hospital administration for transmitting prescriptions from wards to pharmacy; airline administration; stock exchange transactions; Hotel administration for co-ordinating bookings between groups of hotels, etc.

Loudspeaking Telephone

A loudspeaking telephone, which is supplied by the Post Office on a rental basis, can be connected to exchange lines and most types of extensions. The microphone and loudspeaker are built into the equipment so that the user does not have to handle a handset and both hands are free for taking notes, searching through files, etc. It is also useful for small conferences as the people sitting round the desk on which the loudspeaking telephone is placed can all hear what is said by the incoming caller and anyone at the meeting can reply.

TELEPHONE SERVICES

Personal Calls

Should an executive ask for a call to be put through to a specific person in another organization, it is the operator's duty to put this call through to that person. The executive should not be connected until the person requested is on the telephone.

A call may be booked as a personal call on payment of a small extra charge.

A personal call enables a caller to:

1. quote the name of the person to whom he wishes to speak, the names of any acceptable substitutes and the telephone numbers where all or any of them may be found;

2. specify the person to whom he wishes to speak by giving a reference code, title or department or by an extension number, for example:

    (*a*) Reference: 723/EXP/4,
    (*b*) Chief Planning Officer,
    (*c*) Export Department, or
    (*d*) Extension 442;

3. arrange to speak only if two named persons are both available at one particular number;

4. arrange for a person not on the telephone to be brought to a neighbour's telephone, whose number he gives.

In addition to his own telephone number the caller may have his name or particular extension number passed to the called number.

If the personal call cannot be completed at once the originating exchange operator will leave a message at the distant telephone asking the wanted person to ring the personal call operator at the calling exchange as soon as possible. Alternatively, either the caller or the called number may give the time at which further attempts should be made to obtain the person wanted or quote another number at which he may be found.

Personal calls, if not previously completed, are cancelled twenty-four hours after the time of booking.

A personal call fee is payable in addition to the charge for an effective call.

This charge becomes payable as soon as an inquiry has been made at any distant number quoted by the caller, whether the call has been effective or not, but only one fee is payable irrespective of the number of attempts made to complete the call.

The timing of a call does not start until the connexion has been made to the person required, or to an acceptable substitute if the caller decides to speak to someone else at the number called. If the required person or acceptable substitutes cannot be traced, only the personal fee is payable.

If STD is available the caller can obtain the same facility for herself by ringing the number and, if necessary, making an appointment to ring again when the person she wants is available. This will often prove to be cheaper than incurring the personal call fee, but if there is any doubt concerning the availability of the required person, it may prove more economical to use the personal call system.

Fixed-time Calls

A trunk call may be booked in advance to be connected at or about a specified time if the lines are available; a small extra charge is made.

Charge Advisory Service

In order to discover the duration and charge of a telephone call made by the post office telephone operator (not S.T.D.) the caller should ask the operator for ADC (Advice of duration and charge) at the time the call is booked. An additional small fee is made for this service.

Transferred Charge Calls

A charge for a telephone call may be transferred to the called subscriber, if he agrees to accept it. A request for a transfer of charges must be made at the time the call is booked and an additional small fee is payable.

Telephone Credit Cards

A credit card enables a person to make telephone calls from any telephone without payment at the time. Each credit card bears a different number, and when the card holder wishes to make a telephone call or send a telegram he gives his number to the operator. The call is then charged to the telephone account on which the credit card was issued. Calls and telegrams are charged at the appropriate operator rates plus a small fee per call. A quarterly charge is made for each card. Calls made from credit cards are listed separately on the statement, or distinguished by a letter on the telephone account.

Many firms find it useful for their outside representatives to be supplied with telephone credit cards as they can use private telephones without incurring any expense to the owners and can use public call boxes without having to insert coins. The calls must, however, be obtained via the operator. From the firm's point of view it is also a useful control on the telephone calls made as the account indicates which representatives have made the various calls.

Emergency Calls

The procedure for making an emergency telephone call should be clearly understood as in time of trouble, an emergency call efficiently conducted could be a vital factor in saving life.

For the Fire Brigade, Police, Ambulance, Coastguard, Cave or Mountain Rescue Services, dial "999" unless the dial label on your telephone tells you otherwise. It is important to remember that you are connected first, not to the emergency service you require, but to a Post Office operator who will put you through to the required emergency service.

When the operator answers give:

1. details of the emergency service required

2. your telephone number.

When the emergency service answers give:

1. the address where help is needed

2. all other information for which you are asked.

Emergency calls are free of charge.

Temporary Transfer of Calls

Special arrangements may be made with the Post Office for calls to be automatically transferred from one number to another, for example, a doctor, on his holiday or week-end off duty, may have his calls automatically transferred to another doctor's telephone number.

Freefone

This is a telephone service which enables customers, clients, agents or employees to telephone an organization without cost to themselves. It encourages customers to place orders by telephone and it can also be used by representatives and employees to save them the time and trouble of using coins and claiming refunds for calls made to their firm. The calls are made by using a special freefone telephone number. The basic quarterly charge is related to the size of the area covered. The firm is also required to pay the normal telephone call charge plus a small transfer fee for each freefone call.

Miscellaneous Telephone Services

Various additional telephone services are offered by the Post Office, which include directory inquiries, speaking clock, alarm calls, weather forecasts, daily recipes, road conditions, tourist information, Financial Times share index service (updated four times daily) and special activity reports such as cricket test-match results.

Ships' Radiotelephone Service

If the secretary has to make a telephone call to a ship at sea she should ask the local exchange telephone operator for "Ships' Telephone Service", adding, if known, the telephone number and name of the coast station through which the call should be made. Coast stations are listed in the *Post Office Guide*. When connected to the coast station operator, the caller should ask for "Ships' Radiotelephone Call", giving the name of the ship and the name (or designation) of the person required.

Aircraft Telephone Service

A radiotelephone service is available from suitably equipped aircraft to the ground, but it is impossible to locate aircraft from the ground.

Overseas Telephone Calls

Europe

Subscribers with STD on exchanges in several large cities can dial direct to numbers on most exchanges in Belgium, France, Germany, Italy, Luxembourg, the Netherlands, Norway and Switzerland. Subscribers without this facility should ask for "Continental Service".

Information about telephone services with European countries, and about the telephone numbers of subscribers in those countries, is provided free of charge except when it can only be obtained by means of a continental call. If a call is necessary, the caller is charged at the equivalent rate of a one minute conversation between the caller's local exchange and the continental town concerned.

The dialling instructions list the principal exchanges available, the codes to be dialled in order to obtain them and the charges for each country. If an exchange code is not stated, the Continental Exchange operator will verify whether the number can be dialled direct.

When dialling an international number do not pause between the digits as a few seconds' delay between any of the last digits may lose the call.

Countries outside Europe

Calls for countries outside Europe are controlled at the International Exchange, which should be obtained by dialling the appropriate code or by asking for "International Service".

An overseas call may be booked two working days in advance of the day on which it is required. Thus a call required on Friday may be booked on or after the preceding Wednesday, and a call required on Monday or Tuesday may be booked on or after the preceding Friday. It is now possible to dial direct to New York.

The personal call service is available on all operator-connected calls to the continent; and to Canada, South Africa, the USA and certain other countries.

The charges and full details of overseas telephone services are given in the *Post Office Guide*.

Telephone Numbers

It is the intention of the Post Office eventually to convert all telephone dials to figures only and telephones in and around London, Birmingham, Edinburgh, Glasgow, Liverpool and Manchester already use all-figure numbers. The figures before the hyphen are the STD code and those after the hyphen form the local number, for example the telephone number of Sir Isaac Pitman & Sons Ltd is 01–242 1655. The exchange name is replaced by figures which include the STD code.

When it is necessary to quote a telephone number the following rules should be observed:

1. Divide the number into groups of two, allowing a slight pause between each group, e.g. Coventry 495267 would be as follows: Coventry (pause) four nine (pause) five two (pause) six seven.

2. If two similar figures come on each side of one of the pauses, the figures must be separated, e.g. 4992 would be given: four nine (pause) nine two.

3. If two similar figures appear in a group, the word "double" may be used and the figures need not be separately pronounced, e.g. 2644 would be: two six (pause) double four.

4. When the number ends with two noughts "hundred" is used, e.g. 200 would be: two hundred.

5. When the number ends with three noughts "thousand" is used, e.g. 3000 would be: three thousand.

6. When giving "0" say "Oh" and not "nought" which can be confused with "8".

Telephone Alphabet

When it is necessary to emphasize or identify any letter or word it can be done by using the official P.O. alphabetical code, which is as follows:

A for Andrew		J for Jack		S for Sugar	
B „ Benjamin		K „ King		T „ Tommy	
C „ Charlie		L „ Lucy		U „ Uncle	
D „ David		M „ Mary		V „ Victory	
E „ Edward		N „ Nellie		W „ William	
F „ Frederick		O „ Oliver		X „ X-Ray	
G „ George		P „ Peter		Y „ Yellow	
H „ Harry		Q „ Queenie		Z „ Zebra	
I „ Isaac		R „ Robert			

Internal Telephone Systems

The various offices of an organization are usually connected by an internal telephone system or "intercom" which provides an efficient means of communication. A good internal communication system is essential for dealing with inter-departmental business and for conveying information from one office to another.

An intercommunication system may consist of a series of automatic dial telephones operated from a private exchange, similar to the external system; or a multi-cored method in which contact is made from one office to another by pressing a button enabling the sound to be passed through a microphone instead of a telephone hand-set.

An intercommunication system may operate from a central instrument in the executive's office where the caller's voice is amplified and, by pressing a key, the executive can speak to any of his staff, without having to handle a telephone receiver.

An internal telephone has been developed in which the dial is situated in the handset itself. It takes up far less space than a conventional telephone and it can be mounted on the side of a desk or even inside a drawer.

Push buttons are used on some telephones as an alternative to spinning a dial. Push button selection is a quicker and more reliable means of making telephone calls.

Staff may be located whilst they are away from their offices and moving around the premises by loudspeakers operated by the telephonist from the switchboard or by pocket paging. Paging is also usually operated by the telephonist at the switchboard who sends out a call signal when a member of staff is required to receive an urgent telephone call. The member of staff carries a portable receiver in his pocket or clips it to his clothing, and when a call is transmitted from the switchboard, a signal is heard on the receiver which continues until the member of staff reaches a telephone and contacts the telephonist.

In a high-frequency radio paging system when a person is called his receiver emits a calling tone and, once he has pressed the "listen" button he can listen to any message which is passed to him by the operator. Communication, in this system, is not therefore dependent on the use of a telephone.

SOURCES OF INFORMATION ON TELEPHONE SERVICES

1. Telephone Directories:

These list, in alphabetical order, all the telephone subscribers in a locality. There are about seventy telephone directories covering the whole country.

2. Yellow Pages:

These list all business subscribers under their respective trade or profession, for example office equipment dealers, solicitors, etc. Yellow pages are usually to be found at the back of a local telephone directory.

3. Dialling Instruction Booklets:

These list the exchanges that can be dialled, together with the dialling codes and charges.

4. Post Office Guide

This gives a comprehensive guide to all inland and overseas telephone and telegraphic services.

5. Telephone booklets and literature such as "*Telephone Companion*" (a guide to telephone facilities and services for the STD subscribers), "*Using the Telephone*" (a leaflet for students) and "*The Post Office Telecommunication Services at Work*" obtainable from your local Telephone Manager's Office.

QUESTIONS

1. As secretary to a senior executive you are contacted by the firm's telephonist whenever people wish to speak to him on the telephone. How would you deal with these calls? *R.S.A. SD.2*

2. Your employer wishes to speak personally to Mr. T. Perkins, Sales Manager of Bright Metals Limited. Explain the post office facilities which may be used to assist you in making this call.

3. What would you suggest to your telephone operator that she should say instead of the following expressions, which she uses consistently:
   (*a*) (on lifting the receiver) "Hullo";
   (*b*) "Okeydoke" or "O.K.";
   (*c*) (if she cannot hear) "Mr. Who?";
   (*d*) "Hold on, will you?";
   (*e*) "The gentleman you want is out"; or "The gentleman you want is busy";
   (*f*) "Just a minute dear." *R.S.A. SD.2*

4. Draw up a set of rules for the efficient use of the telephone to guide junior clerks who have recently joined your office staff.

5. You receive a telephone call from Mr J. T. Hillery, who asks to speak to your General Manager, Mr W. Reading. What action would you take if Mr Reading was not available to receive the call?

6. Mr J. L. Pickering telephones and asks to speak to Mr A. Brown. You explain that Mr Brown is engaged at a meeting and Mr Pickering decides to leave a message for him. Prepare the message sheet and include the essential points from the following:

The special green card (reference A.492), which you ordered a fortnight ago, is no longer manufactured by John White & Sons. It appears that they have discontinued manufacturing it owing to a considerably reduced rate of demand. Do you want me to order another type of card, or would you prefer me to try to obtain the A.492 quality card from another manufacturer? Please telephone your instructions later today.

J. L. Pickering

7. The Office Manager has been instructed to take steps to reduce the expenditure on telephone calls. Investigate the present position regarding the internal and external telephone calls, and prepare a report on your findings together with your recommendations. *R.S.A. OP.2*

8. Assuming your company has up-to-date equipment, suggest ways in which the Managing Director might communicate with:
   (*a*) other managers in the building;
   (*b*) someone whose work takes him to all parts of the factory;
   (*c*) someone in a provincial branch office. *R.S.A. SD.2*

9. Your employer has received complaints that telephone messages are either not conveyed to the persons concerned or are incorrectly recorded. Clients have also expressed disappointment that the office telephone is not manned during the luncheon period and on Saturday mornings. Examine the situation and write a memorandum to your employer suggesting an improvement in the arrangements for telephone messages. *R.S.A. OP.2*

10. (*a*) In what circumstances might you wish to make use of:
       (i) a telephone answering machine;
       (ii) the transferred charge call service;
       (iii) a telephone credit card;
       (iv) the personal call service?
    (*b*) Explain fully *one* of the above telephone services. *R.S.A. OP.2*

11. Give three ways of making immediate contact with someone in another part of the building. *R.S.A. SD.2*

12. (*a*) In what circumstances is a telephone answering machine useful?
    (*b*) Suggest a suitable pre-recorded message to be received by every caller who is put through to such a machine. *R.S.A. SD.2*

13. (*a*) Give two methods of making a long-distance telephone call.
    (*b*) In each case, how could you find out the cost at the time of making the call? *R.S.A. SD.2*

14. What are the main points to bear in mind when dialling an international telephone number? Name two other ways in which a message can be sent overseas using Post Office facilities. *R.S.A. OP.1*

15. What are Yellow Pages? Why are they useful in the office? *R.S.A. OP.1*

16. (*a*) What is the meaning of the letters STD?
    (*b*) How is the cost of such a call calculated?
    (*c*) How does this cost compare with the cost of calls connected by the operator?
R.S.A. OP.1

Chapter 4
Telegraphic Services

TELEGRAMS

The Post Office telegram service enables brief messages to be sent quickly and efficiently to all parts of the country. In preparing a concise message for transmission by telegram it is important to say as much as possible in the fewest words, because the charge is calculated on the number of words used.

Preparing Telegrams

The following points should be noted in the preparation of telegrams:

1. The message should not be condensed to such an extent that it is ambiguous.

2. Necessary words in the name and address of the addressee should not be omitted, as this is likely to lead to delay in delivery. A telegraphic address should be used whenever it is known.

3. Single words should be substituted for phrases wherever possible. For example:

In the neighbourhood of = nearby
For the time being   = temporarily
A considerable amount of = much

4. All the essential words should be selected and arranged so that, with the fewest possible connecting words, they are clear and convey the correct message.

5. Essential figures should be put into words.

6. Slurred words, such as "can't", "don't", etc., should be avoided as they may easily lead to error.

Telegrams handed over the counter of a post office must be written in pen on the special form provided. If the message is typed, a carbon copy can be made for the file and there is also less risk of the message being misread. The following points should, however, be noted in the typing of telegrams:

1. Words should be typed in block capitals, and three or four spaces should be left between each word.

2. A carbon copy should be taken on either a plain sheet of paper or another telegram form.

3. Where possible, a telegram should be confirmed by letter posted on the same day as the telegram is sent.

4. The address to which the message is to be delivered should include the addressee's name and postal address (or telegraphic address), unless it is sent by telephone or telex which is preferable.

5. If a telegraphic address is used on the telegram the typist should type the full name and address of the addressee on the carbon copy, for identification when it is filed.

6. A good stock of telegram forms should always be available in the office.

7. The sender's name and address should be written on the back of the telegram form.

Note the display of a typed telegram in Fig. 9.

Counting of Words

1. Hyphenated words count as one, e.g. mother-in-law, forty-seven.

2. All the necessary words in an address after the name of the street are charged for as one word. Telephone and telex addresses are charged for as two words, excluding the name of the addressee.

3. Streets are counted according to the number of words they contain, e.g. Regent Street is two words.

4. Approved abbreviations count as one word, e.g. B/L, c/o, a/c.

5. If words are underlined, or brackets or inverted commas used, each underlining, pair of brackets or set of commas counts as one word.

6. Figures are counted at the rate of five figures to a word.

7. Punctuation marks count as one figure.

8. When figures and letters are mixed they must be counted separately, e.g. 25p is charged as two words.

9. A word of more than fifteen letters is counted as two words.

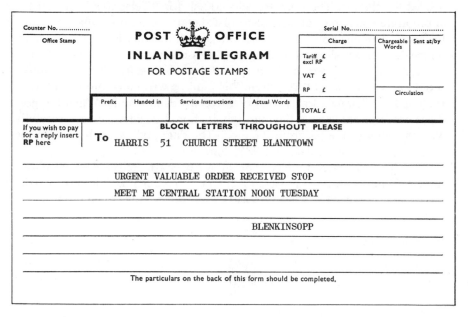

Fig. 9 Telegram Form
(Reproduced by permission of the Post Office)

Current Charges for Ordinary Telegrams

The current charges for ordinary telegrams are stated in the *Post Office Guide*.

Greetings Telegrams

Greetings telegrams are suitable for messages of greeting, congratulation, etc. They are delivered written on special ornamental forms enclosed in a special greetings envelope. They are a little more expensive than ordinary telegrams.

Telegraphic Address

A telegraphic address is used by most businesses. The address generally consists of two words—the name and the town of delivery, e.g. "Jackson, Coventry".

Telephoning Telegrams

Telegrams may be sent by telephone at any hour of the day or night. Even though the message is being telephoned, a permanent record is still needed for the file. The operator should ask for "Telegrams" or dial the appropriate code and number. She must dictate to the post office operator her own telephone number and the message. If delivery is required by telephone the message should contain the addressee's name, telephone exchange name, if any, and telephone number, or, if the appropriate telephone number is not known, the word "Telephone" should be written before the address. It should be dictated clearly, two or three words at a time. When the post office operator reads back the message, it should be checked very carefully with the copy of the telegram dictated. The date and exact time when the telegram was telephoned should be noted.

Telegrams addressed to telephone subscribers are delivered by telephone until 2300 hours. A fully addressed telegram may also be delivered by telephone unless instructions have been received for delivery by messenger.

Sending Telegrams by Telex

If a telegram is sent by telex to a Post Office telegraph office the normal telegraph charges apply. The telex numbers to call are stated in the dialling code cards supplied to telex subscribers. If the message is to be sent to another telex user it must contain the addressee's name, telex number, the name of the post town and the word "Telex". A telegram addressed to a telex address will be delivered by telex at all times during the night or day, provided that the addressee's telex has been left switched on.

Overnight Telegrams

Overnight telegrams are accepted between 0800 and 2230 hrs daily for delivery next day, normally by the first post (except on Sundays and public holidays, when there is no postal delivery). The charges are less than those made for ordinary telegrams.

Prepaid Reply Telegrams

A reply to an inland telegram may be prepaid by the sender up to a limit of £1. A reply telegram form showing on the back the amount prepaid will be delivered with the telegram to the addressee. When a reply-paid telegram is delivered by telephone, the reply voucher is posted with the confirmatory copy of the telegram. The addressee may use the reply voucher in payment or part-payment for a telegram or a telephone account rendered by the Post Office.

Cancellation of Telegrams

A telegram may be cancelled by the sender after it has been accepted for transmission. If the request for cancellation is made before transmission has begun, the charges paid, less a small fee are refunded. If the message has already been transmitted, an official telegram is sent to the delivery office and the normal charge for the telegram made. If the cancellation telegram does not overtake the original before delivery, the sender is informed.

Confidential Telegrams

Special instructions, for example "Confidential" may be written on the outside of the envelope in which the telegram is delivered. These instructions should be written in front of the address on the telegram form and are charged for as part of the message.

Overseas Telegrams

International telegrams may be sent to most parts of the world, to ships in port, to aircraft at airports and to trains at railway stations abroad. The charges and full details are given in the *Post Office Guide*.

TELEPRINTERS

A teleprinter is an instrument, resembling a typewriter in appearance and operation, for sending and receiving urgent messages, in code form, over a telegraph or a telephone line. (See Fig. 10.) It reproduces the typewritten message instantly at one or more points. At these points teleprinters are engaged to receive the message, which is then translated into roman characters and printed.

Telex Service

The main teleprinter communication service in Britain is known as Telex and is maintained by the Post Office. It provides a quick means of communication in printed form among subscribers, combining the speed of the telephone with the authority of the printed word. The printed copy of the message is produced on teleprinters at both the sending and receiving subscribers' installations. Calls may be made to any Telex subscriber in the

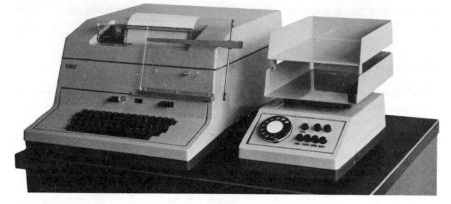

Fig. 10 Telex Teleprinter
(Reproduced by permission of the Post Office)

United Kingdom and to subscribers in certain countries overseas, including the USA. The service is available day and night and messages may be transmitted to a subscriber even though his teleprinter is unattended, provided it has been switched on. The message is then available for attention when the operator returns to the machine. The rental charge covers the provision and full maintenance of the teleprinter, sound reducing cover, table and control unit, and the line to the Telex exchange.

Telex calls are charged according to their distance and duration. Directly dialled inland calls are charged at $1\frac{1}{2}$p per unit. A unit may be of 15, 30 or 60 seconds duration according to the distance of the call. Many of the calls to telex subscribers abroad can be dialled direct, but calls to certain countries have to be made via an operator at the International Telex Switchboard in London. The charges for overseas telex calls which are dialled direct vary from country to country. Current rates are given in a Post Office booklet entitled "International Charges". For overseas calls which cannot be dialled direct the minimum charge is for a period of three minutes.

A correspondent is called by dialling his Telex number. The operator must then wait until the correspondent's answerback code appears on her teleprinter. Every Telex subscriber is given an answerback code for identification purposes. These codes and the Telex numbers are contained in the United Kingdom Telex Directory, which is issued by the Post Office every six months. On receipt of the correspondent's answerback code, the operator sends her own code and then proceeds to send the message. When she has finished she repeats her answerback code and then waits to see the correspondent's code to confirm that the full message had been transmitted.

Punched Tape

Punched tape increases the speed and flexibility of telegraphic communications. A code for the message to be transmitted is punched across the tape, i.e. code signs are represented by punched holes and spaces are shown by leaving the tape unperforated. The code used on punched tape for telegraph purposes is the standard teleprinter code.

Perforating equipment containing a teleprinter-type keyboard is used for preparing the punched tape for transmission and it combines the functions of perforating the tape with typing a printed copy of the message. The punched tape is fitted into an automatic transmitter and the teleprinter is connected to the Telex line. The keyboard is operated to call the required subscriber, and, when the connection has been made, the line is instantly switched over to the automatic tape transmitter. By using automatic transmission equipment an operator can prepare messages on tape before a call is made and then transmit them automatically at about 70 words a minute— twice the normal speed of an operator. The time occupied on the line is kept down to the absolute minimum; a factor of great importance as telex calls are charged on a time basis.

Telegraphic Data Transmission Services

Facilities are provided by the Post Office for transmitting over telephone or telegraph lines information prepared in the form of punched tape ready for use by a computer. These services, which are known as Datel Services, comprise circuits, i.e. the particular type of line, and the necessary equipment to enable punched tape to be transmitted. A head office, in which a computer has been installed may, for example, receive the input information from its branches by one of the Datel services. On receipt of the data from the telephone or teleprinter the head office will feed it into a computer, where it will be read, processed and the results printed. The data from all the branches of the firm can be in the possession of the head office without postal delays and overall up-to-the-minute figures are readily available. Many banks in large cities are using teleprinter or telephone data processing techniques for conveying financial information from their branches to a central computer. By this means all the branches linked to the central computer have their processed results available at bank opening time the following morning.

Telegrams Transmitted by Teleprinter

Telegrams can also be sent from a teleprinter to the Post Office and Cable and Wireless Telegraph Offices for transmission and incoming telegrams can be received directly on to the teleprinter from the telegraph office. Telegrams are then received and sent much more quickly than is possible through the usual channels.

Private Teleprinters

Where an organization does not require the public communication facilities offered by Telex, it may install a private teleprinter service of its own. The machines are installed in the organization's premises and the link between teleprinters may be a short internal line from one office to another in the same building or a line between premises many miles apart. The private lines are hired from the Post Office. When there is more than one distant teleprinter in operation it is necessary for a switchboard to be used to link up the different teleprinters.

QUESTIONS

1. Prepare a telegram to convey the following message in a condensed form:
   I shall arrive tomorrow by the midday train and should be glad if you would be at the station to meet me.

2. Prepare a list of instructions to guide a new employee in the preparation of telegrams.

3. Business letters, telegrams, cables and the telephone all have a part to play in commerce. Discuss their uses, giving examples of occasions when each is specially suitable. *Assoc. Examining Board, G.C.E.*

4. Prepare the following message for transmission by telegram:
   Will you please arrange to attend at this office for an interview with our Mr J. Lycett at 1600 hrs. on Monday next, 14th April, and not, as you were originally informed, tomorrow.

5. Write a cable, not exceeding twenty words in length (excluding names and addresses), to your employer, who is abroad on holiday, informing him of the following circumstances:
   You are the first to arrive at your office one morning, to find the caretaker waiting for you. He is in a state of great agitation. He tells you that he saw a man in a raincoat, with no hat or gloves, and carrying a briefcase, running down the stairs of your building. The caretaker thought the circumstances suspicious, and he had tried the doors of several offices, to find that yours had been forced. When he entered the room he found papers thrown all over the floor, a vase of flowers broken, ink on the carpet, desk drawers open, and the safe-door open. You go with the caretaker, and see that the safe is empty. You know that when you left last night it contained £150 in cash and £50 worth of insurance stamps. You ask him if he has telephoned the police, find that he has not, and do so yourself. The police

arrive, examine the room, and take statements from other members of staff. *R.S.A. SD.2*

6. Explain the following details featured on a Company's headed notepaper:

452 2233 (STD Code 061)
Telex 23721
Cables MANCUNIAN STOCKPORT

In what circumstances would you use these methods of communication? *R.S.A. OP.1*

7. You have travelled to Italy with the Buyer of your Company which imports Italian woollen goods, shoes and jewellery. He still has one important factory to visit when he receives a cable from his Managing Director asking him to return to a sales conference in two days time. Remembering that cables from the continent of Europe are expensive, draft a reply by cable to the Managing Director asking for a further decision. *R.S.A. SD.2*

8. (*a*) What are the uses of the Post Office Telex Service in business?
   (*b*) What are the advantages of using a Telex fitted with punched tape?
   (*c*) Explain the basis on which Telex calls are charged. *R.S.A. OP.2*

9. What would you consider to be the best method of communication to be used by a firm's Head Office in London for each of the following?
   (*a*) A detailed financial document to be delivered the same day to its branch in Manchester.
   (*b*) A message from the Accounts Department to the Central Filing Room requesting a file.
   (*c*) A message to a person in Birmingham (not on the telephone) cancelling an appointment arranged for tomorrow.
   (*d*) An order to be placed with a firm in New York.
   (*e*) Contact with a business associate in Oxford with the intention of influencing his decision on a new project.
   (*f*) A message of complaint to be sent to a firm in Hull.
   (*g*) A congratulatory message to the General Manager's Private Secretary on the occasion of her wedding.
   (*h*) Conveying input information from branches to the firm's central computer at Head Office.
Give reasons for your answers. *R.S.A. OP.2*

10. (*a*) Why is the telegram now so seldom used in business?
    (*b*) Give two alternative methods of sending urgent messages and briefly state your reasons for your choice. *R.S.A. OP.1*

Chapter 5
Reception

The first impression a visitor gains of an organization is influenced by the manner in which he is received at the Reception Office. The office itself should be attractively furnished and designed in every way to impress the caller, and the receptionist must possess the necessary personal qualities and business skills to greet him pleasantly and efficiently.

The receptionist's appearance and manner are very important in creating the right impression and since she provides the first means of communication with the visitor she must have the ability to speak clearly. As the receptionist has to be in contact by telephone with many people throughout the organization she also requires a good telephone manner. She requires tact in order to smooth over difficult situations which may arise such as explaining to a caller that it is not convenient for an executive to see him. In these circumstances she should explain to the caller that the executive is in a meeting or he is away from the office and, if appropriate, an appointment can be arranged on a convenient date for both parties. Alternatively, the visitor may be satisfied in seeing another member of staff who can deal with his business. Skill in handling people and the ability to act tactfully on her own initiative are very important in this essential role of receiving and entertaining callers.

The receptionist requires a comprehensive knowledge of the firm, including its activities, the range of products or services it offers and the role of all personnel. Organization charts, company literature and house journals are useful sources of information which the receptionist may use to keep herself fully informed on these matters.

In a small firm the receptionist will usually combine the work of receiving visitors with operating a telephone switchboard, typewriting and routine clerical work. In a large firm where there is a constant flow of visitors, the receptionist will, however, spend most of her time receiving visitors. In large organizations the reception office may also be responsible for making travel arrangements.

At the beginning of each day the receptionist should be notified of all the appointments made and the movements of executives so that she is able to act without undue hesitancy when visitors arrive.

On arrival visitors are usually asked to sign a visitors book or enter particulars of their visit in a register of callers (see Fig. 11). This provides a useful permanent record of all visitors to the firm.

DATE	NAME OF CALLER	FIRM	TIME OF ARRIVAL	REFERRED TO
197– Jan 1	P.L. Jones	K & S Smith Ltd	0930	R. Evans
" 1	R.C. Ware	} North Eastern	10 15	C. Gillespie
" 1	V. Coleman	} Finance Ltd		
" 1	C. Giles	Giles & Porter Bros	1500	M. Norton
" 1	E. Chapman	Felgate Motors Ltd	1530	R. Evans

Fig. 11 Register of Callers

A visitor from another firm may introduce himself by offering the receptionist a business visiting card such as the one in Fig. 12 below which provides his name, firm and his position in the firm.

Fig. 12 Business Visiting Card

If no card is offered the receptionist should make her own note of these details.

The receptionist should retain the card as it provides the relevant information for informing the appropriate member of staff of the visitor's arrival and for making the necessary introduction. When the visitor makes his request known the receptionist must give him her undivided attention so that he does not have to repeat information. Whilst the receptionist is contacting the requested member of staff or his secretary, the visitor should be seated and offered some reading matter. If there is a delay in arranging for the visitor to be seen by the member of staff it is polite to apologize to the visitor and explain the reason for the delay.

The member of staff, or his secretary, may collect the visitor from the Reception Office or the receptionist may be expected to accompany the visitor to the appropriate office. In this case the visitor must be politely and efficiently escorted to the office he is visiting. If no one is present on arrival at the office, the receptionist must refer the visitor to the secretary or wait with the visitor until the person arrives. Under no circumstances should callers be shown into an executive's room before the executive has been informed. When introducing the visitor, the receptionist must announce his name, title and company clearly. The visitor's name should be given before the name of the executive, but when introducing a man and a woman, it is courteous to announce the woman's name first.

The receptionist should endeavour to use the visitor's name during conversation with him and she should know by name the visitors who call regularly. If a secretary is required to deal with a caller herself, a note of the interview must be typed and taken into her employer's office as soon as possible.

The secretary's personality, tact and discretion are very important when she is called upon to take appropriate action in an emergency such as the one posed in a Royal Society of Arts Secretarial Duties examination given below; the essential lines of action which might be taken are given in the suggested answer.

Question

Mr X calls at your office to see your employer, who has forgotten about the appointment and is now lunching at his club with an important overseas client. How would you deal with the situation? *R.S.A. SD.2*

Answer

1. On Mr X's arrival the secretary should verify the details of the appointment from her diary and her employer's diary.

2. The secretary should apologize to Mr X and explain that her employer has been called away unexpectedly to see an important overseas client. She

should ascertain from Mr X the nature of his business and whether it is urgent or not.

3. Two lines of action could then be taken:

(*a*) If the matter is urgent and a decision must be made by the employer, the employer's deputy should be asked to entertain Mr X to lunch, at the usual hotel, while the secretary contacts her employer at the club.

(*b*) If the matter is not urgent, the secretary should ask the employer's deputy to take Mr X to lunch and see if he can help him in any way. If Mr X prefers to leave the matter until he can talk to the employer, another appointment should be made for him during the next day or two. This should be confirmed in writing or by telephone as soon as the employer has agreed to accept the revised date.

4. Type a memo. of the action taken and place it on the employer's desk for him to see immediately on his return from the Club.

In a well-run office a problem of this kind should never occur, as an efficient private secretary uses her diaries effectively and warns her employer of future appointments.

QUESTIONS

1. Reception duties form part of many secretarial posts and some callers do not have appointments. Describe the secretary's role in:
   (*a*) Receiving callers with appointments.
   (*b*) Dealing with callers without appointment. *L.C.C. P.S.C.*

2. Your firm has an Enquiry Office which houses the switchboard and to which visitors come on arrival. You relieve the receptionist/switchboard operator when she is not there. What steps should you take when a visitor calls? *R.S.A. SD.2*

3. What is the purpose of a receptionist's card index of visitors to a firm? *R.S.A. SD.2*

4. What information should the full-time receptionist of a large firm have on hand? *R.S.A. SD.2*

5. What use would you, as a receptionist, make of the following:
   (*a*) internal telephone directory;
   (*b*) company literature;
   (*c*) a diary? *R.S.A. OP.1*

6. Certain points should be borne in mind when dealing with callers. Mention
   (*a*) three such points in relation to personal calls at the reception desk;
   (*b*) two in respect of telephone calls. *R.S.A. OP.1*

7. What information is normally printed on a business visitor's card? In what ways is this information useful to a receptionist? *R.S.A. OP.1*

8. On 5th June, 197–, the following people called at the Reception Desk of Grosvenor Engineering Ltd.:

Mr Roger Brook of B & C Electronics saw the Managing Director at 10.15 a.m.

At 11.05 a.m. Miss V. Davids requested an appointment with the Personnel Department on private business.

The Marine Department received Mr C. Kavil of A. Peters Ltd. at 4.00 p.m.

Mr G. T. Robinson came at 9.30 a.m. for an appointment in the Diesel Department. (He is a representative of Tabco Ltd.)

Mr D. Samuels of Fitzroy Ltd. arrived at 2.00 p.m. for an appointment in the Sales Department.

Enter the particulars of these callers, in the order in which they arrived, in a Register of Callers. Use the 24-hour time system. *R.S.A. OP.1*

9. An important, but very impatient, man calls to see your employer who can see him either in an hour's time or on another day at a time to be arranged. Explain how you would deal with this caller. *R.S.A. SD.2*

10. What is the purpose of having a secretary to interview callers before they are shown into the employer's office?

Chapter 6
Methods of Payment

The following methods of payment may be used in a business office:

(a) Postage stamps.
(b) Cash (including registration and COD).
(c) Postal orders.
(d) Inland telegraph money orders.
(e) Overseas postal and money orders.
(f) National Giro.
(g) Cheques.
(h) Credit transfers.
(i) Credit cards.
(j) Bills of exchange.

Postage Stamps

Postage stamps are used as a means of payment only for very small sums. Many firms inform their customers that they will not accept postage stamps in payment of their accounts. If they accept them the stamps have to be used in their own postal department or forwarded to the Post Office for repurchase. The sum to be remitted should not usually exceed 5p. Postage stamps are commonly used in payment for brochures, booklets, small items ordered by mail or small refunds.

Cash

Coins and notes may be sent through the post provided they are registered. See page 23 for details of registration. A trader may use cash to settle accounts when a traveller calls, as is frequently done in a small retail business. Offices normally use cash to make small payments necessary for the running of their business, and a petty cash account is kept of these amounts. Wages and salaries are also paid in cash.

Postal Orders

Postal orders are a convenient method of remitting small sums, up to the value of £10, by post. They are issued by the Post Office for 5p, by 2½p steps up to 25p, by 5p steps up to £1 and by £1 steps up to £10. In addition to the face value a poundage is charged.

Up to 4½p in postage stamps may be affixed on all postal orders.

The sender should complete the name of the payee and the office of payment on the postal order. The postal order may be crossed to ensure that payment is made only through a bank. A counterfoil is attached to it, and should be completed and kept for reference. (See Fig. 13.)

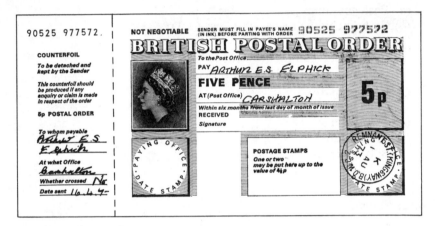

Fig. 13 A Postal Order
(Reproduced by permission of the Post Office)

The payee must sign the postal order and present it for payment at a post office unless it has been crossed, in which case, it should be signed and paid into the payee's bank account.

A postal order is valid for six months from the last day of the month of issue. After the expiration of that period, the order should be referred to the nearest post office or sent to the local head postmaster. If, after the necessary inquiry, payment is authorized, commission equal to the poundage will be charged.

Telegraphic Money Orders

An inland money order for any sum not exceeding £100 may be transmitted to the payee by telegraph. The issuing office sends a telegram of advice to the paying office. The sender must pay:

(*a*) the cost of the telegram;

(*b*) the money order poundage;

(*c*) the charge for any private message that is sent with the order.

To cash a telegraphic money order the payee must take it to the post office named. The payee must disclose to the post office clerk his name and the name of the remitter, and, provided these agree with the post office records, the money will be handed over after the order has been signed by the payee.

Overseas Postal and Money Orders

Postal orders and money orders are issued to most countries within the British Commonwealth and to many foreign countries. Special rates are applicable, details of which are given in the *Post Office Guide*. Payment is made in the currency of the country of payment at the equivalent value of the British currency. When cashing a money order abroad, the payee is required to produce documentary evidence of his identity.

THE NATIONAL GIRO

National Giro is a money transfer banking service operated by the Post Office. It provides a current account banking service through a single organization (the Post Office) with an extensive network of post offices at which money can be paid and withdrawn. Whether the account holder uses the mail service or attends personally at a post office counter, his instructions for payments, transfers or deposits reach the Giro Centre direct and not via the person or company with whom he is dealing. Instructions are processed by computer on the day they are received in the Giro Centre and statements of account and supporting documents are dispatched on the same day, thus providing a 24-hour clearing service.

A business using the Giro system does not lack the information that it would acquire from a remittance sent directly to it with a covering letter, as the Giro forms contain message spaces and the form, as filled in by the remitter, accompanies each day's statement of account when it goes to the firm.

It is also possible for Giro payment orders or transfer forms to be passed direct from remitter to payee. The payment order can, for example, be used in exactly the same way as a cheque and it can be sent, with a covering letter or other document, direct to the payee, but payment is not effected until it has been cleared at the Giro Centre.

Any person over the age of fifteen, business concerns and other organizations are entitled to open a Giro account on depositing a minimum of £1.

Deposits

An account holder wishing to pay money into his own account must complete a deposit form and hand it in with the money to a Post Office. Cheques deposited must, however, be sent direct to the Giro Centre and they are not credited until they are cleared through the bank's clearing house. No interest is payable on money deposited in a Giro account.

Transfers

A transfer from one Giro account to another is made by completing a transfer/deposit form with the Giro number of the account holder to whom the transfer is to be made, the amount to be paid and the remitter's signature, and forwarding it by post to the Giro Centre. Any message relating to the purpose of the payment may be written on the back of the form. The minimum amount which can be transferred is 25p. No charge is made for this service.

Payments

The payment order resembles a cheque and it may be made out to self, to another person or to a company. It can be crossed for payment into a bank account. If it is not crossed, the town where payment is to be made should be specified. An account holder sending a payment of more than £100 is required to specify the exact post office of payment. Payment orders must be sent to the Giro Centre, where they are authenticated and sent on to the payee. A charge is made for each Girocheque payable to someone without a Giro account.

An account holder who has nominated a post office for payments on demand can withdraw up to £20 at either of two post offices nominated, provided he does not do this more often than every other day. Larger sums may be withdrawn by arrangement with a post office.

Giro Systems

The Giro may be used for collecting money and making payments in the following ways:

(1) *The Giro Billing System*

A Giro transfer/inpayment form may be incorporated as part of an invoice. Purchasers who have Giro accounts merely have to sign their names and post the forms to the Giro Centre. Those who do not have accounts can simply take the forms to their local post offices and hand them in with the money and a small fee. Each day all the forms received are processed in the Giro Centre and forwarded to the firms issuing the invoices, accompanied by a statement listing all the transactions.

(2) *Automatic Debit Transfer*

A firm or organization wishing to collect payments in this way must first agree with those of its customers who have Giro accounts that they are willing to have their payments automatically debited when due. When the invoices are sent out to customers they are informed of the day on which the transfer will be carried out and, at an agreed time, the collecting firm will forward to the Giro Centre instructions which must include details of its own account number, the account number of each customer, the amount involved and the date on which each transfer is to be carried out. The transfers are then carried out by the Giro Centre on the due date and on the following day the collecting firm will receive a statement showing details of the transfers made.

(3) *Standing Orders*

Standing Orders, similar to the service provided by banks, may be placed with the Giro Centre for the regular transfer of fixed sums between account holders.

(4) *Periodic Payments without Standing Orders*

An organization collecting periodic payments from customers or members who do not wish to pay by standing order is able to issue books of Giro transfer/inpayment forms preprinted with the collecting firm's Giro number, amount, customer's reference number, the date due and the customer's Giro number (if known). A Giro customer merely signs the form, inserts his account number, if necessary, and sends it to the Giro Centre. A non-Giro customer must take the form with the amount due and a small charge to a local post office.

(5) *Collection from Agents*

Mail order firms may arrange for their agents to use the Giro deposit service to pay in the money they have collected. Each agent is issued with a set of Giro deposit forms containing the firm's Giro number and the agent's reference number, and the amounts collected can be paid in at post office counters with the Giro deposit form.

(6) *Mail Order Transactions*

People who buy goods by post are able to use the Giro transfer or inpayment service. A Giro account holder writes the order in the message space on a transfer/deposit form and sends the completed form to the firm via the Giro Centre. A person without an account can write the order on an inpayment form (see Fig. 14) at a post office and hand in the completed form with the money. The firm receives each day all the orders on Giro inpayment and transfer forms together with the daily statements.

Fig. 14 Giro Inpayment Form
(Reproduced by permission of the Post Office)

(7) *Payment of Salaries, Wages and Occupational Pensions*

The Giro transfer service may be used for the payment of salaries, wages and occupational pensions, provided that employees are willing to open Giro accounts. The Giro payment order service is also a convenient way of paying dispersed employees who do not hold Giro accounts as it is cheaper than using registered post or postal orders.

Giro Directories

Giro directories are published at regular intervals giving details of account holders' names, addresses and account numbers.

BANKING

A bank offers the following services to its customers:

1. It provides facilities to deposit money at interest.

2. Lends money to approved borrowers (bank loans and bank overdrafts).

3. By the cheque system, provides an easy and safe means of payment (current account).

4. Accepts standing orders, i.e. makes regular payment of bills.

5. Direct Debiting.

6. Transfers credit by means of credit transfers or credit cards.

7. Provides facilities for withdrawing cash from cash dispensers (cash cards).

8. Issues gift cheques (certain banks only).

9. Discounts bills of exchange.

10. Provides drafts, letter payments and telegraphic transfers for foreign payments.

11. Issues foreign currency and travellers' cheques.

12. Takes charge of customers' securities, e.g. stock and share certificates, jewellery and other valuables.

13. Provides night safe facilities.

14. Acts as executor and/or trustee.

15. Obtains information for customers concerning investments and makes investments on their behalf.

Various kinds of banking accounts are available:

Deposit Account

A deposit account is an account into which a customer's money is put in order to earn interest. The banker reserves the right of asking the customer to give him several days' notice of withdrawal, but this right is rarely exercised. As the bank has the use of the customer's money for a definite period, it is able to pay interest on the amount invested. The money is not drawn out of a deposit account by cheque, but by submitting a withdrawal form. Usually the depositor will open a current account in addition to a deposit account, and any surplus money above current requirements is then transferred on request to a deposit account so that it may earn interest.

Current Account

A current account is an account into which payments are made and on which cheques are drawn. Money is paid into a current account by the use of a paying-in book or slip and withdrawals are made by cheque. This form of payment is of great importance and is used both for business and private transactions.

Home Safe Account

A home safe account is intended to encourage small savings and is ideal for children. The bank issues a metal safe, into which the customer puts his spare cash. The safe is taken to the bank from time to time, where it is opened and the contents placed to the customer's credit in a home safe deposit account, upon which interest is paid to the customer.

Opening a Current Account

When opening a current account with a bank, a customer will be asked to provide the following:

1. Two references (preferably from other customers who are willing to vouch for the applicant's financial reliability).

2. A specimen signature in the way in which the cheques will be signed. This is necessary for reference where a signature on a presented cheque needs to be verified.

3. If a joint account is being opened, both parties must sign a mandate authorizing the banker to honour cheques with both signatures or with individual signatures.

If a change of style of signature is adopted the bank must be informed.

The bank provides the new customer with:

1. A cheque book;
2. A bank statement;
3. A paying-in book.

Cheque Book

A cheque is a written order to a bank to pay on demand a stated sum of money and bears the name of the person to whom it is to be paid.

The banks provide specially printed cheques, bound up in book form. Each cheque has a serial number which is recorded when the book is issued. Counterfoils are attached to the cheques, upon which particulars on the actual cheque are repeated for record purposes. The cheques are supplied in a variety of sizes and descriptions, but the private customer will normally require a pocket-size cheque.

Bank Statement

The bank statement is a small account sheet, on which the bank enters a record of all the transactions between the customer and itself involving the receipt and payment of money. It is generally supplied in the form of a loose-leaf folder.

The balance of the bank statement is what the bank has in hand of the customer's money in the current account. It may not agree with what the customer thinks should be to his credit because of the following reasons:

1. cheques paid into the bank but not credited;
2. unpresented cheques;
3. bank charges;
4. standing order payments.
5. credit transfers.

A business would make out a reconciliation statement in order to show why the cash book and bank statement balances disagree.

A typical bank statement is given in Fig. 15.

Paying-in Book

A paying-in book is used for recording payments made into a current account. Each page is divided into two or three parts by perforated lines. One part is kept by the bank and the other part(s) is left in the book and retained by the customer as an acknowledgement of the amount paid in. The bank clerk will initial and stamp the customer's copy. The precise details of the money paid in (cash, notes, cheques, etc.) must be stated. (*See* Fig. 16.)

A branch advice system enables a customer to pay money into his own account at any branch of the bank concerned. Moreover, a customer of one bank can pay in at a branch of any other bank. For example, a customer with an account at a bank in Brighton can pay in at a different bank in a small country town where there is no branch of his own bank.

Standing Orders

A customer may give a banker a standing order to pay a certain sum of money periodically from his current account to a person or business.

Lloyds Bank

Statement of account with Lloyds Bank Limited

COLCHESTER

D | Sheet number 5 *

All entries to 22FEB73 inclusive are complete.

S FOREST ESQ
31 ANY STREET
COLCHESTER
ESSEX

Description of entries
BGC Bank Giro Credit
DIV Dividend
D/D Direct Debit
S/O Standing Order
Cheques are designated by the serial number

FOREST S

Account number 0187342

Date	Particulars		Payments	Receipts	Balance When overdrawn marked OD	
1973	Opening Balance				49 67	*
15JAN	CREDIT BY POST			11 03		
		149703	30 00		30 70	*
19JAN	SUNDRY CREDIT			19 28		
		149706	13 65			
		149707	5 42			
		149708	55 05		24 14	OD
22JAN		149711	12 17			
	CASHPOINT CARD 1		20 00			
	CASHPOINT CARD 1		18 00			
		149710	1 50		75 81	OD
25JAN	BANK GIRO CREDIT			266 27	190 46	*
29JAN	DAVIES & NEWMAN	DIV		25 75	216 21	*
30JAN	LEGAL & GENERAL	D/D	9 50			
	LOAN A/C	S/O	15 00		191 71	*
31JAN	KALAMAZOO	DIV		8 51	200 22	*
1FEB	BUCKS CC	DIV		7 14		
	SHELL T & T	DIV		13 21	220 57	*
6FEB		149701	60 00			
	CASHPOINT CARD 1		14 00		146 57	*
13FEB	INVESTMENTS SOLD			209 15	355 72	*
14FEB	LEEDS P B S	S/O	20 50		335 22	*
20FEB		149712	192 36		142 86	*
22FEB	CASHPOINT CARD 1		20 00		122 86	*

The items and balance shown on this statement should be verified and any enquiries directed to the above Branch

Fig. 15 A Bank Statement
(Reproduced by permission of Lloyds Bank Ltd.)

Date 2nd Aug 1973

NOTES: £20		
£10	60	
£5	70	
£1	35	
	3	
COINS: 50p	1	50
SILVER		75
BRONZE		25
TOTAL OF CASH	170	50
CHEQUES, P.O.'S ETC.	225	48
CASHIER'S STAMP AND INITIALS	395	98

5c
R.9.71

Date 2nd Aug 1973 | CODE NO. 30 – 97 – 81 | LLOYDS BANK LIMITED | BANK GIRO CREDIT

CASHIER'S STAMP AND INITIALS

TO: BANK LLOYDS
BRANCH SOUTHAMPTON ROW
ACCOUNT IN NAME OF A. GREY
PAYEE'S ACCOUNT NUMBER 17814127

Paid in by T Grey

NOTES: £20	60	
£10	70	
£5	35	
£1	3	
COINS: 50p	1	50
SILVER		75
BRONZE		25
TOTAL OF CASH	170	50
CHEQUES, P.O.'S ETC. 110 33 / 23 43 / 91 72	225	48
£	395	98

Fig. 16 Paying-in Slip
(Reproduced by permission of Lloyds Bank Ltd.)

The customer does not then have the trouble of remembering the dates of payment and writing and posting the cheques. The instructions, which must be given to the banker in writing, must contain the amount, dates and payee's name and bank. Standing orders are commonly used for paying customers' private financial commitments, such as monthly mortgage repayments, annual subscriptions and insurance premiums, etc.

Direct Debiting

Direct debiting is another method of arranging for a bank to make periodic payments on behalf of its customer. When the standing order method is used the drawer initiates the instruction to make payment, but in the case of direct debiting it is the payee who requests the bank to collect an amount from the drawer's account. This method can be used for fixed amounts at fixed dates or for varying amounts at irregular intervals.

The payee may send the drawer an invoice and, after an agreed interval, arrange for the bank to automatically transfer the appropriate amount of credit. By this process the drawer is given an opportunity to check the amount concerned.

The payee must in all cases have written authority from the drawer in order to arrange for direct debiting to take place.

Credit Transfers (or Bank Giro)

A credit transfer enables the customer to pay his creditors without having to prepare separate cheques for each account. A list, containing the names of the creditors and the amounts to be paid, is sent to the bank once a month together with a cheque for the total amount. The bank then arranges for credit slips to be sent out to the various creditors through their banks. Each creditor participating in this scheme must first be approached and must give written authority for payment to be made to him in this form.

A big saving can be made in stationery, postage and time, and, if an accounting machine or copy writer board system is used, the bank lists, credit advices and the journal are compiled simultaneously.

The credit transfer system can be employed not only by a trader for the payment of his creditors, but also by an individual for transferring money into a bank account of a person or business whom he wishes to pay. The remitter takes the bill into any bank, where he will be required to complete a credit transfer slip, giving his own name and address, the name of the payee, the payee's bank and branch, the amount of money, and the date. The amount of the bill is paid over the counter of the bank with the credit transfer slip and a small charge. The bank clerk will initial and stamp the counterfoil and return it to the remitter as a form of receipt for the money. The credit transfer slips are then sent to the bankers' clearing house, which distributes them to the various banks, and the payee's account is credited with the amount of the bill. After the bank has recorded the payment the slip is sent on to the payee for his information.

By this system payments are made directly into a bank account instead of cash, postal orders, or cheques being handled by the payee. It is also possible for bank customers to have their salaries, commissions, etc., paid straight into their accounts by credit transfers.

Credit Cards

The credit card system enables a person to purchase goods on credit at shops or other establishments which have agreed to participate in the scheme. A card holder may also withdraw cash up to his credit limit without prior notice, from any branch of the bank group participating in the scheme.

The individual is notified of his credit limit, which is the maximum amount that he can owe to the bank at any time. He also receives a plastic credit card which must be submitted to the supplier when ordering goods or services. The supplier makes out a sales voucher in duplicate which is signed by the purchaser and has an impression inserted on it from the credit card. The supplier retains the copy of the sales voucher and issues the customer with the second copy. The Credit Card Centre issue each card holder with a monthly statement of the amount owing and, provided the card holder makes a payment not later than twenty-five days after the date on the statement, no charge is incurred. The supplier deposits the sales vouchers at a branch of the bank and is credited with the amounts less discount.

The scheme has the effect of reducing the amount of cash carried by shoppers and handled by traders and also reduces the number of cheques in circulation, since card holders simply make out one cheque to the bank instead of separate cheques to each of their traders.

Cheque Cards

Certain banks will now issue to their current account holders a cheque card containing the holder's specimen signature and a code number which facilitates the acceptance of cheques by traders. A cheque up to the value of £30, accompanied by a cheque card, will normally be accepted by a trader as he is assured that such a cheque will be honoured by the bank on which it is drawn. Cheque card holders are also entitled to cash cheques up to £30 at any branch of the bank without prior arrangements or any additional charge being made.

This is not a credit card, but a card of authority which makes the cheque a more useful means of payment for the customer and relieves him of carrying substantial amounts of cash.

Cheque cards may also be used for obtaining cash at banks in Europe which display the Eurocheque "EC" symbol, but the foreign currency obtained must only be used for travel purposes. The cheques should be drawn in pounds sterling, maximum £30, out of which the foreign bank will deduct their commission.

Cash Dispensers

Cash cards may be issued to bank customers to enable them to withdraw cash from cash dispensers at any time of the day or night when the banks are closed. At the time when a cash card is issued to the customer he is told his personal number. He has to remember this as it is not recorded on his card or on any document for security reasons. If a cash card is lost or stolen it cannot be used for withdrawing cash unless the personal number is known. To obtain cash the card has to be inserted in a cash dispenser and the appropriate personal number tapped out on the machine buttons, which instructs the machine to issue ten £1 notes. The cash card is also returned for use on another occasion.

Crossed Cheques

Two parallel lines across the face of a cheque constitute a crossing and prevent its being cashed across the counter of a bank. The words "& Co." are commonly written between the lines, but they are not essential. A crossed cheque cannot be paid to anyone except a banker, i.e. the payee must pay the cheque into his banking account and his banker must collect the amount from the drawee banker and place it to the credit of the payee. If a person requires cash for a crossed cheque made payable to him he must either make out his own cheque in the usual way or complete and sign an exchange slip at the bank counter. Crossing does not prevent theft, but it provides a means of tracing the cheque, since the thief must use a bank account to obtain the money.

A crossing without any special directions is known as a general crossing. In the case of a general crossing, the drawee banker must pay the cheque to any banker who presents it for payment. A cheque with a general crossing is given in Fig. 17.

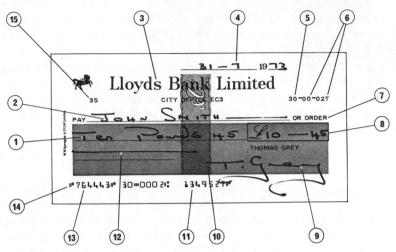

Fig. 17 A Specimen Cheque with a General Crossing
(Reproduced by permission of Lloyds Bank Ltd.)

Special Crossing

A cheque specially crossed must be paid only to the banker named on it and no other; for example, if "Midland Bank Ltd., Warwick" is written between the lines of a crossing, the cheque may only be paid into the Midland Bank at Warwick. An illustration of a special crossing is given in Fig. 18.

Midland Bank Ltd., Warwick

Fig. 18 A Special Crossing

A/c. Payee Only

The words "A/c. Payee Only" are written between the lines of the crossing to ensure that the cheque can only be paid into the account of the person to whom it is made out. (*See* Fig. 19.)

a/c Payee only

Fig. 19 A/c. Payee Only Crossing

Endorsing Over

A cheque which is made out to the payee "or order" may be passed on to a third party in payment of a debt instead of being cashed or credited to the payee's account. The payee will need to endorse the cheque before passing it on to the third party.

Cheques

There are three parties to a cheque:

(*a*) The drawer—the person who draws, i.e. signs a cheque and whose account will be debited.

(*b*) The drawee—the bank on which the cheque is drawn, i.e. the drawer's bank.

(*c*) The payee—the person to whom the cheque is made payable.

A cheque must always be written in pen and contain the points outlined in Fig. 17, the descriptions of which are as follows:

1. The amount of pounds in words.
2. The name of the payee.
3. The name and address of the drawee.
4. The date, written in the order of day, month and year.
5. The national number of the bank.
6. The branch number of the bank.
7. The description "or order" or "or bearer".
8. The amount in figures.
9. The signature of the drawer.
10. A general crossing—if required.
11. Drawer's account number.
12. Lines drawn to close up all blank spaces. The writing should be started well over to the left so that no spaces are left in which additional unauthorized words or figures could be inserted.
13. Serial number of the cheque.
14. Magnetic characters for sorting by electronic computer.
15. Internal sorting number.

"Order" Cheques

"Order" cheques are commonly used and are made payable to "... or order".

The Cheques Act, 1957, states that cheques and drafts paid into the payee's account need not be endorsed. There are exceptions: for example, certain cheques with receipts on the back, post office drafts and cheques paid in by third parties, e.g. a cheque payable to *A* paid into *B*'s account, requires *A*'s endorsement.

A cheque passing through a bank provides sufficient evidence of payment and many businesses no longer issue receipts where payment is made by cheque.

"Bearer" Cheques

"Bearer" cheques are made payable to ". . . or bearer". They do not require the payee's endorsement and the holder or bearer of the cheque is able to cash it or receive credit for it. On endorsement by the payee an "order" cheque is made into a "bearer" cheque.

Open Cheques

An open cheque is one which has not been crossed, i.e. it can be cashed over the counter of a bank.

Post-dated Cheques

A post-dated cheque is one which is dated ahead of the current date. A bank does not credit the customer's account with the amount of a post-dated cheque until the due date.

Stale Cheques

A stale cheque is one which is invalid because it has been drawn for some considerable time prior to presentation for payment. Validity normally expires after six months.

Alterations

If a mistake is made in writing a cheque and the drawer has to alter it, he should sign his name as near as possible to the alterations, as well as in the usual place, as in the example given in Fig. 20.

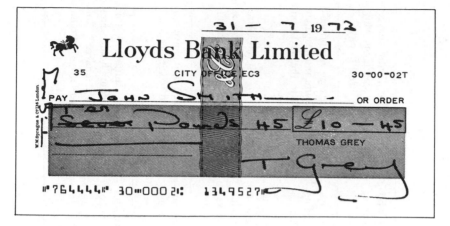

Fig. 20 An Altered Cheque
(Reproduced by permission of Lloyds Bank Ltd.)

Dishonoured Cheques

Dishonoured cheques are those which a banker has, for some reason or other, refused to pay on presentation. The reasons for refusal may be attributed to one of the following causes:

1. Words and figures differ.

2. There are insufficient funds.

3. Irregular endorsement, i.e. the name on the reverse of a cheque does not correspond with the payee's name on the front.

4. Drawer's signature differs, i.e. from that in the bank's records.

5. Notice of customer's death or act of bankruptcy, or that he has been certified as insane.

6. An alteration which requires signing.

7. A garnishee order (a notice sent to a person who owes money to judgment debtors) has been served on the banker.

8. The cheque is post-dated.

9. Payment has been stopped by the drawer.

Usually the bank on which the cheque is drawn marks the cheque with an explanation before returning it to the payee through his bank.

	Cheque	Bank Giro	National Giro
Direction of payment	Sent direct to payee by post.	Sent to drawer's bank who send it, via the Clearing House, to payee's bank.	Sent to Giro Centre; payee informed by statement. May also be sent direct to payee.
Time of payment	The payee will normally receive the cheque within 24 hours if posted by 1st class mail.	Delay of about three days whilst the transfer is being cleared and forwarded to payee's bank.	Giro Centre receive notification in 24 hours and despatch a statement to the payee on the same day.
Receipt of payment in payee's account	Payee must pay in cheque to his bank.	No handling by payee as it is paid by the bank into his account—no security risks.	When sent to Giro Centre there is no handling by payee as Giro pay it into his account —no security risks.
Accounts required	Drawer must have an account, but payee need not have one.	Drawer need not have an account but payee must have one.	Drawer need not have an account and payee need not have one.
Charges	Charge for bank services depending on amount of credit held.	Charge for bank services depending on amount of credit held	Charge for stationery for ordinary account holders and a service charge for Pay-through-Giro account holders.

Fig. 21 An Analysis and Comparison of Cheques, Bank Giro and National Giro

	Cheque	Bank Giro	National Giro
Cheques required	Separate cheque for each creditor.	One cheque may be used for several creditors providing a saving in stationery and postage.	Separate Giro cheque for each creditor but all forwarded to one Centre providing a saving in postage.
Hours of business	Bank hours.	Bank hours.	Post Office hours—longer than banks including Saturday mornings.
For payment of Wages	Safer than payment by cash and easier preparation, but may be inconvenient for employees to pay into bank, and withdraw cash during bank hours.	Safer than payment by cheque and more convenient for employer as all employees are paid by one cheque. Employee is not involved in attending bank for paying giro in but delay of notification of payment by bank (bank statement). Employee is required to attend bank during bank hours for withdrawal of cash.	Similar to a bank giro for security reasons. Paid by employer to Giro Centre but employee must attend post office (longer hours than banks) for withdrawal of cash. Fewer "current account" services available. All employees are paid by transfer incurring no charge on employer.

Fig. 22 An Analysis and Comparison of Cheques, Bank Giro and National Giro

To Stop Payment

The payment of a cheque, after issue, can be stopped by the drawer. The drawer should contact his bank and give the following information:

1. the date of the cheque;
2. the amount;
3. the name of the payee;
4. the serial number of the cheque, which can be obtained from the cheque counterfoil.

QUESTIONS

1. What is the difference between a deposit account and a current account? Under what circumstances would you use each?

2. State the services provided by (*a*) banks, (*b*) the post office, for the payment of money and give examples of the types of transactions in which each is specially useful. *Assoc. Examining Board, G.C.E.*

3. Suggest two methods (other than cash) of paying salaries and indicate what advantages might be gained (i) by employers and (ii) by employees from the adoption of such methods. *L.C.C. P.S.C.*

4. Name three ways of sending money by post. Say in what circumstances you would choose each of them and explain the procedures necessary. *R.S.A. OP.1*

5. (*a*) What is an open cheque?
   (*b*) What effect has a crossing on a cheque?
   (*c*) What is the effect of these particular crossings?

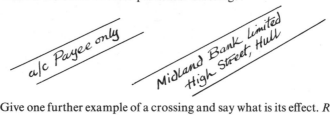

(*d*) Give one further example of a crossing and say what is its effect. *R.S.A. OP.1*

6. (*a*) Describe in as much detail as you can the Post Office Giro System.
   (*b*) Explain the purpose of two documents which are used in connection with Giro transactions. *R.S.A. COS.*

7. (*a*) How much money is needed to open a National Giro account?
   (*b*) What period of notice, if any, is needed to withdraw £10 from such an account? *R.S.A. SD.2*

8. (*a*) What is a Girocheque?
   (*b*) What is the main difference between a Girocheque and an ordinary bank cheque? *R.S.A. SD.2*

9. You have a bill of 50p to pay through the post for a booklet ordered for the office. State what methods of payment would be suitable, giving brief reasons. *R.S.A. SD.2*

10. At present you receive your wages weekly in cash. Your employer suggests that in future you should be paid monthly by means of a credit transfer to a bank account.

(*a*) What are the advantages and disadvantages for you in this method of payment?

(*b*) If you do not wish to open a bank account, what alternative would you suggest? Give your reasons. *R.S.A. SD.2*

11. (*a*) What is a Bank Credit card?

(*b*) How would the card be used by (i) the customer (ii) the seller? *R.S.A. OP.1*

12. (*a*) The Chief Accountant of your firm is considering the possibility of using traders' credits instead of cheques for the monthly payment of creditors. He asks you to assist him by investigating the matter and giving him a report on the advantages and disadvantages of traders' credits, together with details of the changes which would be necessary in the system for making payments. Prepare the necessary report.

(*b*) List other methods of payment which could be used. *R.S.A. OP.2*

13. What is the difference between:

(*a*) a telegraphic money order and a postal order

(*b*) the registration of a letter and using the Recorded Delivery Service and

(*c*) the telegraphic and Telex Services? *R.S.A. COS.*

14. Your firm has just opened a branch in a small town and wishes to open a bank account.

(*a*) If you were instructed to do this, what action would you take?

(*b*) Draft either a cheque form or a paying-in slip, and make specimen entries. *R.S.A. COS.*

15. If you were going for a holiday abroad how would you provide yourself with the necessary spending money? Where would you obtain it? *R.S.A. OP.1*

16. You have two personal accounts at your bank—a current account and a deposit account. Say briefly but clearly what steps you will take:

(*a*) to withdraw £20 from your current account;

(*b*) to withdraw from your deposit account. *R.S.A. OP.1*

17. (*a*) Why are cheques often used in payment of accounts?

(*b*) What effect has a crossing on a cheque?

(*c*) Is it customary to send a receipt if an account is paid by cheque? If not, why not?

(*d*) What action would you take if a creditor told you he had not received the cheque you sent him a week before? *R.S.A. OP.1*

18. (*a*) Explain how the services of a bank can be used in business.

(*b*) Name any other organizations which offer some similar services to those mentioned in your answer to (*a*). *R.S.A. OP.2*

19. State two advantages of using the National Giro. *R.S.A. SD.2*

20. State one advantage and one disadvantage to employees in being paid by each of the following methods:
    (*a*) credit transfer;
    (*b*) cash. *R.S.A. SD.2*

21. Your offices are situated in a house which has a garden at the back. A gardener works at the weekends when the office is closed. He has no bank account.
    Give three ways in which his wages of £3 a week could be sent to him. State which method you consider the best and why. *R.S.A. SD.2*

22. How would you turn the following into cash:
    (*a*) your salary which has been paid by credit transfer;
    (*b*) a telegraphic money order;
    (*c*) an open cheque? *R.S.A. SD.2*

Chapter 7
Filing and Indexing

A large part of the efficiency of an office depends not only on the existence of a reliable filing system but also on the competency of staff in the art of methodical filing and indexing. Filing is carried out for two primary reasons:

1. To preserve correspondence and other documents, i.e. keep them tidy and clean.

2. To have the information contained in the papers available for quick and easy reference.

Correspondence must be filed accurately so that it can be referred to quickly. A document filed incorrectly can be the cause of a delay in a business transaction and even the cancellation of a valuable order. Only when the filing system is efficient can the office function properly, as a delay in locating a paper will have the effect of interfering with and delaying the other sections of the business.

FILING SYSTEMS AND METHODS

Filing systems can be arranged in a variety of ways but there are several considerations to be taken into account in choosing a filing system. It must be:

(a) Quick and simple to operate.

(b) Easily accessible, i.e. the cabinets must be conveniently situated, and the files within the cabinets easy to locate.

(c) Suitable for the particular type of correspondence dealt with; the size, volume and nature of the correspondence must be considered.

(d) Organized to hold current papers only.

(e) Capable of expansion, if required.

(f) Appropriate in size, i.e. not using unnecessary space.

87

In a large organization filing may be organized centrally or departmentally. The points in favour of each of these methods are given.

Central Filing	*Departmental Filing*
1. All files are kept and controlled together in one room.	1. The departmental files are kept in the department and are, therefore, more readily available.
2. A clerk or number of clerks is able to specialize in filing and to administer the system efficiently.	2. The type of filing system may be employed which is most suitable for the correspondence with which the department deals, e.g. an export department would generally use a geographical system, whereas an advertizing department would find subject filing more useful.
3. Accommodation and equipment are economically used in the central arrangement of filing cabinets.	
4. A standardized system of filing can be established throughout the organization.	
5. More effective supervision is possible.	3. Departmental staff will have a better knowledge of the work of the department and should be more expert in filing departmental papers.
6. Files are more complete as all aspects of a subject are filed together and fewer copies of correspondence are required for departments.	4. It is more suitable for confidential files.
7. Effective and efficient follow-up and absent file systems can be organized.	5. The filing system is not so large and therefore is easier to handle.
	6. Departmental code letters may be employed in correspondence and on file titles for easy recognition, e.g. "S" for Sales Department, "A" for Accounts Department, etc.

METHODS OF CLASSIFICATION

General Alphabetical Filing

In the alphabetical method each folder contains the name of a correspondent and is arranged in strict alphabetical order. Guide cards, "miscellaneous" suspension files, or individual letter bars, may be used to divide the letters. The first letter of the surname (not Christian name) is the preliminary guide to the position of the file in the drawer. To determine the exact position of a file, the letters subsequent to the first letter of the surname are the determining factor, e.g. Collins, Thomas should be filed before Cryton, Philip.

Miscellaneous files are generally allocated to most letters of the alphabet for the purpose of holding small amounts of correspondence where individual files are not needed. An index of the correspondence contained in each

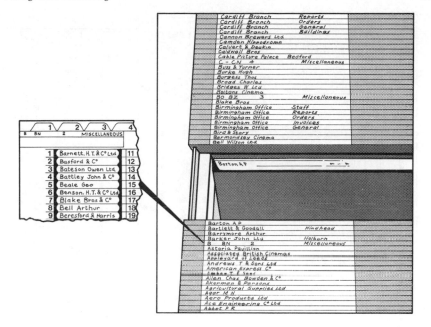

Fig. 23 General Alphabetical Method
(Reproduced by permission of Roneo Vickers Ltd.)

miscellaneous file should be given on the front cover of the file. An example of the general alphabetical method is given in Fig. 23.

Subject Filing

Instead of being filed under the name of the correspondents, letters are filed under subject headings. The subjects are filed in alphabetical order. The primary guides in subject filing give the main headings of the subjects which are relevant to the business, e.g. advertizing, shipping, sole agents, progress, purchasing, management, etc.

Most offices have a certain amount of correspondence which can be filed to advantage by subject. These subjects usually concern the general management of the business and its relation to branches, agencies, trade connexions, etc. The advantage of filing by subject is that all relevant data and correspondence are grouped together for quick and easy reference. (*See* Fig. 24.)

Geographical Filing

In the geographical method correspondence is classified according to the county, town, etc. The principle is identical with that of the general alphabetical and subject methods, except that papers are filed by alphabetically

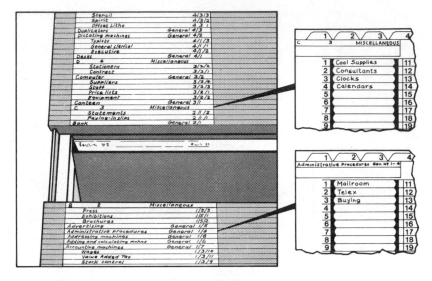

Fig. 24 Subject Method
(Reproduced by permission of Roneo Vickers Ltd.)

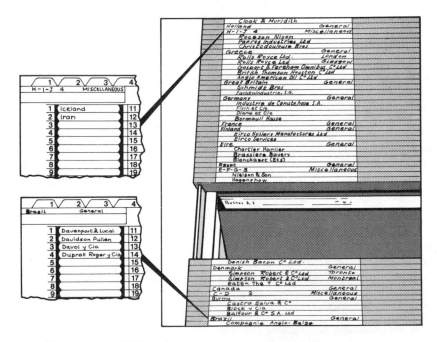

Fig. 25 Geographical Method
(Reproduced by permission of Roneo Vickers Ltd.)

arranged names of counties or towns instead of correspondents or subjects. This enables all correspondence relating to a country or town to be grouped together and individual files to be allocated to the agents or representatives. Obvious uses for geographical filing are in transport and export offices, planning departments and sales departments, where it is frequently necessary to group papers in district or territorial order. An illustration of this system is given in Fig. 25.

Numerical Filing

Files are arranged numerically, each correspondent being allotted a number. Index cards or index strips are required to connect the numbers with the names. Each index card contains the name of the correspondent and his allotted file number, and is arranged in alphabetical order in an index-card drawer.

When a certain file is required, the name of the correspondent is located in the index-card drawer, under the appropriate letter of the alphabet, and the number of the file ascertained. The numbered file can then be found in the appropriate filing cabinet.

Fig. 26 shows an example of the numerical method.

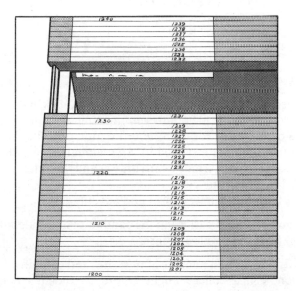

Fig. 26 Numerical Method
(Reproduced by permission of Roneo Vickers Ltd.)

The advantages and disadvantages of the alphabetical and numerical filing methods are given below:

Method	Advantages	Disadvantages
Alphabetical	1. A convenient method of grouping papers by firm, subject or location. 2. A direct and quicker method of filing without the need for a separate index. 3. Less cost in materials.	1. Difficulty may be experienced in locating common names. 2. Uncertainty of file location when subjects are used. 3. Difficult to assess space requirements for expansion.
Numerical	1. Numbered files are more easily found than alphabetical files and are less likely to be misplaced when they are returned. 2. The file number may be used on letters for reference. 3. Capable of indefinite expansion as new files are placed at the back of existing files. 4. The index card or strip may be employed for other purposes (see below).	1. Reference to an index causes a delay in locating a file. 2. More costly in materials and time taken to maintain the system. 3. Transposition of figures can be serious in misplacing papers and files.

A Card Index

A card index should provide an accurate and quick means of locating information, especially the file number in the numerical method of filing.

A separate card is used for each item (i.e. title of a file, book, client or patient), and the cards are arranged in strict alphabetical order. The cards are generally kept in a special index-card drawer and the letters of the alphabet are subdivided by projecting guide cards.

Index cards have the following uses and advantages:

1. Cards can be handled easily and the continuity of the alphabetical index is not affected by withdrawals and insertions.

2. The cards may serve a number of purposes and contain a large amount of information, e.g. a college might record a student's name, address, number, fee paid, date admitted, length of course, examinations passed, date left, employer's name and address, etc.

3. The information can be typed on to the cards.

4. Where classification is necessary for any special purpose, coloured cards and indicators can be used for easy identification.

5. Financial records may also be combined with other information on the cards and this is particularly useful where payments are made by instalments.

6. The index can be used to maintain a mailing list of names and addresses.

7. A note can be made when a file is taken away from the filing cabinet, and a clip-on metal signal fitted to the card.

Terminal Digit Filing

This is a variation of the numerical method of filing illustrated in Fig. 26. Files are arranged according to the last pair of digits of a number instead of the first as in the traditional numerical method. File numbers are broken down into groups of digits, e.g. 489 63 21 and all files ending with the same two numbers are grouped together behind a primary guide. The section allocated for 21 will, for example, contain file numbers 21 6321 4896321 721 and all numbers terminating with 21. Within the 21 section of the filing cabinet the files will be further subdivided into a secondary section according to the two digits preceding the final pair. The file number referred to above, would, therefore, be placed in the 63 section. The files are then arranged numerically within the secondary section according to the digits at the beginning of the number. For example, 4896321 will be placed immediately before 4906321.

The main advantages of terminal digit filing are that the files can be located quickly because lengthy file numbers are broken down into smaller groups, sorting is made simpler and there is less likelihood of files being misplaced. If files have to be removed or additional files inserted they do not affect the continuity of the system.

Decimal Filing

This is a numerical method which is very often used for subject division: a good example is the Dewey decimal method which is adopted by libraries for classifying books. Whole numbers are allotted to the main subjects, for example a Publicity Office might use the following basic numbers for its principal subject headings:

50—Advertising
120—Literature
200—Exhibitions
250—Materials, etc.

Sub-sections are indicated by the digits following the whole number and the decimal point: those below might be used in connexion with advertising:

50.1—Direct Mail
50.2—Press
50.3—Television
50.4—Cinema
50.5—Showrooms

A further sub-division of files in connexion with the Press would result in numbers being allotted as follows:

50.21—*The Times*
50.22—*The Guardian*
50.23—*The Daily Mail*
50.24—*The Daily Telegraph*

When a new file has to be added to the system it will usually be related to an existing subject and can be inserted in the appropriate place by adding a decimal point.

By the decimal method of filing it is quite easy to recognize from a file reference on a letter the topic to which it relates and the location of the file in the cabinet.

Chronological Filing

This is where the documents are filed according to their dates in numerical order. Chronological filing is not often used as a basic system, but it is the normal method of filing papers within files.

The Combination of Alphabetical and Numerical Methods

The alphabetical methods can also incorporate reference numbers, as illustrated in Fig. 24. Each letter or part of a letter is given a number, and a further number is allocated to each file as it is made, for example, if letter C is numbered 3 and there are seven files in the group, the last file to be opened is numbered 3/7. In this method the files are alphabetically arranged and the numerical aspect is secondary and is purely there as a reference for correspondence.

Another method combines the alphabetical and numerical systems but without using individual index cards. The files are arranged in alphabetical groups and are numbered within these groups. Each letter, or part of a letter, has a guide card which also gives an index of the numbered files in that letter group. A guide card, for example, covering the alphabetical range

Aa–An would be numbered $A.1$ and the first file, Allen Bros., would be numbered $A(1)/1$. The next file received, Adcock, T. J., would be numbered $A(1)/2$ and placed next to Allen Bros.' file. The files need not necessarily be in alphabetical order within the division. The next file, even if it was Abbington, would take the number 3 position.

SYSTEMS OF FILING

Vertical Filing

In this system, the papers or documents are placed into files, which are arranged vertically (upright). The files are effectively displayed with title strips or labels on the top edges. Papers can be placed in or taken out of the folders without the folders having to be removed from the filing cabinet. The files can be stored in cabinets, drawers, racks and shelves.

Suspension Filing

Folders or pockets may be suspended vertically from metal runners fitted inside cabinet drawers (*see* Fig. 28). These metal runners and chassis rails suspend the pockets in such a manner that they are held clear of the bottom of the drawer. The files are thus protected from a considerable amount of wear and tear, and, no matter how heavily they are loaded, retain their neat and tidy appearance.

The actual correspondence is filed, not directly into the suspended pockets, but in inner folders. The pockets may be connected together to form a "concertina" arrangement. This prevents loose papers from being mislaid underneath the pockets. The "concertina" can be broken at any point for the insertion of an additional pocket to maintain an alphabetical method.

The titles, which must be clearly given on both the pocket and the inner folder, may be displayed in a number of ways. Upright tabs or flat strips are in common use. The cards for the tabs or strips are supplied in perforated lengths to enable them to be prepared on a typewriter. The cards are completely covered and their titles kept clean and legible with shields of cellulose acetate or similar material which melts under extreme heat but does not burst into flame. Celluloid is rarely used because of the risk of fire. The cards are supplied in a variety of colours for classification purposes.

Duplicating stencils required for future use are commonly filed in a cabinet specially made for the purpose, and using the vertical suspension system. Clear labelling and indexing are essential to ensure that old stencils can be found quickly and easily.

Lateral Filing

Lateral filing is a system of storing files side by side, rather like books on a shelf. The files are generally suspended from rails placed laterally in cupboards, racks or on open shelving. They are fitted with title holders which can normally be adjusted for the required angle of vision. Where accommodation is limited, lateral installations are ideal, as space does not have to be allowed for the opening of drawers and they can be built up as high as the ceiling will allow (*see* Fig. 27).

Shelf filing has the same advantages as the lateral system but the files, instead of being suspended from rails, are arranged securely along open shelves.

The advantages and disadvantages of the lateral and vertical systems of filing are given on page 97.

Plan Filing

Plans and drawings may be stored horizontally in flat drawers or vertically in storage cabinets where the drawings are arranged in an upright position. Vertical cabinets contain compartments with wave-like dividers enabling large drawings to stand erect without buckling. A vertical plan cabinet occupies less than a third of the floor space of a horizontal cabinet of equal capacity. Each compartment has its own indexing strip so that the drawings can be easily identified (*see* Fig. 29).

Box Files

Where there is a limited amount of correspondence or where a particular group of papers, documents, etc., has to be kept in a separate container, a box file may be conveniently and effectively used. The boxes are made of cardboard or metal. The papers are either fitted into the box by means of a loose-leaf book or held in place by a spring clip. The loose-leaf type is called a lever-arch file.

Pending Files

A pending file may be used to contain the daily correspondence and routine papers that so often encumber an executive's desk. The papers may be filed alphabetically or in other categories, such as "For reply", "In abeyance", "General Manager", "Personnel Manager", "Personal", etc. The file may be of a box type or a flat tray type with each section heading clearly visible.

System	Advantages	Disadvantages
Lateral *Fig. 27 Lateral Filing*	1. Saving space as there is no need to allow for opening drawers. 2. Can be built up higher than vertical cabinets. 3. Can be accommodated in alcoves which would not be suitable for vertical cabinets. 4. Larger range of files can be viewed at one time.	1. Difficulty in reading file titles in a vertical position. 2. Files may become dusty because of the large opening. 3. Location of files from a height can be a hazard.
Vertical *Fig. 28 Vertical Filing* Illustrations reproduced by permission of Flexiform Ltd.)	1. The files are more compact and there is less chance of losing documents, particularly if files are suspended. 2. Papers can be inserted and replaced without removing the file. 3. The titles can be read clearly. 4. Cabinets have greater protection from fire and dust.	1. Extra space is required for opening drawers. 2. More expensive equipment. 3. Only one person at a time can have access to a filing cabinet.

Microfilming

Microfilming is a process developed for bulk copying of loose-leaf records. Correspondence, financial records, engineering drawings, extracts from books or magazines or other documents are copied on to films for filing purposes. When reference is made to the filmed documents, the film is fitted into a viewer, reader or projector where the documents can be seen in enlarged form. The microfilm is prepared in three stages:

1. the original documents are photographed;

2. the film is developed;

Fig. 29 A Plan Filing Cabinet
(Reproduced by permission of Roneo Vickers Ltd.)

3. the processed film is read and analysed.

This process has the following advantages:

1. It saves space and weight as bulky correspondence files are reduced to rolls of film. For example, 1 cu. ft. of space can hold the films needed to record 1 500 000 cheques and a roll of 16 mm. film 100 ft. in length can accommodate about 8 000 A4-sized documents or 24 000 cheques.

2. Documents can be sent abroad at reduced postal rates.

3. There is little risk of misplacing information or losing records.

4. Film is more durable than paper and provides a much more permanent record.

5. The film can be enlarged on to paper, thus providing quick and accurate duplicate copies of the original documents.

The installation of the costly equipment which is necessary for carrying out the microfilming process is only an economical proposition in large offices where vast quantities of documents are handled and filed daily. In addition, the necessity of using a viewer every time reference is made to a document may also prove inconvenient in certain circumstances.

Aperture Cards

Microfilming techniques are used in making aperture cards which are 80 column punched cards with microfilms mounted on them. The punched holes denote the contents and reference number of the microfilm and are used for quick sorting and retrieval of the cards when they are required for viewing or for reproducing paper copies. An example of an engineering drawing preserved in this manner is given in Fig. 30 below.

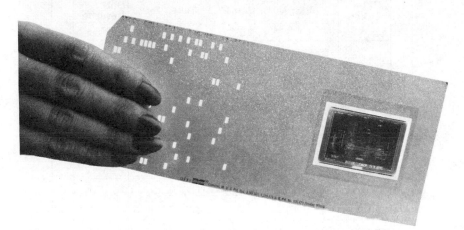

Fig. 30 Microfilm Aperture Card
(Reproduced by permission of Kodak Ltd.)

Absent Folders

One of the most frequent sources of delay and annoyance in filing is to find that a folder has been removed from its place in the cabinet, and a lengthy, irritating search all over the office is necessary to trace it. This can be avoided by the insertion of an "Absent" marker in the place of the folder removed for reference as illustrated in Fig. 31.

An absent card can be used, which records the number or name of the folder, the initials of the person to whom it is issued and the date. It remains in the cabinet until the folder is replaced, providing a check on the whereabouts of the folder.

Another system is the suspended absent wallet. In this particular system the wallet is suspended with the pocket from which a folder is removed. A completed docket showing the number or name of the folder, the name of the person to whom it has been issued, the department concerned and the date, is placed in the wallet and retained until the folder is returned. This absent wallet, whilst providing a check on the whereabouts of the folder, has the further advantages of:

1. providing a receptacle for the receipt of papers whilst the folder is out;

2. determining at a glance which folders are out, and, if required, enabling their recovery to be made without delay.

Date Taken	Folder Nº or Name	Taken By	Date Returned
ABSENT			

Fig. 31 The Absent Folder
(Reproduced by permission of Roneo Vickers Ltd.)

Follow-up System

There are several systems which can be used satisfactorily for following up correspondence, and one very effective system is given here. A follow-up system is used to ensure that a matter is not overlooked. If, for example, an executive writes a letter on the 11th of the month, he may wish to send a further letter on the 21st if a reply has not been received. When the executive signs the letter on the 11th of the month, he completes a memo form, attaches it to the copy of the letter in question, enters on it the date when the letter is next wanted, and places it in his filing tray. The filing clerk fills in the name of the correspondent and, if necessary, the subject matter, and then detaches the form, which is filed in the appropriate monthly pocket of the "follow-up" filing cabinet. The letter itself is then filed away in its proper file with other correspondence, where it can be found at any time it is wanted.

The "follow-up" filing cabinet drawer contains twelve pockets, titled January to December; the pocket for the current month contains a file which is subdivided by thirty-one daily insert sheets. The memos are placed in the appropriate monthly pocket and are subdivided on a daily basis when the month becomes current. The system can have a separate pocket for each day of the current month if the quantity of papers requires it.

Each day the filing clerk extracts any memo forms from the current daily insert, finds the papers or letters to which they refer, couples the forms and letters and passes them to the individual whose initials appear on the form. After appropriate action, the executive places the form and the papers back in the filing tray with, if necessary, a further date marked in for follow-up, and the whole process is repeated. Appointments for future dates and many other items can be dealt with by this system, which is almost automatic in operation. Note the information recorded on the memo form and the arrangement of the pockets in the follow-up system given in Figs. 32 and 33.

VISIBLE RECORDS

Cards or forms are arranged to overlap in such a manner that their edges are exposed to view. The exposed portions carry, in addition to the title, various control features which summarize essential details contained in entries on the records.

Visible Card Records

The cards are housed in flat trays, in such a manner that while they overlap each other, the title of each is clearly visible. The trays are kept in cabinets which are normally made of steel, with locking devices to safeguard confidential information. Colour markers or indicators may be affixed to the cards to focus attention on vital facts. Sixty to seventy cards can be accommodated in each tray, and as many as twenty-one trays fitted into a single cabinet. Transparent plastic shields are generally fitted over the exposed portions of the cards, to protect them from dirt and to provide a suitable carrier for the coloured markers. (*See* Fig. 34.)

Visible Loose-leaf Records

These are similar in principle to visible cards. The sheets, which are smaller in size than the covers, are held by punched holes on one edge of the book. The holding mechanism enables the sheets to be fitted into the book in such a way that they overlap one another. The books are, of course, portable and can be locked away when not in use. As with ordinary loose-leaf books, the forms can be inserted or extracted easily without interfering with the continuity of the records.

Fig. 32 Follow-up System
(Reproduced by permission of Roneo Vickers Ltd.)

TICKLER MEMO			DATE 27/1/--		
NAME *Charles Broad & Co Ltd*			PHONE		
ADDRESS			LETTER DATE 26/1/--		
SUBJECT					
REMARKS *Renewal of Transport Contract*					
RETURN TO *R. Johnson*	ON *9/2/--*	*9/3/--*	*7/4/--*		
	ON				
	ON				

Fig. 33 Follow-up System Memo
(Reproduced by permission of Roneo Vickers Ltd.)

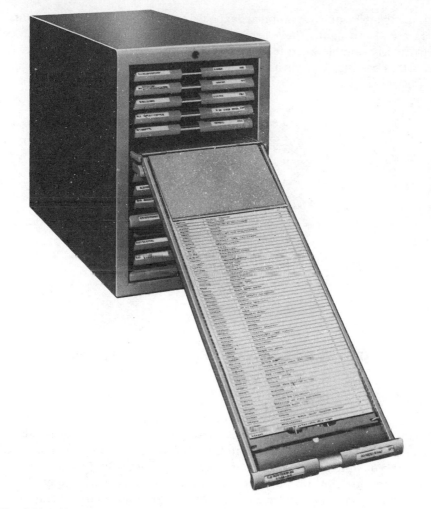

Fig. 34 Visible Card Records
(Reproduced by permission of Roneo Vickers Ltd.)

Loose-leaf records may also be filed in binders and held into position by posts, prongs, or thongs. Binders are recommended for filing bank paying-in slips, copies of invoices, minutes of meetings, copies of orders, petty cash vouchers, and receipts.

Vertical Visible Card Records

These are held loosely in a container so that they can be extracted and replaced easily. The cards stand upright in cabinet drawers or boxes, and the name and other control features are exposed to view. Loose papers, accounts, etc., are placed immediately behind the appropriate cards. This system is particularly suitable when it is necessary to remove the papers completely from the container, e.g. when an entry is made on a typewriter or an accounting machine.

Fig. 35 Rotary Indexing Equipment
(Reproduced by permission of Rotadex Systems Limited)

Rotary Indexing Equipment

Rotary indexing equipment (*see* Fig. 35) is used for holding a large number of index cards or line reference strips in rotating wheel cabinets or stands so that the information contained in the records is within easy reach of the clerk. This type of equipment enables one operator to have access to many more cards than is possible with the vertical card index, less space is required and the information can be extracted from the records much more quickly. The cards are housed in separate containers within the circumference of a wheel mechanism, and the wheels are simply rotated to bring the required card to the top of the cabinet.

Rotary equipment may also be used for housing line reference strips containing individual references to addresses, telephone numbers, prices, or measurements.

Strip indexing Equipment

In most offices there is a need to find certain items of information, such as names and addresses, telephone numbers in current use, current commodity prices, etc., frequently and quickly, and the line reference equipment strip-indexing method is the most efficient and practical. The information in the container is visible to the clerk without her having to search through sheaves of papers, books or loose cards. Individual references, each on its own strip, can be pinpointed instantly.

Each item of information is recorded on a separate strip, and these are built up one above the other in suitable carrying devices, so that all the information contained in them is visible. The strips are generally supplied in sheets which can be passed through a typewriter. Additions, amendments and deletions can be made without affecting the continuity of the records.

Strips are available in a number of different shades, which facilitates colour classification. In addition, various forms of signalling devices can be employed. The strips may be housed in panels, wall fitments, books, stands, revolving units or cabinets. An illustration of strip indexing is given in Fig. 36.

The advantages of the visible record cards are:

(*a*) The records can be seen at a glance; it is not necessary to fumble through many cards.

(*b*) The visible portion of the card lends itself to various effective control features.

(*c*) The cards are less likely to become dirty as transparent plastic shields are fitted over the exposed portions.

(*d*) Arrangement and rearrangement of records is simple and speedy.

Edge-punched Cards

Edge-punched cards combine a card record system with a rapid process of sorting. The cards are supplied with a series of punched holes round the edges, each hole representing a specific item of information. A personnel record card might, for instance, contain holes for such information as sex, year of birth, education, qualifications, department, trade, or profession. A card is prepared for each employee and the holes are converted into slots (*see* Fig. 37) to indicate the relevant facts. For example, the card for Mary Jones, a shorthand-typist in the accounts department, would be slotted at the positions for female, shorthand-typist and accounts department. To select information from the cards a steel needle is passed through a particular position and the cards which have been slotted in that position fall away from the remainder of the cards. It is therefore very easy and quick to secure the cards for all the shorthand-typists employed in a company, or alternatively all of the staff employed in the accounts department. Edge-punched cards may be employed for a wide range of office systems, including vehicle records, estate agents' clients records, sales analysis, etc. The main

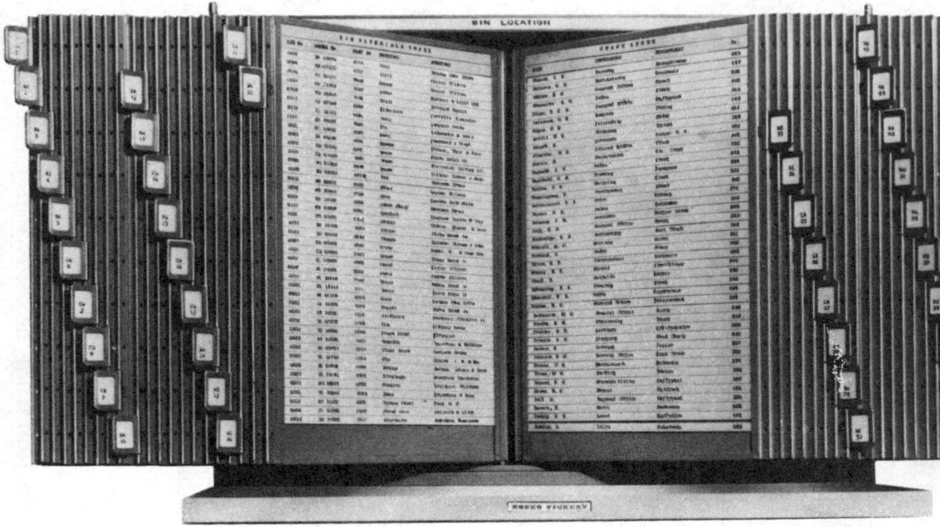

Fig. 36 Line Reference Equipment Strip Indexing
(Reproduced by permission of Roneo Vickers Ltd.)

Fig. 37 Edge-punched Cards
(Reproduced by permission of The Copeland Chatterson Co. Ltd.)

advantage of this system of sorting is that no expensive machinery is required.

Slotted cards in which the whole area of the card is used is a more comprehensive system, and one which may be employed for sorting and selecting a much larger amount of information.

General Rules for Filing

1. File neatly and methodically by:

(*a*) sorting and grouping all correspondence before filing (sorting equipment is referred to on page 172) and

(*b*) placing the papers on to the files squarely, so that all the edges are perfectly straight.

2. Ensure that the correspondence is placed in the correct file.

3. Place the correspondence in the files in the correct sequence of dates so that the most recent document is on top.

4. Avoid large bulky files. Correspondence which is old and not currently required should be separated from the current file and either destroyed or

placed into a "dead" file. The "dead" files should be stored away in a strong room or store cupboard and indexed. A note of the "dead" file number should be made on the current file so that reference can be made to the old correspondence, if necessary.

5. Do not remove individual papers from a file. If an individual paper *must* be removed, a note stating the date, name of correspondent, and name of the person holding the paper, should be placed in the file.

6. When there is insufficient correspondence from one source to justify opening an individual file, place it in a "Miscellaneous" file.

7. If a file is temporarily removed for reference, complete an absence marker or card.

8. Have adequate cross references of file titles either on the covers or on an index card; for example, Chief Constable of Blankshire, Lt. Col. Jenkins should be indexed under "Chief", "Blankshire" and "Jenkins".

9. File daily so that the filing system is always up to date.

10. Observe the following points when placing files and index cards in their cabinets or drawers:

(*a*) The surname is placed before Christian names, and if the surnames are the same, the first Christian name determines the position, e.g. Jackson, John would be placed before Jackson, Thomas.

(*b*) If the Christian and surname are embodied in the name of the firm, the surname is written first, followed by the Christian name and finally the remainder of the name; for example, Leonard White and Co. should be filed under "White, Leonard, and Co.".

(*c*) If a company has several names, the first name is taken as the surname for filing purposes, e.g. Messrs. May, Jones and Jenkins should be filed under "May".

(*d*) When "The" is the first word of the name, it is either omitted, or placed at the end, for indexing purposes, as follows—High Pressure Tools Limited, The.

(*e*) In hyphenated names, the first name is used, e.g. in Smith-Ryland use Smith.

(*f*) Titles are placed after the surname and before the Christian names, e.g. Champion, Sir G. H.

(*g*) Names beginning with Mac, Mc, or M' are treated as if they were spelt "Mac".

(*h*) Names beginning with "St." are treated as if they were spelt "Saint".

(i) In names such as De La Rue, De La Mare, etc. the prefix is regarded as part of the surname and indexed as if they were one word, e.g. Delarue.

(*j*) Nothing comes before something, i.e. a name without an initial precedes a name with an initial, as in the following names:

(1) Roberts.
(2) Roberts, A.
(3) Roberts, A. A.

(*k*) Names which consist of initials are placed before full names, e.g. B.R.S. (Parcels) Ltd. precedes Brown Bros.

FILING METHODS

The following chart shows the most suitable methods of filing various business documents. It should be noted, however, that it is necessary for each filing requirement to be studied individually in its true environment, taking into account quantities, contents, sizes, etc., and that the subjects are dealt with in general terms only.

Documents	Recommended method of filing	Remarks
Accounting records	Vertical visible card cabinets (indexed alphabetically under the names of the debtors or creditors)	This method enables the book-keeper to extract and replace the record cards easily from the cabinet when making entries.
Original application forms completed by staff when joining the firm	Visible loose-leaf record books	The books should be locked in a cupboard or cabinet when not in use.
Art work	*Large*: horizontal or vertical plan cabinets *Small*: lateral or vertical (subject or numerical)	
Bank paying-in slips	Loose-leaf post binders in date order	
Blueprints	As for "Art work"	
Catalogues	Lateral or vertical (alphabetical)	File under the name of the firm or the name of the product offered by the firm.
Computer print-outs	Loose-leaf Post binders for use with sprocket-punched continuous stationery (*see* Fig. 38) Indexed under subject and date	

Computer tapes	Lateral cabinet with racks fitted for tape containers (see Fig. 39) Indexed numerically	Cross referenced with an alphabetical card index system.
Records of current prices	Visible record equipment—strip indexing—indexed under the name of the product	
Dictating machine discs or belts	Lateral or vertical—placed in pocket folders or document cases	The date of the dictation and the name of the dictator should be stated on the front of the belt or disc and on the front of the folder, and it should be filed in date order.
Insurance policies	Lateral or vertical (numerical)	The method of indexing is generally that of an index number in combination with the name of the insured and branch of insurance, i.e. House, Life, Motor-car Policy, etc.
Copies of invoices	*Current*: post or prong binders in numerical or date order *On completion*: transferred to a permanent locking post binder	The completed binders are stored on shelves in cupboards or in filing cabinets. Where large numbers of documents have to be filed the microfilming process is ideal.
Used master sheets for a spirit duplicator	Lateral or vertical (alphabetical, alphabetical/numerical or subject)	Master sheets will not normally be stored for long periods of time because of the relatively short life of the dye impressions. They can, however, be stored for reference purposes in the same way as general correspondence. The sheets should not be folded or creased in any way.

FILING METHODS (*cont.*)

Documents	Recommended method of filing	Remarks
Microfilms	Trays in metal cabinets to accommodate 16 mm. or 35 mm. films in their boxes or aperture cards. Indexed numerically	Cross referenced with an alphabetical card index system.
Minutes of meetings	Loose-leaf post binder fitted with locking device—filed in date order	Business meeting minute books must always be of the loose-leaf type to allow sheets to be extracted from the book for typewriting.
Names, addresses and telephone numbers in frequent use	Strip indexing (alphabetical)	
Copies of orders	As for " copies of invoices "	
Petty cash vouchers	Loose-leaf post binder—filed numerically	The vouchers are given serial numbers before being entered in the Petty Cash Book and then they are filed in serial number order.
Photographs	As for " Art work "	
Large-size plans	Vertical or horizontal plan cabinets (subject or numerical)	
Price Lists	As for "catalogues"	
Punched cards	80-column card trays in metal cabinets (*see* Fig. 40) Indexed under subject and date	Trays are designed to allow access to all cards without removal from the cabinet.

Document	Method	Notes
Receipts	As for "petty cash vouchers"	
Completed share transfers and record of share-holders	Loose-leaf thong or post binder	Every company having fifty or more members should, unless the Register of Members is in such a form as to constitute in itself an index, keep an index of the names of the company's members. A loose-leaf binder can be correctly indexed and can form a Register of Members.
Shorthand notes of confidential meetings	Lateral or vertical—filed in the order of the dates of the meetings	The cabinet containing the files should be kept locked and supervised personally by the secretary.
Confidential staff records	*Correspondence*: lateral or vertical. *Cards*: visible cards housed in flat trays. Filed alphabetically under the names of the staff or numerically under their works numbers	Because of the confidential nature of the records the filing cabinets in which they are kept must be locked when not in use.
Used stencils wanted for further use	Lateral or vertical (numerical/alphabetical)	The stencils must be protected by semi-absorbent covers or placed in storage folders with protective wax sheets. The type of indexing is dependent on the matter contained in the stencils, the quantity kept and the equipment available, but invariably a combined numerical and alphabetical system is satisfactory.
X-ray plates	As for "Art work"	

Suitable Methods of Filing Various business Documents

Fig. 38 Computer Print-out Binder
(Reproduced by permission of Twinlock Limited)

Fig. 39 Computer Tape Rack
(Reproduced by permission of Flexiform Ltd.)

Fig. 40 80-column Punched Card Trays
(Reproduced by permission of Flexiform Ltd.)

QUESTIONS

1. Outline the procedure to be taken by a filing clerk when:
   (*a*) a paper may be correctly filed under more than one letter of the alphabet;
   (*b*) a member of another department wishes to take out a file. *R.S.A. OP.1*

2. Draw up simple rules for a new employee, who, under your supervision, will deal with the filing of correspondence.

3. When opening a new filing system, what would influence you in your choice between alphabetical, numerical, geographical or subject methods of indexing? *R.S.A. SD.2*

4. You work in a firm which has grown from one department to four departments over the past year. Previously only you and your employer handled all correspondence. Now, correspondence is going out from four different departments, each department keeping its own files. As a result letters cannot easily be traced. Write a report on how you would arrange a central filing system and what rules you would make for its use. *R.S.A. SD.2*

5. What circumstances would cause you to recommend to your employer that he should spend a considerable sum in converting his card index of customers to a modern visible system? Information is at present recorded on 5-in. by 3-in. cards stored upright in wooden drawers. *R.S.A. SD.2*

6. You cannot continue to accumulate duplicate copies of certain orders; yet reference must be made to these for some months after they are made. Suggest a method of dealing with this problem. *R.S.A. SD.2*

7. Discuss the advantages and disadvantages of (i) centralized filing and (ii) departmental filing. What do you consider to be the most important general rules to be observed for the efficient working of any filing system? *L.C.C. P.S.D.*

8. How would you store for future use:
   (*a*) used master sheets for a spirit duplicator,
   (*b*) stencils,
   (*c*) dictating machine discs,
   (*d*) maps? *R.S.A. SD.2*

9. Place the following in what you consider to be the correct form and order for indexing:
   Walter d'eath and Co. Ltd.
   The Hornsey Public Baths
   Delany and Brothers
   O'Brian and Co. Ltd.
   Pat O'Brien
   Stephen de la Mere
   Lady P. Morris
   The British Pen Company
   A. B. McBride

A. D. MacBride
B. M'Bride
Borough of Blackwater
London County Council
20th Century Printers Ltd. *R.S.A. SD.2*

10. On taking up a new appointment you find that the filing indexing systems are unsatisfactory. Draft your report and recommendations, mentioning briefly, in addition to ordinary correspondence, any five of the following:

Blue prints; catalogues; completed share transfers; petty cash vouchers; staff records; criminal case histories (in a solicitor's or barrister's office); record of shareholders (in a company having several thousand shareholders); used stencils; records of retailers (in a company having a large outside sales staff); bank paying-in slips. *L.C.C. P.S.D.*

11. A great many stencils, relative to varying subject matter, are prepared in your office for circulation to the many branches of your company and its associated companies. Describe a method for overcoming the inconvenience frequently caused by inability to trace copes of the duplicated matter when required some weeks/months after dispatch. *L.C.C. P.S.D.*

12. (*a*) Place the following names of individuals, professional bodies and trading organizations in the order and form in which you would index them:

L. M. MacIntyre
The British Plastics Co. Ltd.
1970 Express Services
Borough of Bexley
A. M. McBridie
St. John Courtney Salon
E. A. Sanford & Co. Ltd.
Dennis O'Donovan
Stephen Watts-Owen
Henry Levene & Co. Ltd.

(*b*) Draw up a typical "Out" guide and discuss its importance. *R.S.A. COS.*

13. What is meant by lateral filing? What are (i) the advantages and (ii) any disadvantages arising from its use? *R.S.A. SD.2*

14. It often occurs in certain firms that letters and other documents which have been filed cannot be found when urgently wanted. Suggest reasons why documents may be temporarily lost and the changes that should be made to ensure greater efficiency. *R.S.A. SD.2*

15. (*a*) Arrange the following names in order for alphabetical filing:

Hoyland District Council	Dr. T. J. O'Connor
Department of the Environment	Royston Parkin & Co.
D. R. Donnison	Royal Insurance Co. Ltd.
Corona Soft Drinks	Old Denaby Motors
Grants of St. James's (Northern) Ltd.	Frank Corker (Contractors) Ltd.

(*b*) Why are index cards necessary in numerical filing? Give an example of the layout of the card you would use. *R.S.A. OP.1*

16. Prepare a report to your Office Manager on the advisability of transferring all the departmental filing systems to a central filing department. Set out clearly in your report the advantages and disadvantages to your organization of the two systems. *R.S.A. OP.2*

17. (*a*) Explain the uses and advantages of visible card records.

(*b*) Design a visible record card for use in a personnel department. Your illustration should also indicate (i) the information conveyed on the visible edge and (ii) the use of signalling devices. *R.S.A. OP.2*

18. The Head of your Department has asked you to examine some new systems of filing and recording information with the object of saving office space and at the same time having the records available for quick and easy reference. In a memo. to your Head of Department explain the features of (*a*) microfilming; (*b*) lateral filing and (*c*) one other method which you consider should be introduced. *R.S.A. OP.2*

19 The filing clerk complains that he is short of space for storing current correspondence and that the files are becoming very bulky and difficult to handle. He also experiences difficulty in locating papers in the files (indexed under subject headings) after other members of the staff have been engaged on filing. Examine the filing clerk's complaints and prepare a report to the Office Manager setting out your findings and making recommendations to improve the efficiency of the filing system. *R.S.A. OP.2*

20. Your firm has acquired a small fleet of delivery vans. Your employer wishes you to set up a new card-index system which will show all details of the vehicles, monthly mileage, maintenance and repairs, and names of drivers. Advise him as to the type of equipment you wish to use. He has seen index-cards incorporating marginal punched holes to indicate certain information in place of written entries. Explain why you would or would not, adopt this type of card. *R.S.A. SD.2*

21. How would you indicate in your filing system:

(*a*) that you had removed a file from the filing cabinet;

(*b*) that a letter filed in file 77 also referred to the subject matter dealt with in file 88? *R.S.A. SD.2*

22. (*a*) Discuss the advantages and disadvantages of alphabetical and numerical systems of filing.

(*b*) Name *three* other classification systems and say in what circumstances you would use each of them. *R.S.A. OP.2*

23. "Edge-punched cards combine a card record system with a rapid process of sorting."

(*a*) Explain the meaning of this statement.

(*b*) State the uses of edge-punched cards.

(*c*) Describe briefly any other methods which are available for sorting information in offices. *R.S.A. OP.2*

24. What effect is mechanization having on filing procedures? Select any one procedure to illustrate your answer. *R.S.A. OP.2*

25. Describe a simple method of operating a bring forward (follow-up) system for correspondence in the office. *R.S.A. OP.1*

Chapter 8
Office Memory Aids

The secretary cannot be expected to remember the large number of details necessary in the day-to-day working of her office, including her employer's engagements and appointments and future planning of her duties. She should be certain therefore to make a note in her diary, not only of every engagement and appointment arranged for her employer, but of work to be done on future occasions. The secretary will normally have two diaries to keep up-to-date—her employer's and her own. She should see that all entries which affect her employer are entered in his diary as well as in her own.

When making entries in the diary, the secretary should:

(*a*) Always write clearly and with a pen—provisional appointments may be entered in pencil first and inked in when they are confirmed.

(*b*) Note the time, name of contact, place and any other relevant information as briefly but comprehensively as possible.

(*c*) For social engagements, make a note of the reception or cocktail time—say, " 1930 for 2000 "—and also any particular information on dress.

(*d*) Enter the appointments in the correct order of occurrence during each day.

(*e*) At the end of each day, make a careful check of each diary to ensure that all items have been dealt with and all appointments kept.

A typical day's page in the secretary's diary is given in Fig. 41.

Booking of Appointments

When booking appointments, the secretary should:

(*a*) Keep in mind the routine office matters with which the employer probably prefers to deal at certain times of the day.

(*b*) Allow the necessary travelling time between appointments.

(*c*) Remember that meetings can extend beyond their estimated finishing time, and allow for this by mentioning the difficulty, if necessary, to the person requiring an appointment, unless he is so important that the employer would wish to leave his meeting to keep the appointment.

```
DIARY

Friday, 2 August 19--

Time          Place          Business

0930          -              Agenda for Staff Meeting

1000          Board Room     Staff Meeting

1045          -              Reserve seats for Tuesday
                             26 August, 1200 hrs train
                             Birmingham to Euston for
                             Mr and Mrs X

1100          Office         Typewriter Mechanic

1130          Office         Appointment: Mr S Jenks
                             to see Mr X. File -
                             Housing - 1294/ST

1200          Bank           Petty Cash - £25

1400          Office         Staff Meeting Minutes

1445          Dentist        Mr X's appointment

1600          Bloxham        Reception at 1900 hrs
                             Remind Mr X
```

Fig. 41 Diary

(*d*) As a rule appointments are made by telephone. On the same day write a letter confirming the telephone conversation. A copy of the letter will be made, providing a permanent record of the conversation and booking for the file. A note of the action taken should then be given to the employer for his information.

(*e*) When writing to an hotel, address the letter to "The Manager".

Hotel addresses and descriptions are contained in the:

(i) *Hotel Guide* (prepared by The British Hotels and Restaurants Association).
(ii) *A.A.* and *R.A.C. Handbooks* where hotels are classified by stars.
(iii) *R.A.C. Continental Handbook* and *Guide to Europe*. (The *A.A.* also issues a foreign touring guide.)

(*f*) When making social appointments, which include the employer's wife, either during the day or the evening, make sure that each appointment is convenient to her before accepting on her behalf.

(*g*) If the employer's wife is a business or professional woman, there is a possibility that she may require the presence of her husband at various functions connected with her own activities, and constant, careful corroboration with her is necessary in the booking of the employer's own engagements. The degree to which this is necessary depends very largely upon the employer's preferences concerning his own and his wife's social engagements.

Appointments Cards

If the employer is away from his office for a whole day, attending various functions and appointments, he may require his secretary to prepare an appointments card. This should be a convenient size for him to carry around, and should be accompanied by any necessary invitation cards or files of correspondence. Fig. 42 is an example of an appointments card.

```
APPOINTMENTS


Tuesday, 24 June 19--

   1030 hrs              Sales Conference at Blanktown
                         Branch Office.  (14 High Street).
                         Agenda enclosed.

   1300 hrs              Lunch at Queen's Hotel with
                         Blanktown Branch Manager and
                         Mr T G Wey (New Zealand Agent).

   1430 hrs              Interview with Solicitor (11 Cole
                         Row) regarding Lease of Holiday
                         Villa at St Isam.  File attached.

   1600 hrs              Meet Sir John and Lady Bond from
                         Elmpet Airport.  Rooms have been
                         reserved at Longton Manor Hotel.

   1930 (for 2000)       Dinner at Longton Manor Hotel.
                         Dress: Formal.  Invitation card
                         enclosed.  Flowers for Mrs X have
                         been ordered for 1900 hrs.
```

Fig. 42 Appointments Card

Plastic Year Planners

Large plastic calendars provided with spaces for every day of the year can be used for planning appointments, meetings and other business activities. By this means it is possible to see at a glance a year's activities and to plan engagements methodically on one single sheet. Self-adhesive coloured signals can be used to highlight significant dates.

Other Memory Aids

Other methods of keeping appointments and dates constantly under review include the preparation of a typed list of engagements placed on the employer's desk daily or weekly; a monthly or weekly appointments card displayed on the employer's desk; indexed memory aids (*see* below); and an efficient follow-up system, described in Chapter 7, "Filing and Indexing".

Indexed Memory Aids

An indexed memory aid system consists of suspended folders for each day of the month, and twelve folders bearing the names of the months, which are held in a steel cabinet. When a matter requiring attention on a future date arises or when appointments are made, an entry is made on a card and placed in the appropriate file. The folders are then referred to every day, and after a day's entries have been dealt with, that file is placed at the back of the month's files. If a matter requires action in a month, or even several months' time, an entry is made on a card and placed in the file for the appropriate month. On the first day of that month the cards are sorted and placed in the appropriate day files for the current month. Matters which might easily be forgotten are currently kept in view, and the system is quick and easy to operate.

QUESTIONS

1. Explain the uses of a diary for business purposes, and give a typical page with at least eight entries.

2. Your employer has a full day ahead of him tomorrow, which will take him from one appointment to another, away from the office, with little time to spare. He asks you for a note of his appointments. Give this to him in the most useful form. *R.S.A. SD.2*

3. Your employer has a great many business and social engagements. Assume that you are responsible for his appointments diary; what are the chief factors to be borne in mind? *L.C.C. P.S.D.*

4. Discuss means by which you can ensure:
    (*a*) that your employer keeps all the appointsments made for him, and
    (*b*) that he deals with all matters that he has put aside for attention on specific dates? *R.S.A. SD.2*

5. On returning to your office after a day's absence you find the following message left for you by your employer. Write the letters as instructed.
    Miss A: I shall not be in the office in the morning. Please write to the City Hotel and reserve a room for Mr and Mrs Brown, who are arriving on Friday next from New York. Get that letter off at once. Then write a letter for my signature to Mr Cook at The Modern Works, telling him of Mr Brown's visit and saying that I should like to accept Mr Cook's offer to show Brown over the works on Saturday morning. Find out if they work a normal programme on Saturday mornings; if

not, it had better be some other time, as the Browns will be here for a week only. *R.S.A. SD.2*

6. A colleague of your employer celebrated his silver wedding anniversary in March. In February your employer asked you to remind him to write a letter of congratulation on the appropriate date. You forgot to do so. Your employer was naturally extremely annoyed and, as this was not the first time such a situation had arisen, told you to devise a "fool-proof" reminder system. What did you suggest? *R.S.A. SD.2*

7. When your employer returns from her holiday, she will want to know what has taken place in her absence, and what appointments you have made on her behalf. How would you prepare this information for her? *R.S.A. SD.2*

8. Your employer, a very busy Executive, has many business and social engagements and he relies entirely upon you to keep his diary.
List the important points to be borne in mind in doing this and state how you would keep him advised of day to day appointments. *L.C.C. P.S.C.*

9. Your employer asks you to cancel one of his business appointments for the following day. How would you do this? *R.S.A. SD.2*

10. An employer has a desk diary and so does his secretary. What are the advantages of each having a diary? *R.S.A. SD.2*

Chapter 9
Office Equipment

TYPEWRITERS

The typewriter is an indispensable item of equipment in the office, and there are very many styles and models manufactured. These may be manually or electrically operated, portable, noiseless or even capable of typing braille.

In most offices where several typewriters are in daily use, a contract is placed with a firm of specialists in typewriter maintenance to send a mechanic to service the machines periodically. However, the mechanic cannot guarantee continuous smooth operation without the co-operation of the operator and it is, therefore, necessary for the typist to see that her typewriter is kept in the best possible condition so that it will always produce first-class work. For this purpose a servicing outfit should always be available and it should contain a hard type-brush, a soft long-handled dusting brush and a duster.

Ten Points on the Care of the Typewriter

1. Brush the type with a hard brush every morning.

2. Dust and clean the machine regularly, and wipe the roller.

3. Clean underneath the typewriter to avoid dust rising into the machine.

4. When removing the cover, make sure that it is not caught up in some part of the mechanism.

5. Always cover the machine at night, and whenever it is not in use.

6. If the typewriter has to be moved, lift it by the base from the back, and never by any other part. Before lifting, lock the carriage in the centre position by bringing the margin stops together; this will prevent the carriage from running from one side to the other if the machine is tilted.

7. Never leave a typewriter:

   (*a*) near a hot radiator, or
   (*b*) where it may be knocked off the desk by a passer-by.

124

8. Always use a backing sheet to protect the platen when using a single sheet of paper. The backing sheet will also improve the appearance of the typewriting.

9. When erasing, move the carriage fully to the left or right, using the margin-release key, so that the rubber shavings drop on to the desk and not into the type basket.

10. If the typewriter is not functioning properly, examine it and try to discover what is wrong. If the faulty part cannot be repaired easily or if the cause is not apparent, the machine should not be used until an experienced mechanic has attended to it.

Correction of Errors in Typewriting

1. Always read through typed matter carefully before removing it from the typewriter, as it is far easier to correct an error before the sheet has been taken out of the machine.

2. Move the carriage fully to the right or left to prevent eraser shavings falling into the type basket.

3. To determine whether the space for the correct letter is in the right position, disengage the ribbon carrier by means of the stencil switch, and tap the letter required gently.

4. If a dark typewriter ribbon is being used, first erase gently with a soft pencil eraser and then finish with a harder typewriter eraser.

SPECIAL PURPOSE TYPEWRITERS AND DEVICES

Several devices have been developed to assist the typist in producing work more easily and more effectively. Some of these are described in the following paragraphs.

Front Feed Device

The front paper feed is a development in the design of the mechanism at the front of the platen, which enables invoices to be inserted from the front, while the day-book sheet is held in the machine by the normal feed. This mechanism is also used for the writing of receipts, cheques and other documents of which a summary may be required.

A similar device is used in a contract writer which is a modified electric typewriter used for typing successive documents whilst retaining a journal sheet in the carriage. The journal sheet is not affected whilst the other documents are being inserted or removed, yet during typing the line space moves simultaneously for both journal sheet and document. The typewriter can be used without any adjustment for normal typing when not being used for documentation.

Card Holding Attachments

This is a development which enables stiff cards to be fed into a typewriter and curved around the cylinder. It consists of a special platen with a metal channel. The edge of the card or label is placed in this channel, and the platen turned backwards until the card is in the correct typing position. The card is then held firmly in position whilst typing is carried out. This addition to the typewriter is designed to make it possible to type on the extreme top and bottom edges of small cards and labels.

Continuous Stationery Machine

The paper is fed in from the rear of the machine and can be torn off in sets as the typing on them is completed. The carbon paper remains interleaved in the next set of forms which automatically follows on and remains in the machine at the appropriate position for typing. It helps the typist to increase output by making it unnecessary for each set of invoices to be interleaved with carbon, and for the carbon to be removed after each invoice has been typed.

Carbon Ribbon Equipment

This equipment consists of a spool carrier fitted to the left-hand side of the typewriter, and accommodating a roll of carbon paper or acetate ribbon (about six hundred and fifty feet) with a take-up spool situated in a similar position on the right-hand side. A special ribbon centre guide and side guides are also fitted to give the necessary guide and position to the ribbon. The carbon paper ribbon produces sharp and clean impressions of the typed matter, and it is ideal for private secretarial work.

Roll Holder and Knife with Rapid Feed

This special purpose typewriter is fitted with a roll holder, bail bar paper knife and a rapid-feed device. The roll attachment accommodates paper in continuous form and a paper knife is provided on the bail for separating each form as it is completed. The rapid paper feed is used when it is required to commence the first typing line on a series of documents at an equal distance from the top of each page. The distance set is variable, and once the adjustment has been made, the document can be fed into the correct typing position by a single movement of the rapid feed lever.

Dual Unit Typewriter

This typewriter is primarily designed for the typing of scientific and mathematical formulae when narration and mathematical or scientific symbols are mixed. The typewriter consists of two type units built side by side with a carriage, which can be easily removed from unit to unit.

Hectograph Carbon Roll Typewriter

This typewriter has been designed to produce master sheets for use on spirit duplicating machines. The hectograph carbon is supplied in seventy-five-foot rolls, and passes round the platen of the typewriter, carbon side outwards, and is wound on to a roll again after use. The paper feed is designed to keep the master copy away from the carbon until the impression is made. The carbon moves one space each time the carriage is returned by the line space lever, although the master sheet is free to move independently.

Special hectograph carbon ribbons may also be used for preparing spirit master sheets.

Dual Tabulator

A typewriter which has a tabulator with a dual setting mechanism is now available. When tabulator stops for a second set of headings or columns are temporarily required, the first setting can be retained while the second stops are used. The original set can be brought back into use quite simply by moving a lever.

Electric Typewriters

In all electric typewriters the features normally operated by the typist, i.e. key depression, carriage return, line spacing, tabulator, etc., are electrically controlled. These electrically-operated actions enable operators to type with very little physical effort and with much less fatigue than with the manually operated typewriters.

As a result of the reduced physical effort involved in operating electric typewriters, operators are able to type quickly for much longer periods than are possible on the manual machines. As many as twenty carbon copies can

Fig. 43 The Typing Element (or Golf ball)
on the IBM Selectric 82
(Reproduced by permission of IBM United Kingdom Ltd.)

be taken at one time, which makes the machine useful for a variety of tasks such as invoicing, preparation of balance sheets, departmental memos. The electrically-controlled impression provides a sharp, even striking of the keys which is ideal for cutting stencils and preparing masters for duplicating reproduction processes.

One electric typewriter, the IBM Selectric 82, commonly known as the golf ball typewriter, has dispensed with type bars and uses a small cylindrical head (*see* Fig. 43) which contains all of the usual characters. When the keys are operated the typing head, not the carriage, moves and is revolved to the printing point required. This typewriter takes up less space on the desk as there is no movement of the carriage. If the typist strikes two keys almost simultaneously, the typewriter stores the second stroke until the first has printed.

The typing element (or golf ball) can be removed and a new one of a different type style inserted in a few seconds which makes it very useful for typing documents where a variety of type styles and sizes are required. This typewriter also uses closed ribbon cartridges (*see* Fig. 44) so that the ribbon can be changed quickly without handling the ribbon itself. The selective ribbon system gives the typist a choice of two "one-time" ribbon types.

Fig. 44 IBM Ribbon Cartridge

One of these, a film cartridge ribbon contains a plastic film which provides up to 120 000 character impressions; the other cartridge ribbon is a self-regenerating paper ribbon which allows several impressions to be made from the same area of ribbon and provides a total of 580 000 impressions.

Proportional Spacing

Proportional spacing, in which the width of space between characters varies with the size of the character, is provided on some electric typewriters, for example, the characters **i l j** occupy less space than, say, **m** and **w** and provision is made for this. Proportionally spaced characters improve the appearance of a passage and are easier to read.

Magnetic Tape Typewriters

A magnetic tape typewriter records on a magnetic tape the material which is typed and corrections are made by typing over the incorrect material. If a second draft is required any alterations to the original tape are typed and recorded on a second tape, reference being made to the lines of type affected. A composer is then used to merge the two tapes and produce a correct copy. Justification of margins, tabulating, centring and indentation can all be performed by selecting the appropriate buttons on the composer control panel. Any number of top copies can be automatically produced at a speed of about 14 characters per second from the corrected draft on the magnetic

Fig. 45 IBM Magnetic Tape Selectric Typewriter and Composer
(Reproduced by permission of IBM United Kingdom Ltd.)

tape. A magnetic tape typewriter and composer console are illustrated in Fig. 45.

Magnetic Card Typewriters

This typewriter uses a re-usable magnetic card for recording the typing of a first draft, and a separate card is used for each page of typescript. If it is necessary to amend or update the draft, the alterations are made by locating the line and the word on the magnetic card and typing in the revision. To type out the full amended copy, the typist presses a button and the machine types out the corrected version automatically at a speed of up to 180 words per minute. The card can be stored in a filing system for reference and re-use whenever required. This attachment is particularly good for producing reports, legal documents, export correspondence, offset-litho masters and any work of a repetitive nature requiring high quality reproduction. Any frequently used letters and paragraphs may be recorded on magnetic card and reproduced as often as they are required.

Further developments in the use of magnetic cards enable this device to be used as a computer terminal to store and retrieve data and, by using the telephone service, data recorded on magnetic cards can be transmitted to a branch or firm in another part of the country.

Varitypers

The Varityper produces typewriting which looks like printers' type. Once the machine has been programmed to the required line width, the operator types out the line and the justifying mechanism calculates the correct word spacing. The line is then retyped and the machine automatically inserts the correct amount of word spacing. Two type founts can be used in the varityper at one time. A large number of type styles are available, and the founts for these can be changed simply and quickly; foreign languages, chemical and mathematical formulae are included. An illustration of a Varityper is given in Fig. 46. It is possible to insert italics in the middle of a paragraph, or certain sections can be reproduced in a bolder face for special emphasis. The Varityper looks like a typewriter and is operated in much the same way but it has no type bars. There is a standard keyboard, space bar and carriage return lever. The Varityper will produce "masters" suitable for any method of reproduction, e.g. offset litho or stencil duplicator, etc. It enables the typist to produce originals of price-lists, service manuals, specifications, etc., equal in appearance to professional type-setting at a much lower cost.

Flexowriter

This is an electric typewriter of the automatic type which is capable of punching holes in tape, reading the tape and reproducing typewritten material from it. Letters and other business documents can, therefore, be automatically typed from a punched tape. The Flexowriter may be used in various ways, including billing and documentation where the same information has to be accurately reproduced on to several documents, automatic data processing and preparing data for transmission by teleprinter or telephone in the Datel services (see page 57).

Fig. 46 Varityper
(Reproduced by permission of Adressograph-Multigraph Ltd.)

Justowriter

This is similar to the Flexowriter in being capable of preparing and reproducing punched tape, but the operation is performed on two machines. The material is typed and punched tape produced on the first machine which, at the same time, records the amount of space required in each line to justify the margin, i.e. to make all the lines of type end at a specified point on the scale. The tape is transferred to the second machine which automatically reproduces typewritten matter but with a completely justified margin. This machine, with its facility for justifying margins, is particularly good for preparing masters for duplicators and for displaying information on forms, brochures, etc.

QUESTIONS

Typewriting

1. What steps would you take:
   (a) to keep your typewriter in good working order, and
   (b) to prevent carbon paper from becoming creased?

What would you suggest if you were asked to improve the quality and to increase the number of carbon copies which you obtain from one typing? *R.S.A. SD.2*

2. Your typewriter is about to be replaced and you are asked to state your preference as to type, carriage, etc., on the machine to be supplied. Give reasons for your choice, mentioning all the features you wish to find incorporated. *R.S.A. SD.2*

3. Draft an avertisement suitable for insertion in a trade journal advertising for sale an unwanted office typewriter in good condition. *R.S.A. SD.2*

4. Your employer wishes to send out 1 000 letters, with a facsimile signature, on headed notepaper, to look as nearly as possible like individually typed letters. How would you propose to deal with this? *R.S.A. SD.2*

5. You work in a small branch office which may not buy any new equipment without applying to Head Office for permission. You badly need a new typewriter. Prepare a letter, for the signature of the branch manager, making a case for the purchase of this typewriter. Head Office is usually unwilling to spend money on your branch, since you are making very little profit. *R.S.A. SD.2*

6. In what ways do some modern typewriters differ from those used ten years ago? What are some of the purposes of the punched or magnetic tape produced when using certain kinds of typewriters? *R.S.A. SD.2*

7. Give four reasons to support the theory that electric typewriters are more efficient than manual typewriters. *R.S.A. SD.2*

8. In what ways do any four of the following special-purpose typewriters differ from standard typewriters:
   (*a*) magnetic tape typewriter;
   (*b*) typewriter with front feed device;
   (*c*) Vari-typer;
   (*d*) Flexowriter;
   (*e*) dual unit typewriter. *R.S.A. OP.2*

9. List the responsibilities you consider the supervisor of a typing pool has:
   (*a*) to her employers,
   (*b*) to her typists. *R.S.A. SD.2*

10. (*a*) In what ways does an automatic typewriter differ from an electric typewriter?
    (*b*) What uses are being made of the automatic typewriter in offices? *R.S.A. OP.1*

DUPLICATING

Typists, shorthand typists and private secretaries are generally expected to know how to prepare stencils and master sheets and undertake the work of duplicating. It is important, therefore, for them to be conversant with the stencil, spirit and offset litho processes.

THE STENCIL PROCESS

The matter to be reproduced is cut into a stencil which consists of a sheet of special wax tissue. The stencil may be cut by a typewriter (the ribbon of the typewriter being disengaged) or it may be cut by hand, using a stylus pen. It is also possible to reproduce stencils covering a very wide range of subjects, including photographs, drawings, forms, etc., by photographic and electronic processes in which special stencils are prepared either by the manufacturers, or by the user, if he wishes to purchase the necessary equipment.

Whatever the type of stencil used, the inking process operates in the same way: the ink is fed through the stencil and on to the paper. Semi-absorbent paper is normally used for this form of duplicating, although with care, almost any weight of paper may be used. If it is necessary to use a paper which does not absorb the ink, interleaving sheets should be placed between duplicated sheets. This can be done by hand or by means of a special interleaver attached to the machine.

OPERATING PROCEDURE

Preparation of Stencil

1. Ensure that the type characters of the typewriter are perfectly clean before cutting the stencil.

2. Insert the carbon paper between the stencil backing sheet and the stencil, with the carbonized surface towards the stencil.

3. Insert the stencil into the typewriter and adjust the stencil so that it is in line with the type guide.

4. Disengage the ribbon by means of the stencil switch, so that the type bars strike directly on to the stencil.

5. Type with a sharp even touch in order to cut the stencil cleanly, giving slightly heavier pressure to letters such as "m" and "w".

6. Take care with punctuation marks and strike "o", "e" and "c" with slightly less force to avoid making perforations.

7. If there are any loose characters, smooth them down to close the perforation.

8. If a mistake is made in typing, hold the stencil clear of the carbon with a pencil and paint over the error with correcting fluid. Allow this to dry and type in the correct letters, leaving no trace of the error.

9. On completion of the stencil, check the type-written matter thoroughly with another typist,

10. Before commencing the next task on the typewriter, clean the keys with a stiff brush, as the type tends to become clogged up with wax after cutting stencils.

Note: A plia film (a special plastic transparent sheet) may be used to cover the stencil whilst it is being typed. This protects the stencil and keeps the type bars free from wax.

Fixing Stencil to Cylinder

1. Lower the stacking tray.

2. Open the cylinder cover.

3. Remove the carbon paper from stencil.

4. Anchor the head of the stencil on to the duplicator and then, turning the handle slowly, allow the stencil to fall into position on the cylinder, smoothing out any creases as it revolves. Ease out small creases sideways. To adjust large creases, lift stencil and reposition.

5. Tear off the backing sheet.

6. Clip the bottom of the stencil under the tail flap.

7. Close the cylinder cover.

Insertion of paper

1. Fan the paper to allow the air to separate the sheets and place it in the feed tray.

2. Adjust the paper feed side rail guides, if necessary.

3. Lower the paper weights.

4. Adjust the stacking tray side and end guides.

5. Raise the feed tray ready for duplicating.

Trial Run Adjustments   1. Take the paper for the first copy through the machine and study it carefully. This first copy provides the operator with a clue to any further adjustments which may have to be made before beginning the run, e.g. more space at the top of the document or at one of the sides. Paper should be used economically, particularly in the trial turns at this stage.

2. Replenish the ink supply if necessary.

Duplicating   1. Set the counter for the number of copies required.

2. Connect the electricity and switch on.

3. Use the control levers as directed in the manufacturer's manual.

Tidying and   1. Disconnect the electricity.

Completion   2. Take off the stencil by detaching it at the heading, and if it is likely to be required again, blot it and place into a filing folder for storage.

3. Drop the feed tray.

4. See that there is no paper still going through the machine and replace all unused paper in its packet.

5. Leave the cylinder handle in the "off" position and carry out all of the stacking operations.

6. Dust the machine so that paper fluff is removed.

7. Replace the dust cover, as this protects the machine from dust and damage.

Safety Precautions

1. In the case of all electrically operated machines:

(*a*) The plug should be regularly inspected.
(*b*) Avoid having a trailing flex which may be a hazard for the operator or other staff passing by.
(*c*) Always switch off the machine when not in use and remove the plug.

(*d*) If the machine is not functioning properly, do not tamper with the electrical parts but call on the services of a mechanic.

2. Never operate a duplicator with the cylinder uncovered. Modern machines do not operate with the cylinder exposed—a safety requirement of the Offices, Shops and Railway Premises Act 1963.

3. The machine can be stopped at any time during duplicating by moving the control lever to the "neutral" position or by pressing the red emergency stop button.

Maintenance

1. Regular servicing is essential.

2. Dust regularly and keep metal parts clean by rubbing over with a cleaning fluid.

3. Ensure that all levers are in the "off" or neutral positions.

4. Cover the machine when it is not in use.

Materials and Ancillary Equipment

1. Stencils:	standard—for normal typing.
	pre-cut—used for forms or letter headings.
	tracing—translucent.
	drawing—blue coated for hand-writing.
	brush—for use with acid-brush stencil ink for posters.
	electronic—for reproducing diagrams and photographs.
2. Pliafilm:	As referred to in preparation of stencil.
3. Ink:	Supplied in tubes.
4. Paper:	Semi-absorbent.
5. Correcting fluid:	for making corrections.
6. Stylus pens and backing plates:	for handwriting.
7. Blotting folders:	for storing stencils.

8. Cardboard tops: for affixing to stencils to hang in vertical filing cabinets.

9. Electronic Stencil Scanner: This is a machine as illustrated in Fig. 47, which produces a facsimile stencil of an original drawing or photograph for duplicating. The stencil is cut by a sparking stylus which produces a facsimile. As an electronic eye (photocell) travels along the rotating copy it emits signals from which a fine wire stylus cuts holes of varying size in the stencil according to the density of the copy.

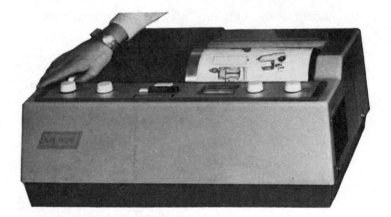

Fig. 47 Electronic Stencil Scanner
(Reproduced by permission of Gestetner Duplicators Ltd.)

Applications

For reproducing up to 5 000 copies of various business documents, including circular letters, reports, minutes of meetings and agenda for distribution, menus, house magazines, instruction manuals, etc.

Advantages	Disadvantages
1. Large number of copies repro-duced (up to 5 000) copies. 2. Good quality reproduction. 3. Ease with which photographs and drawings can be reproduced with electronic stencils. 4. Stencils can be stored and re-used. 5. Cheap copy paper. 6. The stencil duplicator is relatively easy to operate and is usually operated by a typist.	1. The absorbent paper is unsatis-factory for handwriting. 2. Separate runs and separate sten-cils are required for two or more colours. 3. Once used, masters cannot be altered. 4. Expensive for a few copies in view of the cost of stencils.

THE SPIRIT PROCESS

In this process, as the name implies, spirit is used as the duplicating medium in place of the ink used with stencil machines.

A master copy (half-art paper coated with china clay) is prepared from a transfer sheet coated with an aniline dye and providing a mirror impression. The image is transferred from the master to the copy paper (now in positive form), spirit being used to dampen the copy paper and allow a small coating of the dye to be deposited on to the copies.

Masters and copies can be of varying sizes, in fact there are spirit machines which permit the copying of work that varies in size between 25·4 mm × 76·2 mm (1 in × 3 in) and 432 mm × 762 mm (17 in × 30 in). There are both hand and electric machines and papers up to 432 mm × 356 mm (17 in × 14 in) in size can be fed automatically.

Any work that is written, drawn or typed as a "master" can be reproduced in up to seven colours in one operation on to various thicknesses of paper or card. The master can be filed like an ordinary piece of paper and further copies taken later. If necessary, masters can be posted from office to factory, or branch office overseas to head office in this country. In this way both sales orders and factory or works orders can be taken from one typing.

OPERATING PROCEDURE

Preparation of Master   1. A hand-written master is prepared by writing on the master sheet with a ball-point pen or sharp pencil and the transfer sheet (known as hectograph) is placed

underneath with the carbonized surface facing upwards. It is preferable to use a backing sheet to provide
a smooth surface, but only normal pressure should be
used for writing.

2. For preparing a typewritten master the typist
should use a normal touch and she should ensure that
the type characters on her typewriter are perfectly
clean. It is not necessary to disengage the ribbon for
preparing spirit masters.

3. Leave a sufficient margin on all four sides of the
master paper.

4. If an error is made, it is necessary to remove the
carbon impression on the glossy side of the master.
The following methods may be used:

(*a*) A soft erasure (made specially for the purpose)
will absorb the carbon and, at the same time,
replace the original surface. Although it leaves
a dirty mark, this will not show up on the copies.

(*b*) A correcting fluid may be painted very thinly
over the error and this replaces the clear china
clay backing.

(*c*) A sharp instrument may be used to scrape away
the carbon, but the disadvantage with this
method is that it may also scrape away the china
clay backing on the master.

After the incorrect material has been removed, the
correction should be made, and for this it is necessary to insert a piece of unused transfer sheet behind
the master, so that the carbon content of the alteration
will be the same as for the rest of the master. Type or
write in the correction.

5. On completion of the master, check it thoroughly
with another typist. Be careful not to handle the
carbonized surface of the master.

Operation of   1. Prime the felt pad with fluid by pumping the
Duplicator   fluid control lever several times.

2. To test that the felt pad is sufficiently damp for duplicating set the pressure control at "1" and hand-feed one sheet of paper through the machine without inserting the master at this stage. Turn the handle twice, starting and finishing at the "6 o'clock" position. If the paper is evenly damped, the machine is ready for use. If it is not evenly damped, pump more fluid to the felt pad.

3. Check that the feed tray mark "v" is set at "8" and is in line with the mark "v" on the perspex tray also set at "8"—or other number required for the size of paper being used.

4. The master is fixed to the roller with the dye surface uppermost. With the handle in the neutral position, open the master clip on the drum by moving the lever to the left.

5. Insert the master by dropping it into the open clip of the drum, ensuring that it is straight against the paper guide and that the dye side of the master is on the outside of the drum towards the perspex tray.

6. Close the master clip by moving it to the right, which fastens the master to the roller.

7. Hand feed one sheet of paper, with the fluid control at "1" and pressure control set at "1" and use it as a trial copy for making any necessary adjustments.

8. Adjust the top and bottom margins, if necessary, by turning the vertical registration control wheel on the left side of the machine.

9. Adjust the side margins, if necessary, by moving the paper guide bars at each side of the paper feed tray, or if only a minor adjustment is required turn the horizontal adjustment knob at the right hand side of the feed tray.

10. Lift the corner separators by moving back the red knob on the right of the feed tray.

11. Fan the paper thoroughly to allow the air to separate the sheets and place it in the feed tray,

watermark side upwards. Ensure that the paper guide bars are close to the paper and that the paper is tight up to the corner separators. No more than 150 sheets should be placed into the machine at a time.

12. Release the knob to lower the corner separators.

13. Drop the automatic feed wheels onto the paper and turn the wheels until the paper curls a little.

14. Set the counter at 000 so that this will indicate the number of copies run off.

15. Turn the handle twice for each copy, keeping check on the counter for the number required. For quantities of fifty or more the pressure control will have to be moved to higher numbers and the fluid control may need a higher setting depending on the density of the master. (A used master will require a higher density of fluid.)

Tidying and Completion

1. Remove the master by moving the master clip to the left. The clip should then be returned to the closed position.

2. Return the fluid control lever to "0".

3. Return the pressure control lever to "0".

4. Ensure that the handle is returned to the "neutral" "6 o'clock" position.

5. If adjustments were made on the feed tray and perspex tray return the controls to the normal positions.

6. Remove spare paper from the feed tray and the duplicated copies from the stacking tray.

7. Store away unused paper and other materials in their correct places.

8. Replace the dust cover, as this protects the duplicator from dust and damage.

Maintenace

1. Cover the machine when not in use and dust regularly, paying special attention to the pressure roller and drum.

2. Ensure that the pressure and fluid levers, and the master clip are "off" when the machine is not in use.

3. Switch off electricity and remove plug before cleaning and whenever the machine is not in use.

4. Do not overdamp the machine as this will shorten the life of the master.

5. Remove staples or clips on masters before placing them on to the roller, as they may damage the machine.

6. Place the master in the drum clip evenly, otherwise it may crease.

Materials and Ancillary Equipment

Paper: for masters   — one-side art paper with china clay coating.
          for copies   — non-absorbent paper.
          transfer sheets — coated with aniline dye (available in seven different colours).

Backing Sheets: for preparation of masters.
Fluid: duplicating spirit.
Correcting Equipment: correcting fluid.
                            Eraser.
Master packs: Prepared by heat transfer machines for the reproduction of drawings and diagrams.

Applications

As transfer sheets or carbons can be obtained in a variety of colours, spirit duplication has many uses. Complete copies can be taken of minutes, reports, accounts, price-lists, drawings, diagrams, and all forms of commercial documents. It is particularly good for internal memorandums and circulars as the copies are cheap and quick to produce.

Billing and documentation of all kinds can be performed by spirit duplication, as it is not only possible to reproduce complete copies of the information placed on the "master" copy, but to select specific information from any part of the original. For example one "master" copy could supply the information for an invoice with copies for accounts, statistics, file, etc.; delivery advice note, packing note, consignment note, stores copy, traveller's copy, labels, tags and envelopes. Only one typing is required for all these documents, and once the "master" is checked, complete accuracy is ensured throughout.

Data Selection

Items of data can be selected from computer print outs on a multi-purpose spirit duplicator incorporating the latest developments in selective data reproduction by push button control. It offers a simple means of reproducing on office or factory routine forms, selected data from an original prepared by a computer or other means, on master paper, without the risk of errors in transcription.

Advantages	*Disadvantages*
1. Easy and quick preparation of masters and operation of machine.	1. There is no standard quality of reproduction as the master deteriorates with use.
2. Cheap for 20 to 100 copies.	2. Copies fade if exposed to light for any length of time. It is unsuitable for displayed notices if required for a period of over six months.
3. Several colours can be reproduced simultaneously.	
4. The copy paper is good quality and suitable for handwriting.	3. There is a limit to the number of copies secured from one master, and if more than two hundred and fifty copies are required, it is advisable to use either stencil or offset litho duplication.
	4. The quality of work reproduced resembles carbon copies and is not comparable with stencil and offset litho duplicating.

THE "OFFSET" LITHO PROCESS

The master for the offset litho process, which may be either a metal or paper plate, can be prepared in one of the following ways:

(a) Typing with a typewriter fitted with a litho ribbon;
(b) Writing or drawing with special inks or carbon paper;
(c) Using photographic or electrostatic copying processes;
(d) Using electronic scanners.

Whichever method is used in producing the image it must contain a greasy substance. The master, fitted round a plate cylinder, is dampened with water, which the greasy material refuses to accept, but which is retained by the non-greasy areas. The master also comes into contact with an inking roller, the ink being accepted by the greasy image area and repelled by the moistened areas. The image on the master, which has attracted the ink, is offset in negative form on to a rubber blanket which in turn is offset on to the copy paper in positive form. The principle involved in this process is illustrated in Fig. 48.

Direct image and photographic are the two main groups of plates used in offset litho duplicating. A direct image plate is one in which the image is applied directly, i.e. by a typewriter or by hand drawing. A photographic plate receives its image photographically through a film and the image areas are greased during subsequent processing prior to duplicating.

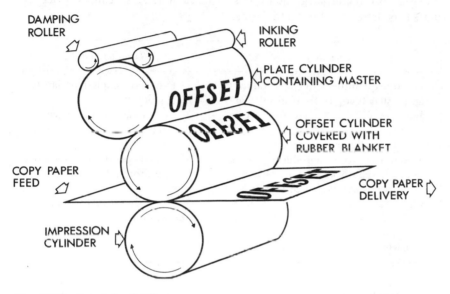

Fig. 48 The Principle of Offset
(Reproduced by permission of Gestetner Duplicators Ltd.)

When typing offset paper plates special silk film, nylon or cotton offset ribbons should be used. Paper and acetate carbon ribbons may also be used on suitably adapted typewriters. The typist should maintain a firm, even touch on the typewriter, just sufficient to give a clear impression. On no account should the characters be embossed through the plate. She should handle the plate carefully by not fingering the typing areas of the plate and preventing grease or dirt from appearing on it.

An offset eraser should preferably be used for making corrections. Medium pressure should be applied to remove the greasy part of the image, leaving only a faint "ghost" image. The typist should not scrape the surface of the plate, since this will damage the coating and prevent satisfactory duplicating. The correct passage should be re-typed using exactly the same pressure as before when using a fabric ribbon, but on typewriters fitted with paper or acetate ribbons it may be necessary to give each character a double stroke when typing the correction.

Applications

Almost any type and weight of copy paper can be used for this process of duplicating. Copies of a high quality can be obtained and it is particularly good for producing large quantities of circular letters, leaflets, price lists, parts lists, letter headings and forms.

Advantages	*Disadvantages*
1. Large quantities can be reproduced; up to 50 000 copies from metal plates and about 2 000 copies from paper plates. 2. Very good quality reproduction. 3. Suitable for reproducing office forms. Large stocks need not be kept as metal plates can be stored and re-used when required. 4. Good quality copy paper can be used. 5. A cheap method of duplicating particularly for large quantities.	1. Expensive capital outlay for machinery. 2. Additional office space required for duplicating and stores for materials. 3. Skilled operators are required for the more advanced applications. 4. Not economical for short run applications.

Colour Duplication

The spirit process, as explained on page 139, is capable of providing colour duplication by the use of coloured transfer sheets in the preparation of the "master" copy. It is also possible to carry out the colour duplication in the stencil process by changing the ink and the cylinder. In some machines it is only necessary to remove the cylinder and replace it with a similar cylinder containing another colour of ink. In others, however, it is necessary to carry out extensive cleaning of the machine before using another colour.

When it is desired to carry out a piece of work which contains a number of colours, it must be remembered that with the stencil process as many stencils as there are colours will be required, each separate stencil being prepared for only that part which has to be reproduced in that particular colour. Each colour must register where it is intended to appear on the copy.

Any number of colours may be used together in offset litho duplicating, provided a plate is made for each, and each requires a separate run through the machine. Coloured work of a very high standard can be achieved, but, as with the stencil method, the operator must ensure that each colour registers in the exact position on the copy.

COPYING MACHINES

Duplicating and printing processes produce copies of documents, whereas copying processes produce replicas of an original.

One of the great advantages of copying by machine is, of course, the obtaining of a copy quickly and without the possibility of any copying errors which may happen no matter how good the copy-typist may be.

The machines are electrically operated and the "master" (or original) from which the copies are photographed does not have to be prepared in any special way; there is no need for carbons, stencils or special paper; there is usually no limit to the number of copies which can be taken at any time, nor does the quality deteriorate; alterations or corrections can be made without any difficulty.

Copiers are either rotary or flat bed types. The originals for rotary copiers are processed inside the machine and they must, therefore, normally be single copies. A flat bed machine is one where the original is copied on top of the machine under a cover and this enables books and magazines to be copied as well as valuable documents which could be damaged inside a rotary machine.

The essential features of the main copying processes are given in Fig. 49.

Storage and Care of Materials

Care must be taken in the storage of photocopying materials and in general it is advisable not to order large stocks which may deteriorate. Most copying papers and chemicals require a cool dry place for storage and light sensitive negative papers should always be well covered and not exposed to light. The points referred to on page 136 concerning electrical apparatus should be observed when using copying machines. Staples and other paper fasteners should be removed from originals before inserting them in heat copiers and these copiers should also be given adequate cooling time before switching them off at the end of a copying assignment.

Laminating

Machines are available for laminating papers or cards for protection against moisture, dirt, grease and tampering. The document is placed in a machine with a heat process which seals it between layers of transparent film. It is used for notice board notices, valuable documents, sales literature, book or record dust jackets, menus and any papers or cards which require protection against wear and tear.

Name	Process	Suitable for offset master	Suitable for dyeline trans-lucency	Principal features and applications
DRY PROCESSES				
Electrostatic and Xerographic	In the xerographic process the original, which can be single or double-sided, is placed face downwards on a scanning screen and projected on to a selenium-coated plate charged with electricity. A fine powder which is charged electrostatically is covered over the plate and when the copy paper is brought into contact with the plate the image is attracted to it, forming a direct positive image. The image on the copy paper is then fused by heat to retain it permanently. Paper is automatically fed through the machine and copies can be produced at the rate of six a minute. The electrostatic process is similar except that the paper is coated with zinc oxide charged electrostatically and the image is coated with powder and fused to the paper by heat.	Yes	Yes	Good quality copies are obtained, but it is only economical for large quantities of copying. Suitable for most copying requirements from originals in any colour.

Process	Description			Notes
Heat Transfer/ Thermal (Thermographic)	This process uses a copy paper which is sensitive to heat. The heat created by infra-red rays is applied to the image, causing it to darken in direct positive form on the copy paper.	No	No	Simple and quick operation, but it uses inferior paper, will only copy originals containing a carbon content and some colours will not copy. It is useful for preparing spirit masters, thermal stencils for use on a stencil duplicator, overhead projector transparencies and for laminating documents.
Dual Spectrum	This process uses light which transfers the image from the original to an intermediate paper of light sensitive material. The intermediate paper image is then transferred to the copy paper by heat which produces a black on white copy.	No	No	This is more versatile than the thermographic process because it copies non-mineral inks and can also be used for copying from books as it is supplied with a flat exposing unit.
WET PROCESSES **Diazo (Dyeline)**	The original, known as a translucency, must be on transparent or translucent paper. It is placed in contact with dyeline paper and exposed to light. The light bleaches the paper white except for the areas covered by the image. The image is finally developed by a wet chemical or vapour.	Yes	Yes	This process is used for copying large drawings and is also suitable for reproducing documents which require frequent updating, such as statements. It can only be used to copy single-sided documents which must be translucent.

Name	Process	Suitable for offset master	Suitable for dyeline translucency	Principal features and applications
Direct Positive/ Autopositive	From translucent originals it produces a positive black on white copy without requiring a negative. From originals which are opaque or having an image on both sides a reverse image (negative) is obtained first and positive copies processed from it. A wet process using developer and stabilizing solutions.	No	Yes	A photographic process suitable for most copying requirements in any colour but rather expensive.
Gelatine Transfer (Verifax)	A negative, known as the matrix, which has a coating of gelatine, is exposed from the original. The matrix is entered into an activating solution and the image is transferred to the copy paper. Between 6 and 15 copies can be secured from one matrix.	Yes	Yes	A cheap process for small quantities but variable quality of reproduction as the temperature affects its performance.
Reflex	A negative is made first by exposing the original to light and developing and fixing it by normal photographic means. Any number of prints can then be taken from the negative.	No	Yes	Good reproduction qualities but diffused lighting is essential and it is an expensive process.

Transfer Diffusion	Exposure of the original is made on to a negative material, but unlike the reflex process, the negative is processed inside the copier to produce a positive copy. The original is sandwiched between the negative and copy papers and, after exposure to light, the original is removed and the negative and copy paper pass through a combined developer and fixer. The two sheets are pressed together by rollers and after being peeled apart reveal a positive print. Normally two copies can be obtained from one negative, but if multicopy materials are used, up to 15 copies may be taken.	Yes	Yes	Similar to reflex—both of these processes are particularly good for high quality copying required for example in legal documents and extracts from books.

Fig. 49 Copying Processes

QUESTIONS

Duplicating and copying

11. You have been made responsible for a new duplicator, which is to be used by personnel from other departments. Draft instructions, in the form in which they are to be displayed in the office, for the use and care of the duplicator. *R.S.A. SD.2*

12. State the most efficient manner of obtaining the following, taking into account economy of money and time:
    (*a*) Six additional copies of a closely typed A4 sheet;
    (*b*) Fifty copies of a circular letter, for internal use, now in rough manuscript draft;
    (*c*) As in (*b*) but 500 copies required;
    (*d*) One thousand copies of a two-page typed document, which includes a diagram. *R.S.A. SD.2*

13. The Office Manager complains to you that duplicated matter given to him for distribution is very poor in quality. He shows you that the work is patchy, that some of the words are missing altogether, and that there are ink smears on all copies. How do such faults arise, and what action should be taken to prevent them? *R.S.A. SD.2*

14. In your office there are a spirit duplicator and an ink duplicator, but no addressing machine. Each month you send to the same fifty addresses a small booklet. To avoid typing individual envelopes, how can you use the machinery at your disposal? *R.S.A. SD.2*

15. Describe steps to be taken in dealing with preparation and dispatch of a four-page bulletin to 1 000 people in:
    (*a*) an organization where there are frequent dispatches of this size,
    (*b*) an office where this occurs infrequently. *L.C.C. P.S.D.*

16. There are many different types of office "photo-copiers". For instance, some are dry and some are wet. Describe two different systems with their advantages and disadvantages. *R.S.A. SD.2*

17. Your employer visited the Business Efficiency Exhibition and was very impressed by the offset litho duplicators he saw. He asks you to compare offset litho with the stencil and spirit duplicators at present in use in your office. Prepare a tabulated statement making comparisons of the three machines under the following headings:
    (*a*) Duplicating process (state the materials you would use).
    (*b*) Applications, i.e. its suitability for the production of:
        (i) Black typewritten work,
        (ii) coloured typewritten work,
        (iii) handwriting/drawing,
        (iv) photographs.
    (*c*) Quantities produced.
    (*d*) Type of paper employed for copies.
    (*e*) Other remarks. *R.S.A. OP.2*

18. (*a*) Describe the various ways in which photo-copying machines can be used in the administration of an office.

(*b*) List the factors to be taken into account when selecting the most appropriate photo-copying process. *R.S.A. OP.2*

19. (*a*) Explain *in detail* how you would obtain one copy of a printed document from an office copier.

(*b*) Name the type of machine you would use and say why you would choose it.

(*c*) What are the advantages and disadvantages of photocopying? *R.S.A. OP.1*

20. State, with reasons, whether you would or would not suggest using a photo-copying machine in the following circumstances. If you would not recommend using a photocopying machine, what other machine would you use, assuming its availability?

(*a*) Ten copies of a two-page report which is required for internal use. It is in draft form and needs retyping.

(*b*) 200 copies of a three-page report which is to be sent to customers. It is already in its final form.

(*c*) Six copies of a page of a book which is required for internal use. The page must not be torn out.

(*d*) A customer's letter which has to be dealt with by three departments. *R.S.A. SD.2*

21. What masters are required for the following:

(*a*) an ink duplicator;

(*b*) a spirit duplicator;

(*c*) an offset-litho machine;

(*d*) dyeline? *R.S.A. SD.2*

22. (*a*) Give two materials of which offset-litho plates can be made.

(*b*) Give two ways in which offset-litho plates may be prepared for offset-litho printing.

(*c*) Give two advantages of using an offset-litho machine instead of a stencil duplicator. *R.S.A. SD.2*

23. Select any method of photo-copying and give information under the following headings:

(i) method of producing a copy

(ii) advantages over other methods

(iii) disadvantages of the method

(iv) cost per A4 copy

(v) an example of a job for which the copier would be suitable. *R.S.A. OM.*

24. Your firm requires 500 copies of a four-page catalogue to be duplicated from already prepared stencils. The amount of value-added tax on each item in the catalogue appears in the right-hand column on all pages and is to be shown in red.

Using these headings explain how you would deal with the task.

(i) Quantities and types of materials required

(ii) Preparation of duplicator and method of running off

(iii) Assembling catalogue and additional equipment used

(iv) Cleaning and filing the used stencils

(v) Packing up equipment and materials. *R.S.A. OM*.

25. (*a*) What is:

(i) the transfer diffusion method of photocopying;

(ii) the chief use of the dyeline copier;

(iii) the type of copier on which one may dial the number of copies required;

(iv) a thermal stencil?

(*b*) Give a brief account of the work of a scanner and mention the duplicating process in which it can be used. *R.S.A. COS*.

26. How would you correct errors:

(*a*) on a wax stencil,

(*b*) on a spirit master? *R.S.A. SD.2*

27. Your firm has agreed to make available to your department a sum of money which will enable you to purchase either an electrically operated ink duplicator or a good photocopying machine.

What considerations would you take into account when deciding which machine would be most suitable for your work? *R.S.A. SD.2*

28. List the steps you would take in the preparation of a spirit master. If the final product is to be in two or more colours, how is this achieved? *R.S.A. SD.2*

29. (*a*) Make a list of instructions designed to guide your office junior in cutting a stencil on a typewriter.

(*b*) How is grafting on a stencil carried out? *R.S.A. SD.2*

30. (*a*) Describe three ways in which a stencil can be prepared for ink duplicating.

(*b*) Explain the limitations of each of the three ways described in (*a*) above. *R.S.A. OP.1*

DICTATING MACHINES

Recording machines use either a non-magnetic or a magnetic medium.

NON-MAGNETIC MEDIA

The non-magnetic recording process is similar to the process used in gramophone records; a stylus cuts modulations into the recording material and when it is required to reproduce the sound a pick-up is passed over the modulated grooves. An advantage of this medium is that the amount of dictation recorded can be seen clearly. A permanent record is made, and corrections must be noted on an indicator slip. The permanency of the recording is important, as there is no danger of the recording being cleared before it has been transcribed by the typist. The responsibility for making corrections is passed on to the typist as the dictator simply draws the typist's attention to any corrections which have to be made. The typist must make a note of such amendments and implement them at the correct points of the dictation. Index slips are essential to indicate to the typist corrections, information regarding the length of the letters, additional copies required, etc.

Plastic Belts

Plastic belts provide non-erasable permanent recordings. The playing time of a belt is about fifteen minutes, which, on an average, results in approximately one and a half hours of typing. By using an index slip the dictator and typist are able to locate positions of dictated passages on the belts. The belt weighs very little, is small and can be posted in an ordinary envelope. The plastic belt is particularly useful where a permanent record has to be retained in a filing cabinet.

Discs

Plastic discs, like other non-magnetic media, provide a permanent record. The playing time is about twenty minutes. The discs can be resurfaced by a special heat process to enable them to be re-used.

MAGNETIC MEDIA

Recording machines using magnetic media do not provide a permanent record, and corrections are made by the simple process of talking on top of the original dictation. The tapes, sheets, etc., can be used indefinitely as new recordings take the place of previously dictated material.

Sheets

The sheets used in these machines are made of magnetically coated plastic or paper. They are coated only on one side; the other side is left free for notes. The paper sheets, which are inexpensive, can be filed in the same manner as ordinary correspondence. Magnetic sheets are useful for sending messages through the post, as they can be folded into a DI size envelope and sent at the ordinary postage letter rate. Folding and even crumpling do not damage the recording. The sheets will record about twelve minutes of continuous dictation. A copy of a recording can be obtained by placing two sheets on to the machine instead of one.

Plastic Belts

A plastic belt will take up to fourteen minutes' recording, and after the dictation has been transcribed, the belt can be cleaned with an eraser magnet. The area of recording can be seen clearly on the machine and this enables the dictator and typist to locate the position reached and assess the length of the dictation. Belts can also conveniently be dispatched by mail and folding does not affect the recording.

Tapes

Tape recorders use a magnetically-coated plastic tape capable of recording at least thirty minutes' dictation.

Discs

Discs coated with magnetic material are used for dictation times ranging from six to twenty minutes. The discs are supplied in several colours; this is useful for identification purposes.

Posting Recorded Material

Sheets and belts containing recorded messages are suitable for sending through the post to agents, representatives, etc., and they help to eliminate much shorthand and typewriting work. There are, however, disadvantages of which the student should be aware in posting recorded material; for example:

(*a*) In most systems no record can be kept of the communication.

(*b*) Recording media are not recognized legally.

(*c*) A noise, such as a door slamming, makes the dictation inaudible, and this may not be discovered by the dictator.

Remote Dictation System

A remote dictation system consists of a recording machine or, as is usually the case, several recording machines which are situated in the typists' room. The machines are operated remotely from several dictating units allocated throughout the offices. This system is particularly useful in a large office where it is not economically practicable to provide individual dictating machines for all who require dictation facilities. Each dictator has access to a microphone, or some other form of recorder, from which the dictation is immediately transmitted to the point of transmission (the typists' room).

The dictation system can be linked either to a **PABX** or **PBX** telephone network or a separately wired circuit, and contact is made to a central bank of recording units by dialling a special number on the telephone.

A more even flow of dictation can normally be expected from a remote dictation system and this makes the even distribution of the typing easier.

Dictation

The following points should be observed in the recording of dictation:

1. Keep the volume of voice as low as practicable.

2. Hold the microphone fairly close to the mouth.

3. Do not speak too quickly or in jerks, but speak into the microphone at the speed which is used for dictating to a shorthand typist.

4. Speak clearly and deliberately, using a steady, conversational rhythm in phrases of about five to ten words.

5. Spell out foreign and unusual words, using the phonetic alphabet.

6. Avoid clipping words with the "On–off" switch.

7. If a correction is made, refer to it on the index slip.

8. State the exact requirements clearly *before* dictating a letter or report; the date the letter is to be typed, the number of copies required, enclosures, etc.

9. Indicate the start of a new paragraph by the word "paragraph".

10. It is advisable to dictate the full stops, question marks, colons, semi-colons, dashes, exclamation marks, brackets and quotation marks.

Transcribing

The following points should be observed when transcribing recorded dictation:

1. Pay attention to any special instructions and corrections accompanying the record.

2. Letters required urgently by the dictator should be typed, checked and returned to him first of all.

3. The size of each letter must be assessed before typing, to enable the correct size of paper to be used.

4. Any doubtful points in the dictation should always be checked with the dictator or another responsible member of staff.

5. Consult a dictionary whenever there is any doubt about the spelling of a word.

6. Insert the proper punctuation marks and allow adequate paragraphs.

7. Every transcription must be accurately typed and the utmost care must be taken in checking letters, etc., before they are removed from the type-writer.

8. Take very great care of the transcribing machine and always cover it when not in use.

ADVANTAGES AND DISADVANTAGES OF RECORDED DICTATION

The advantages and disadvantages of employing machines for dictating purposes should be clearly understood, and the vital factors are set out below.

Advantages of Recorded Dictation

1. There is a saving in a shorthand typist's time because, when she is receiving her dictation by shorthand, the employer's flow of dictation is interrupted by the necessity to think of his next phrase or by the interruption of telephone calls or visitors. When a machine is used for dictation, the typist can be employed on other work whilst the dictation is being given.

2. Belts, sheets, etc., carrying dictated material can be mailed, and in this case even the work of typewriting is eliminated. The addressee must, of course, have a recording machine of the same kind.

3. Dictating machines can be used to record the entire proceedings of a meeting, discussion or lecture, although when more than one person is speaking it is sometimes difficult to distinguish voices.

4. The employer is able to dictate at any time he chooses; for example, at lunch time or after his secretary has gone home. If he has a portable machine, he can dictate even whilst he is travelling.

5. The shorthand typist does not have the experience of having to decipher a badly written outline, as, with a dictating machine, any unfamiliar word can be played over and over again until it is understood.

Disadvantages of Recorded Dictation

1. When a machine is used, the personal contact between the employer and his secretary is lost. As she takes down dictation in shorthand, the secretary is often able to assist her employer with queries.

2. After dictation to a shorthand writer all queries and doubtful points have been answered.

3. On many of the dictating machines correction is impossible, and on others it is rather difficult.

4. The shorthand typist's notebook provides a valuable record of the correspondence dictated, and reference can easily be made to previously dictated matters.

5. Many employers cannot be troubled to operate dictating machines and find shorthand efficient and quick.

6. A recording machine does not indicate the name of the person speaking, and for this reason it is at a disadvantage at a meeting where several people are speaking. Chiefly because of this, the record of the proceedings will not be entrusted to a machine in our courts of law, where the work is undertaken by the Shorthand Writers' Association. This is also true of the report of the proceedings in the Houses of Parliament, where the *Hansard* shorthand writers take a full and accurate verbatim record for printing and distribution the following morning.

7. Recorded dictation can be transcribed by a pool of typists, but the work dictated to the private secretary is of such a nature that shorthand is essential. Brief instructions are given, discussion takes place, and much is left to the discretion of the private secretary.

8. The disadvantages of posting recorded material, as mentioned on page 156, should be noted.

9. If a dictating machine is to operate efficiently very good dictators are needed.

10. It is much more difficult for the typist to correct the employer's English and it is also more difficult if she has to look up any information previously dictated for inclusion in a letter.

11. It is uneconomic if the saving of time on the part of the typist results in the employer taking longer to dictate with a dictating machine.

QUESTIONS

Dictating

31. Your employer travels to many branches. It is his habit to dictate letters and reports on to tapes, discs or belts (according to equipment available at branches), and to post the recorded matter to you for transcription. What equipment is necessary in your office, and what rules should your employer observe? *R.S.A. SD.2*

32. You are allowed to choose a dictating machine for your office. State the type of machine you would prefer, giving reasons for your choice. *R.S.A. SD.2*

33. In your office there are two dictating machines. When they were bought it was intended that one should be used by two executives for their dictation, and the other should be used by one typist-transcriber. However, sometimes both men want to dictate at once, and sometimes more than one transcriber works at the same time. This means that the two machines are frequently passed from person to person, and much irritation is caused because accessories, as, for example, a foot control or a microphone, are missing. Search usually reveals that they have been put in somebody's desk drawer, and a great deal of time is wasted tracing the necessary parts before dictation or transcription can begin. It is proposed in future that you shall be responsible for the dictating equipment, and you are expected to devise some system whereby the borrower signs for what he or she takes. The equipment consists of the two machines, four spools of tape, two microphones, two head-sets, two foot-controls, and correction pads. List any rules you would make, and show how you would keep any chart or book, if you think one necessary. *R.S.A. SD.2*

34. What instructions should be given to a typist who joins your firm and will be transcribing from a dictating machine? *R.S.A. SD.2*

35. What is the value, to a large business organization, of a centralized dictating system? *R.S.A. SD.2*

36. You are an audio-typist. When you transcribe, you expect to get certain instructions:
    (*a*) at the beginning of the whole dictation;
    (*b*) at the beginning of each letter;
    (*c*) during the course of the dictation of a letter;
    (*d*) at the conclusion of either a letter or the whole dictation.
 Make a list of these instructions, divided as above, in a manner which you consider would help you most when transcribing. *R.S.A. SD.2*

37. When a person dictating to a dictation machine makes a mistake, what should he or she do in the case of:
    (*a*) a magnetic recording machine;
    (*b*) a non-magnetic recording machine? *R.S.A. SD.2*

38. Dictating machines have been introduced into your organization. The representative of the firm supplying the machines has shown the staff how to use them.
 You are the only experienced audio-typist in the organization and you are asked

to write some simple instructions (which do not include the mechanical aspect of the machines) to guide the other transcribers. Write the rules covering the points of importance. *R.S.A. SD.2*

39. Mr Spencer and Mr Adams are busy surgeons.

(*a*) Mr Spencer dictates his letters to his secretary as and when he can. Sometimes he is not free to deal with correspondence for two or three days at a time.

(*b*) Mr Adams dictates his letters to a dictation machine. Sometimes he does this in his consulting room, when he is free; sometimes he dictates at home and leaves the tapes on his secretary's desk early in the morning on his way to the hospital. State the relative merits of each system of dictation from the points of view of both the employer and the secretary. *R.S.A. SD.2*

40. The firm for which you work proposes to install a system of audio-typing. In a report to the firm's Personnel Manager discuss the effects of such a change on the shorthand-typing staff and suggest ways in which their goodwill and co-operation might be obtained. *R.S.A. OP.2*

ADDRESSING MACHINES

Addressing machines are available which use as their printing medium stencils, hectograph masters or metal, foil and plastic plates. In each, repetitive information is placed on to a "master", which, in order to reproduce the information, is passed through a machine which records the information very much more quickly than handwriting or typewriting and with absolute accuracy. It is similar to a duplicator in providing duplicate copies but instead of producing a large quantity of copies from one master it duplicates one, or as many as are required from a large number of masters.

Stencils

Stencil-operated addressing machines work in much the same way as stencil duplicating machines. The stencils, which are prepared on a typewriter, are made of impregnated fibre mounted on a cardboard frame. The frame may be narrow to carry the stencil only, or may have space at the top for a label which contains a copy of the information on the stencil, or which can be used as a record of mailings, payments, etc. The stencils can form a very useful index and a suitable system of guide cards arranged alphabetically, geographically or by trades will simplify classification. A special attachment is fitted to the typewriter to enable it to type the stencil cards.

The stencils are cheaper and lighter than metal plates but they are not so durable. The inking process can be messy and time consuming, but it produces a good quality copy.

Hectograph Masters

Hectograph-spirit addressing machines employ the principle of spirit duplicating referred to on page 139. Hectograph dye paper is used when typing the "masters", which are supplied in continuous form. The master sheets are perforated for easy separation and are fitted into plastic frames, which can be obtained in various colours for special indication.

The masters are very cheap and easy to produce, but the quality of reproduction varies with use and there is a limit to the number of copies obtained from one master. A feature of this process is the ease with which coloured impressions can be made.

Metal and Plastic Plates

Metal and plastic-plate addressing machines work from embossed plates, which print through an inked ribbon to give a facsimile typewritten impression. The plates are prepared on embossing machines; the most effective one is an electrically-operated machine with a typewriter-style keyboard.

Figure 50 illustrates a large addressing machine on which production speeds up to 2 000 impressions per hour can be achieved when feeding forms by hand. This machine, called an automatic data writing machine, with its large work top area, has been designed for payroll preparation, production control forms, credit transfers, direct mail, advertising, etc. A very good impression can be obtained from a metal or plastic plate and more than one copy can be made by using NCR or carbon paper. The metal plates are, however, heavy and the machines tend to be rather noisy. The plates are expensive to make and there is a delay in receiving new and amended plates from the manufacturer if an embossing machine has not been purchased.

Foil Masters

A foil master is a paper-thin strip of metal alloy which can be embossed on an ordinary typewriter. The foil masters are supplied with eight foils in one strip, perforated for easy typing and separation. Each foil holds up to eight lines of 40 characters in elite type. The embossed foil masters are fitted into carriers which may take the form of ledger cards or record cards. The masters, when fitted into the machine, print through a plastic ribbon to give a facsimile typewritten impression, similar to the metal plate machine. This is a cheap and easy method of preparing plates. No special equipment is required in their preparation and the plates are light and clean to handle.

Fig. 50 Automatic Data Writing Machine
(Reproduced by permission of Addressograph-Multigraph Ltd.)

Addressing Machine Devices

1. Automatic or hand feeding.

2. Controls to print one copy, skip (i.e. pass through the machine without printing) and repeat.

3. Foot pedal control allowing the operator to use both hands for feeding materials into the machine.

4. Programming for automatic selection of cards.

5. Numbering and dating attachments.

6. Automatic counter for recording the number of impressions made.

7. Masking device for cutting out information which is not required.

8. Signature plate attachment.

Applications

Addressing machines can be used for a wide range of office systems. In addition to addressing envelopes they may be used for heading invoices, statements, delivery notes, advice notes, credit transfers, circular letters and pay documents and envelopes.

QUESTIONS

Addressing

41. For what purposes, other than that of addressing envelopes, can an addressing machine be used? Is it possible, using an addressing machine (i) to address more than one envelope to the same address, and (ii) to address envelopes only to selected addresses from among the stencils or plates? Give reasons for your answers. *R.S.A. SD.2.*

42. Your employer is considering purchasing an addressing machine and he asks you to supply the answers to the following questions:

(*a*) For what purposes, other than that of addressing envelopes, can an addressing machine be used?

(*b*) Can the stencil, master or plate be used for any other office functions?

(*c*) Is it necessary to purchase a special purpose typewriter for preparing the stencils, masters or plates?

(*d*) What are the differences in the printing medium between the stencil, spirit and metal plate machines?

Write a report clearly setting out the answers to the questions. *R.S.A. OP.2*

43. Choose any type of addressing machine and explain how you would do the following:

(i) make a plate or card

(ii) use the plate or card to address an envelope

(iii) file the plate for future use

(iv) ensure that the cards or plates always correspond to your firm's mailing list requirements

(v) keep the addressing machine in good working order. *R.S.A. OM.*

44. You become secretary to your local coin collectors' club. It has about fifty members and notices are sent out each month. You find that all envelopes are typed or written by hand. You consider this a great waste of time.

Write a letter to the chairman of the club suggesting an improved system. *R.S.A. SD.2*

ADDING AND CALCULATING MACHINES

Adding/listing Machines with Small Keyboard

The keyboards on these machines comprise ten keys only—one key for each digit, nought to nine. The compact arrangement of the keys allows them to be operated by touch as in typewriting.

The machines are equipped with a carriage to hold a tally roll or other kind of form on which the calculations are printed, and they are constructed for either manual or electrical operation. Totals are obtained on the manual machines by depressing the total key and operating the handle, but on the electric machines the total is obtained by merely depressing the total motor-bar. On most machines full totals are automatically printed in red, and are identified by an asterisk, and subtotals or " Carry Forward" totals are also printed in red, but without an asterisk. Most models have the credit balance feature which indicates the amount of credit when the sums subtracted are greater than the sums added. Credit balances are identified by a "Cr." sign.

The machines are capable not only of adding and listing, but also of calculations involving subtraction, multiplication, division, discounts and percentages.

Before beginning the calculations, the operator must make sure that the machine is cleared. Figures are entered on the keyboard by depressing, in succession, the appropriate keys in the same order as the figures would be read. Whenever an amount consisting of pounds only is entered two noughts must be entered at the end of the "run". Amounts consisting of pence only are entered in the correct position without the need to insert noughts, except for amounts which contain noughts. Many machines do not have facilities to insert half pence, but where there is a half pence key it will only print in the position immediately following the pence column.

Adding/Listing Machines with Full Keyboard

With the full keyboard the amounts are first set up on the keyboard by reading the figures from left to right and depressing the appropriate keys. The sum is then transferred to the adding register and printed on the tally roll at the back of the machine by pulling the handle, or in the case of an electric model by depressing the motor-bar.

The keys are divided into separate columns, which correspond to the ruling of a ledger account, for pounds and pence. When the keys are depressed, the sum on the keyboard can be examined before it is listed. Several keys can be set up on the keyboard at the same time by using two or more fingers and reading the entire amount and not one figure at a time. The noughts are printed automatically without operation of the keys. With this type of keyboard it is possible to correct an error before operating the machine, as the keys which have been depressed are visible. They remain down until the motor-bar is touched or the handle pulled. If a mistake has been made in one column, the error can be corrected by depressing the correct key in that particular column, or the whole amount set up on the keyboard can be cancelled by pressing the error key. Adding and listing machines are operated either by hand or electrically. Machines can be obtained which will deal with weights and measurements, if required.

Adding/listing machines can be used for balancing cash, adding cash sales, checking invoices, taking out trial balances, adding pay rolls, checking till rolls, stocktaking, preparing statements, checking P.A.Y.E. records and pay envelopes, reconciling bank statements and preparing sales day-book and analysis, etc.

Key-driven Adding/Calculating Machines

The distinguishing feature of key-driven adding/calculating machines is that when a key is depressed the number is immediately registered in the sight dial. There is no operation of a lever or motor-bar during a calculation, as when the operator depresses the key its value flashes instantaneously in the front dial. When another key is depressed, its value is then added to the first. These machines are used for wages, invoices, and stock record calculations, and where considerable numbers of long additions have to be performed. The machine performs all four processes of arithmetic, and is available for either manual or electrically-powered operation.

Some machines are fitted with a second accumulating memory register. If two or more groups of additions are to be totalled the operator depresses the "plus" bar after each group addition. This clears the group total from the front dial and automatically accumulates it in the rear dial. The operator can then carry out another group addition, and when a grand total is required the "plus" bar is depressed and the grand total appears in the rear dial. Direct subtraction is also a simple process with the memory dial calculator. The operator registers a subtract item or totals a group of subtract items in the front dials. The subtract key is depressed, and instantly the total is subtracted from the grand total in the rear dial, thus providing an automatic net total.

It should be noted, however, that the results of these machines are not recorded on a list, as in the previous examples.

Light-weight electronic calculators are now being used in preference to the electric calculators as they are much easier and quicker to operate, much more portable and take up less desk space.

Rotary-operated Calculating Machines

Rotary-operated calculating machines perform automatically addition, subtraction, multiplication and division at very high speeds. They are also capable of calculating square roots, cube roots and other involved mathematical problems. They are set either by a lever or a key, and in both machines the results of the calculations appear in the dials.

To operate the lever-set machine the figures are set up by placing the levers against the appropriate numbers in the setting mechanism, which may take the form of a barrel. The amount is then transferred to the product register by turning the crank handle on the right-hand side of the machine.

On the key-set machine there is a keyboard with rows of keys numbered nought to nine in a series of columns and the figures are set up by the depression of keys.

The Printing Calculator

The printing calculator automatically adds, subtracts, multiplies and divides, and also lists all the factors and results of the calculations on a tally roll. The tally roll is useful for providing printed proof of the accuracy of the calculations and also for attaching to the document for future reference and checking. Because the individual totals are recorded on the tally roll a series of calculations can be carried out in one run. Printing calculator machines are all electrically operated and are capable of multiplication and division, accumulative multiplication, multiplication followed by division, adding and subtracting whole numbers or decimals and calculating percentages, exchange rates, discounts and interest.

MANIFOLD BILL BOARDS

Manifold bill boards (or copy writer boards) are used for entering and posting several documents simultaneously. The entries are made by hand and the copies are produced by the use of carbon paper. Statements can be prepared on a manifold bill board at the same time as the entries are made in the ledger and journal. This eases the situation at the end of the month, as the statements are ready for sending out immediately the last ledger posting for the month has been made. One advantage of this method of book-keeping is that there is a greater accuracy of working as the possibility of error in posting from one record to another is eliminated.

Manifold bill boards can be used for a wide variety of accountancy purposes. They may, for example, be employed in preparing, in one operation, the following sets of documents:

1. Purchase Accounts: Bought ledger, proof sheet, and remittance advice note.

2. Pay Records: Payroll, individual earnings record and pay slip.

3. Cash Records: Cash book, customer's receipt, and bank paying-in slip, or cash book, cheque, and bank advice.

ACCOUNTING MACHINES

Mechanization of the production of routine accounting records is a necessity in the business world today. Accounting machines are invaluable in providing management with an up-to-the-minute source of information, and in effecting an enormous saving of time, money, and labour in all departments of business. They are capable of performing several book-keeping entries automatically by a single operation, thus relieving the book-keeper of much routine work. Most accounting machines combine the essential features of a typewriter and an adding/listing machine. These machines make entries on ledger sheets and statements simultaneously, and their great advantage in a busy office is that all statements are ready for sending out immediately the last ledger posting for the month has been made. Typical applications of accounting machines are the following:

1. Posting to a sales ledger where three records are prepared simultaneously—the ledger, statements and journal.

2. Entering in one operation the customer's receipt, copy receipt for posting to the sales ledger, the cash received sheet and two copies of the bank paying-in slip.

3. Preparing cheque and payments cash sheet.

4. PAYE accounting including the employee's earning record, the pay slip for the employee, the pay roll and the pay envelope.

The use of magnetic cards with accounting machines has increased their speed and versatility. The cards can be used to store information such as account numbers, names and addresses and balances. When a ledger card is placed in the console, the magnetic data is read, checked and fed to the processor. During processing, the card is updated both visually (on the front) and magnetically (on the reverse side of the card). Entries are made by feeding in magnetic cards and by the operator keying in the new data on the keyboard. Calculations are carried out automatically at high speeds and the results are printed out on continuous stationery or on working documents such as invoices, statements, sales ledger and sales journal. The retention and up-dating of data on the striped magnetic cards relieves the operator of much of the repetitive operating required on accounting machines without this facility. The information stored on a striped card for a typical payroll accounting operation might, for example, consist of the clock number, social security number, name of employee, hourly rate or salary, union dues, savings deductions, insurance deductions, earnings to date, savings deductions to date, insurance deductions to date, income tax paid to date and week code.

PUNCHED-CARD SYSTEMS

The fundamental steps in a punched-card system are:

1. creating the records by punching and verifying the records;

2. sorting the records;

3. tabulating the information contained on the cards.

Punched cards (*see* Fig. 51) are used to provide the input figures and to record the results produced by the machines.

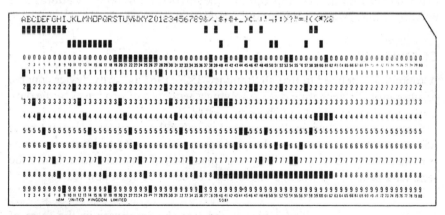

Fig. 51 A Punched Card

The punching, sorting and tabulating operations are similar whatever the purpose for which the machines are required, and the only differences between one application and another are in the design of the cards, and the ways in which the various functions of the tabulator are employed. Punched card systems are capable of much of the repetitive routine calculation involved in the accounting and secretarial work of commerce and industry, for example they can be used for the record-keeping functions of business involving general accounting, expenditure control, sales accounting, sales analysis, purchases accounting, costing, production control, payroll, invoicing, stores accounting, market research, statistics, depreciation and plant records, hire purchase, and stock control.

Invoices, time sheets, orders, etc., are replaced by cards of a uniform size, on which the information is recorded by punched holes. After the cards have been punched and the accuracy of their punching verified, they are available for the production of the various accounting records and tabulated statements which may be required. The cards are sorted automatically by means of the punched holes. They are placed in the feeding magazine of a sorter and a row of sensing pins is fitted over the column to be sorted. The machine is set in motion and the cards are moved along to the sensing pins. The passage of the cards is interrupted for a fraction of a second while the pins descend.

The pin corresponding to the punched hole passes through it and causes the appropriate receiving box to open and receive the card. One box is provided for each of the nine punching positions in each column, and one for rejected or unpunched cards. Accounting and statistical records are produced from the card by means of a tabulator which senses the cards and prints the information on appropriate documents; automatically adding and printing totals, balances and grand totals.

COMPUTERS

A computer is defined in British Standard 3527:1962 as "Any device capable of automatically accepting data, applying a sequence of processes to the data and supplying the results of these processes".

Computers were originally designed to solve the complex calculations of scientists and mathematicians, but their use in present-day business situations is more concerned with handling vast quantities of business data, hence the term data processing which is often used to describe such applications.

There are five main parts to a computer:

1. **Input** — the data which is fed *into* the computer in the form of punched cards or paper tape; magnetic tape; direct typing (either console typewriter or terminal devices); printed characters (as on cheques).

2. **Output** — the information which is produced *from* the computer as the end product which may be in the form of printed

matter (e.g. lists, invoices, etc.). Output may also be in the form of cards, tape or discs to be used as input for another operation, or may be displayed visually similar to TV.

3. **Storage** — the computer's "memory" which allows data to be stored, worked upon and up-dated, i.e. new information replaces the information previously stored.

4. **Calculating** — the arithmetic unit capable of performing calculations at very high speed by means of binary arithmetic.

5. **Control** — a means by which the other parts of the computer are co-ordinated and applied as directed by the program.

Computer Applications

Computers are capable of performing all of the accounting machine and punched card installation applications referred to earlier but at very much higher speeds without human intervention and with the ability to handle more complex data. In a sales ledger application, for example, the computer is able to compare the amounts of invoices with the credit limit of customers and in stock control, comparisons of stock levels can be made with pre-determined minimum figures drawing attention to the items which require re-ordering.

Other typical computer applications include payroll, bought ledger, production planning, costing and budgetary control, hire purchase transactions, market research and statistical information for management control.

Using the Computer

Before a computer can be put to work a great deal of preparatory work must be undertaken which involves the analysis of the existing office systems and the design of new computerized systems. Each system is made up of a number of programs which are composed of a series of detailed instructions, e.g. read a punched card; subtract stock issue from stock balance, etc. Part of a program used for the sales ledger application referred to above might contain the following instructions:

ADD INVOICE TOTAL TO OLD-BALANCE GIVING NEW-BALANCE IF NEW-BALANCE IS GREATER THAN CREDIT LIMIT WRITE EXCESS LINE WRITE NEW LEDGER RECORD.

Computer Staff

Data Processing Manager — responsible for all aspects of computer administration and operations.

Systems Analyst Programer — concerned with designing and analysing office systems for computerization and programing them.

Data Preparation Operators (or Key Punch Operators)

Control Clerks

File Librarians

Computer Operators

— concerned with the operation of the computer, including the preparation of input data.

SORTING DEVICES

Documents

Correspondence should be sorted and classified before filing, and a document-sorting cabinet is a valuable aid to arranging the names or subjects into alphabetical order; a suspended folder is provided for each letter of the alphabet, and the documents are placed in or behind the appropriate folder.

Flap sorters are commonly used for sorting documents for filing. The flaps are hinged to a steel base and arranged in such a manner that they overlap each other with the titles of each being clearly visible. The titles will generally contain the letters of the alphabet, but numbers, subjects or other classifications may be used. Papers, as they are sorted, are placed under the appropriate flaps and are held securely in position. The filing clerk can sort a large number of documents whilst remaining seated and the compact arrangement of the sorting device avoids unnecessary reaching or other tiring movement.

Punched Cards

Automatic sorters are used for punched cards. *See* page 169 relating to punched-card systems.

Cash

In banks, wages departments and stores, large amounts of cash and notes must be counted speedily and accurately. Mechanical means of performing this task have become a necessity, and a wide range of equipment capable of handling and counting coins and notes has now been devised. Some are capable of carrying out several operations of counting and sorting, e.g. one counting machine is capable of counting mixed silver at the rate of £1 200 per hour. Machines capable of counting and preparing wage packets have also been developed. These machines will feed coins rapidly and accurately into a chute, at the base of which is placed a wages packet or other container to receive them.

Change-giving machines are also in common use today, especially in railway stations and places of entertainment. These machines are capable of paying out any combination of coins by pressing one or more keys as required.

LATEST DEVELOPMENTS

Office machinery is rapidly changing and developing and it is important that the secretary keeps her employer fully informed of the latest trends. She should take a keen interest in the excellent illustrated leaflets and booklets which the manufacturers supply and visit business efficiency exhibitions and the showrooms of office equipment dealers.

QUESTIONS

Accounting and other Machines

45. Your firm, quite a small one, has been doing its accounts by hand. A salesman has tried to sell your employer a book-keeping machine with a small keyboard (i.e. 10 keys). Another salesman has recommended using a 3-in-1 system on Billing Boards.

Your employer asks you whether you know anything about either of these and asks you to write out notes for him stating how both types of equipment could be used. Set out your notes in the form of a simple report. *R.S.A. COS.*

46. (*a*) What are the uses of a punched card installation?

(*b*) What information would you expect a punched card, used for invoicing, to contain?

(*c*) Describe briefly the principal stages of a punched card system. *R.S.A. OP.2*

47. Describe the various means which are available to enable calculations to be made quickly and accurately. What factors would you take into consideration when selecting the most appropriate means for your office? *R.S.A. OP.2*

48. The figures given below were printed on an adding and listing machine. What do you learn from them?

```
        245.89  +
        305.22  +
         00.06  +
         00.06  −
          1.10  +
TOTAL   552.21  *
```

R.S.A. SD.2

49. Your employer is considering purchasing a calculator. Supply the answers to the following questions in memorandum form:
    (*a*) In what specific ways will a calculator be of use in the office?
    (*b*) What is the difference between an adding-listing machine and a calculator?
    (*c*) What is meant by: (i) a key-driven calculator, and (ii) a rotary-operated calculator? *R.S.A. OP.2*

50. What are the uses of:
    (*a*) a Vari-typer,
    (*b*) continuous stationery and form-feed equipment,
    (*c*) an adding and listing machine? *R.S.A. SD.2*

51. (*a*) What types of office machinery and equipment are likely to be used by an organization employing an office staff of 300, all housed in the same building? and
    (*b*) "There is, today, a tendency towards over-mechanization." Discuss this statement. *L.C.C. P.S.D.*

52. Your company, which has difficulty in obtaining additional staff, is faced with the following problems:
    (i) Insufficient time to enter increased output of mail in the Post Book.
    (ii) The shorthand-typists are unable to cope with correspondence in the time available.
    (iii) Accounting and calculating machines are heavily overloaded and the system is unable to produce up-to-date figures when required.
    What machinery or equipment would you suggest installing to ease one of these situations? Give your reasons. *R.S.A. COS.*

53. Your Office Manager has asked you to attend a business equipment exhibition and examine some of the latest machinery and systems. Prepare a report of your visit, giving details of four items of recent development. *R.S.A. OP.2*

54. Name the types of machine in connection with which the following items of equipment might be required:
    (*a*) a stylus pen;
    (*b*) a belt which cannot be cleared by re-recording;
    (*c*) a tally roll;
    (*d*) a master sheet with a shiny side. *R.S.A. SD.2*

55. In setting up a new office, what equipment do you consider necessary to cover the work listed below? Briefly state the reasons for your choice. There will be two partners' secretaries, one shorthand-typist, two typists able to use dictating machines and one clerk.
    Routine correspondence, memoranda, etc.
    Important correspondence and confidential work.
    Minutes of meetings.
    A large amount of material requiring two or three copies.
    A monthly circular letter to be sent to about 400 agents in this country and abroad. *L.C.C. P.S.C.*

56. Discuss the ways in which the mechanization of offices today is affecting secretarial staff. *L.C.C. P.S.C.*

57. List five hazards in the use of machines in the office and state the precautions to be taken against these. *R.S.A. OM.*

58. Name three machines that use punched paper tape. *R.S.A. SD.2*

59. Electronic computers are being used increasingly in offices. Give a list of office functions for which a computer can be used and outline the advantages of using a computer as compared with other methods. *R.S.A. OP.2*

60. Name three office procedures for which computers are now being used by some organizations. What are the advantages of using computers for these purposes and what factors should be considered before deciding to computerize any given procedure? *R.S.A. OP.2*

61. (*a*) Name two types of office machine which use continuous stationery. Describe the type of continuous stationery used and its advantages.

(*b*) Name one office machine which uses a tally roll and describe the advantages of this type of stationery.

(*c*) Name one office machine which uses semi-absorbent paper and describe the disadvantages of this type of paper. *R.S.A. OP.1*

62. (*a*) List the machines used in an automatic punched-card installation and explain the function of each.

(*b*) Why are many automatic punched-card installations being replaced by electronic computers? *R.S.A. OP.2*

63. Name and explain the uses of three keyboard machines (other than typewriters) which you might find in an accounts department of a medium-sized organization which did not have the use of a computer or automatic punched card equipment. *R.S.A. OP.2*

Chapter 10
Sources of Information

A large part of the efficiency of the good secretary lies in her ability to know where certain information may be obtained, and her readiness to check doubtful points instead of allowing them to slip into letters and documents without verification. She should make herself familiar with all the books of reference connected with her work, and she should know where to obtain the book if it is not kept in her office and what it contains.

A list of the most important reference books for general purposes follows.

Telephone Directories

Telephone directories are published for the large cities and for county areas. Names, addresses and telephone numbers of subscribers can be obtained from them.

Classified telephone directories and yellow pages attached to the ordinary directories are useful for extracting names and addresses of those engaged in a particular profession or trade. They are indexed under the headings of the trades and professions, arranged alphabetically, and give names, addresses, telephone numbers and associated advertisements.

Street Directories

Street directories are published for specific areas (e.g. *The Post Office Directory* is published for London and each county) and give the names of streets and the responsible occupiers of each house, office, shop and flat. These are arranged under the headings of streets in alphabetical order and there is also a private residents' section in which the names of the residents are arranged in alphabetical order. Trades and professions are also listed.

Post Office Guide

The *Post Office Guide* gives details of postal, telephone and telegraphic facilities; inland and overseas postal rates; methods of posting different types of matter; particulars of foreign mails with rates and dates of posting for places abroad, and savings, remittance and other services. It is renewable annually, usually in July; regular supplements are sent free of charge on application to the local postmaster.

Special leaflets, giving current airmail charges, are also obtainable from the Post Office.

English Reference Books

A good selection of English reference books should include:

1. A good dictionary.

2. *Roget's Thesaurus of English Words and Phrases*, in which words are arranged according to their meaning, as distinct from a dictionary, where they are arranged in alphabetical order.

3. Fowler's *Modern English Usage* for assisting with awkward points of grammar and usage generally; Partridge's *Usage and Abusage* is an acceptable alternative.

Books for Travel Information

1. Timetables are published by British Rail giving detailed routes of trains and the names of all stations at which they stop. These guides provide sufficient information for the secretary to compile a timetable of trains travelling anywhere in Britain. Boat services connected with British Rail are also covered. A continental edition is published for places abroad.

The *ABC Railway Guide* gives only the time of departure and arrival of trains between London (or the town of issue in a local *ABC*) and the station of destination. Details of stations on the route and changes to be made are not given. The names of stations are arranged in alphabetical order, and, in addition to the train times, the *ABC* gives details of fares; the county in which a town is situated; populations; distance of towns from London; and early closing days.

2. The *Automobile Association Members' Handbook* (two-yearly) and the *Royal Automobile Club Guide and Handbook* (yearly) are useful for information about road travel, hotels, etc. The handbooks give the following information:

(*a*) full details of all the services offered to members, which include free breakdown service, legal advice, technical advice, telephone service, travel abroad, route maps, vehicle inspection, appointed garages and hotels;

(*b*) detailed maps of Great Britain;

(*c*) brief details about towns, including county, population, early closing day, distances from London and other places, appointed garages and hotels.

3. *ABC Coach and Bus Guide.*
4. *ABC Shipping Guide.*
5. *ABC World Airways Guide.*

Forms of Address

The following books will assist the secretary in ascertaining decorations, honours and qualifications, and placing them in their correct sequence. They will also provide correct forms of address and a variety of other information concerning eminent people:

Black's *Titles and Forms of Address*
Debrett's *Peerage and Titles of Courtesy*
Who's Who[1]
Kelly's *Handbook to the Titled Landed and Official Classes*
Burke's *Genealogical and Heraldic History of the Landed Gentry*

British Qualifications

British Qualifications is a useful guide to educational, technical, professional and academic qualifications in the United Kingdom giving descriptions of qualifications and the addresses of professional bodies.

Publications Guide Books

For details about newspapers or publications relating to any particular trade or profession reference should be made to *Willing's Press Guide* or the *Newspaper Press Directory*.

A trade journal is a magazine published weekly or monthly relating to a particular trade, e.g. *Mine and Quarry Engineering, Wool Record and Textile World, Colliery Guardian*. It specializes in the trade news, keeps its readers informed of the latest developments and provides them with a large selection of advertisements.

---

[1] *Who's Who* contains biographies of living eminent people and *Who Was Who* provides a record of eminent people who have died. There are several other forms of *Who's Who*, such as *International Who's Who, Who's Who in America, International Year Book and Statesmen's Who's Who, Who's Who in Art, Who's Who in the Theatre, Who's Who in the Motor Industry, Who's Who in Trade Agreements*, and *Authors' and Writers' Who's Who and Reference Guide*, etc.

Whitaker's Almanack

Whitaker's Almanack is a comprehensive reference book containing information on a large number of topics, including:

1. The calendar year.

2. Important information of world affairs, including largest cities, British and foreign embassies, rulers of foreign countries, etc.

3. Detailed information about the United Kingdom, including its past and present sovereigns, the Royal Family, the Peerage, the Privy Council and parliamentary procedure, Cabinet Ministers and a complete list of Members of Parliament, the order of precedence in Great Britain, the Bank of England, the Law Courts and the churches.

4. Statistical information regarding population, housing, crime and divorce, labour, agriculture and fisheries, railways, etc.

5. Sections dealing with England, Wales, Scotland, Northern Ireland, Isle of Man and Channel Islands, as well as all the countries of the British Commonwealth of Nations; the area, population and governments of the British Commonwealth of Nations, the European Economic Community, the United States of America, the United Nations, and foreign countries.

6. Miscellaneous information including Nobel Prize Winners, literature of the year, publishers and books published, music and poetry of the year, drama and films, broadcasting, art and other exhibitions, sport, trade unions, banking and finance, professional fees, postal regulations, weights and measures, etc.

Whitaker's Almanack is renewable annually in December.

Pears Cyclopaedia

This a compact and useful handbook with sections dealing with a variety of subjects, e.g. English dictionary, events, gazetteer, office compendium, prominent people, synonyms and antonyms, ready reckoner, legal data, etc.

Government Reports

Hansard is the official report of the proceedings in Parliament, and is useful if a secretary, on behalf of her employer, wishes to obtain details of a debate in Parliament on a particular topic, or on a bill in which her employer may be particularly interested. It is a verbatim report, i.e. it is reported word for word. Reports are made of the proceedings both in the House of Commons and in the House of Lords.

All Government Reports are published by Her Majesty's Stationery Office, which has branches in most of the large towns and cities in Great Britain.

Year Books

A year book is generally in the form of a diary and gives full details of a particular organization, e.g. a county council usually prepares a year book which gives the dates of its meetings, a list of members of the council and chief officers, standing orders and other information which is helpful to its members.

The Municipal Year Book and Public Utilities Directory

This provides information about local authorities in England and Wales. The area, population, rates, and names of chief officers are given for each county council, district council, etc.

Directory of Directors

This directory is published annually and gives a detailed record of all directors and their joint stock companies.

Stock Exchange Official Year Book

This book provides information regarding companies, securities, investments, etc.

Kelly's Directory of Manufacturers and Merchants

This directory lists manufacturers and suppliers arranged alphabetically under the headings of goods and services.

Guide to British Enterprise (Dun and Bradstreet Ltd.)

Lists the names, registered addresses, subsidiary or parent companies, field of activity, names of directors and nominal capital for a selection of prominent firms in the United Kingdom.

Directory of British Associations

A directory listing the addresses, activities and publications of trade and professional associations, societies, research organizations, chambers of trade and commerce and trade unions.

Statistics

The Annual Abstract of Statistics, which is a publication of the Government Statistical Service (HMSO), gives annual statistics covering a wide range of activities, including area and climate; population; social services; public health; housing; justice and crime; education; labour; manufacturing and external trade; transport; overseas finance; central and local government; bank and index of retail prices.

Statistical data is also supplied in the *Monthly Digest of Statistics. A Statistical Year Book* (Annuaire Statistique) published by United Nations supplies International statistics.

Dictionary of Acronyms and Abbreviations

A dictionary giving the meaning of initials and abbreviations in common use.

Employment Legislation

Croner's Reference Book for Employers is designed to provide employers with information on the various Acts of Parliament and regulations relating to the employment of persons in factories, offices and shops. A monthly amendment service is provided in order to keep the information up-to-date.

Lists for the Services

The *Army List* gives details of War Office commands, regiments, battalions, officers, etc., an alphabetical index of officers and other useful information concerning the organization of the army.

Lists are also compiled for the air force and navy.

Law List

The Law List gives details of judges, magistrates, county court registrars, solicitors, barristers, etc.

Crockford's Clerical Directory

A directory giving information about the clergymen of the Church of England, their parishes and livings, etc.

Similar clerical directories are prepared for the other religious denominations.

Medical Directory

This is a directory of qualified medical practitioners. There is also a *Dentist's Register* and a *Register of Nurses.*

Ready Reckoner

A ready reckoner is an essential reference book for an office, providing a quick means of arriving at answers to calculations involving multiplication, discounts, percentages, etc.

Technical Terms

In offices dealing with such matters as engineering, scientific research, electrical, radio and television equipment, printing and so on, it is advisable to have an appropriate dictionary of technical terms. Technical dictionaries include the *Authors' and Printers' Dictionary, Black's Medical Dictionary, Chamber's Technical Dictionary, Dictionary of Legal Terms, Dictionary of Scientific Terms, Short Dictionary of Architecture,* etc.

Place Names

A good gazetteer or world atlas is useful in the office for verifying the spelling of names of towns, counties, etc.

Reference Libraries

Reference libraries hold a large stock of all kinds of reference books and the secretary should certainly visit her local library to see and examine the reference books on view.

TRAVEL INFORMATION

If it is necessary for the employer to make frequent business trips, often at short notice, sometimes using his motor-car and sometimes travelling by train, boat or aircraft, it is essential that his private secretary should be fully conversant with the preparations necessary. The four principal methods of travel—road, rail, sea and air—are dealt with giving (*a*) the reference books and other sources of information which should be available in the office and (*b*) the final preparation which must be made in each case.

Road

Reference Books and Sources of Information

1. *AA* or *RAC Handbook*.
2. *ABC Coach and Bus Guide*.
3. Telephone numbers of the employer's garage, mechanic and nearest *AA* or *RAC* office.
4. Road maps.

Final Preparations

1. Arrange for the appropriate road maps and route plans to be available.
2. Verify the weather conditions in the area in which the employer is travelling.
3. Confirm the booking of hotels.
4. Prepare his itinerary, and include telephone numbers of hotels, appointments, meetings, etc., and have a clear understanding of the times and places where the employer may be contacted.
5. Collect and hand to the employer all the documents required.
6. See that the employer has his personal requisites, including suitcase, car and AA/RAC keys, driving licence and insurance certificate.
7. Prepare a supply of office stationery to enable the employer to write letters, reports, etc., during his travels.
8. Discuss outstanding matters.

Rail

Reference Books and Sources of Information

1. British Rail *Guides*, plus a regular supply of the supplementary issues concerning train times.
2. Telephone numbers of the nearest railway stations.

Final Preparations

1. Confirm the time, station, platform of departure of train and the time of arrival at destination.

2. Obtain the ticket for the journey plus one for a reserved seat and/or sleeping berth if applicable.

3. Make arrangements for the employer to be met at his destination.

4. Points 3 to 8 under the heading of "Road".

Sea

Reference Books and Sources of Information

1. *ABC Shipping Guide*.

2. Current visa, passport, baggage, export licence, health and insurance regulations.

3. Telephone number of the local travel agency office.

4. Telephone number of employer's bank for arranging currency and travellers' cheques, etc.

Final Preparations

1. Verify the name of the quay from which he is leaving.

2. Obtain his tickets.

3. See that the employer has his passport, visa, vaccination certificate and any other documents required.

4. Check that adequate labels have been affixed to his baggage, and prepare labels for the return journey.

5. Obtain foreign currency and travellers' cheques.

6. Make arrangements for him to be met at the port of destination.

7. Points 3 to 8 under the heading of "Road".

Air

Reference Books and Sources of Information

1. *ABC World Airways Guide*.

2. Current visa, passport, baggage, export licence, health and insurance regulations.

3. Telephone numbers of the nearest air-line booking office and private charter office.

4. The telephone number of the local travel agency office.

5. The telephone number of the employer's bank for arranging currency, travellers' cheques, etc.

Final Preparations

1. Verify the air terminus from which the employer is leaving, details of the time by which he must present himself there and the actual take-off time.

2. Obtain his tickets.

3. See that the employer has his passport, visa, vaccination certificate and any other documents required.

4. Check that his baggage does not exceed the maximum weight.

5. Obtain foreign currency and travellers' cheques.

6. Make arrangements for him to be met at the airport or air terminus.

7. Points 3 to 8 under the heading of "Road".

Preparation of an Itinerary

An example of an itinerary is given in Fig. 52.

The following points should be noted in the preparation of an itinerary:

1. A card of a convenient size must be used so that it can be handled easily; it should be no larger than a postcard.

2. Make a note of any special reservations, such as a sleeping berth, which have been made for the journey.

3. As towns frequently have more than one railway station, make sure that trains arrive and depart from the same station, or that sufficient time is allowed for changing from one station to another.

4. In all timetables Sunday trains and sometimes Saturday trains are shown separately, and the secretary must be very careful to see that she is looking at the correct section for the day on which her employer is travelling.

5. Code letters in the guide books must be referred to, noted thoroughly and mentioned in the itinerary; for example, "Light refreshments available".

6. Ensure that the information is being taken from the current edition of the timetable, as considerable changes are made between the summer and winter services.

7. When looking up times of trains in a timetable, you would do well to work backwards from the station of destination to the station of departure, e.g. if you are looking up the time of a train from Leamington Spa to Truro, look in the index to stations for the name "Truro". Under the heading "Truro" will be a further list of stations. Note the station nearest or most convenient to the town of departure and refer to the table indicated.

```
ITINERARY


Saturday, 16 August 19-- and
Sunday, 17 August 19--



Depart   Leamington Spa (General)        1613 hrs
Arrive   London (Paddington)             1820 hrs

         Dinner at The Dorchester        1900 hrs

Depart   London (Paddington)             2350 hrs
Arrive   Truro                           0705 hrs

Note:    (1)   Sleeping berth (Reference 14a)
               has been reserved from Paddington
               to Truro.

         (2)   Light refreshments are available
               on the night train.
```

Fig. 52 Itinerary

TITLES AND FORMS OF ADDRESS

An employer expects his secretary to take very great care over the verification of titles, decorations, qualifications and forms of address contained in his correspondence. When in doubt, she must always look up this information in one of the reference books mentioned on page 178.

If the employer is in communication with a large number of titled people his secretary should be in possession of a comprehensive reference book on the use of titles, such as Black's *Titles and Forms of Address*.

Care must also be taken in placing decorations, honours, and qualifications in their correct sequence so that they are arranged in the order of their importance; the most important appearing first, e.g. Air Vice-Marshal T P Lines, CB, CBE, DFC (The CB is a higher honour than the CBE, and therefore precedes it.)

The correct order of precedence for notable persons in Great Britain is given in *Whitaker's Almanack*.

OTHER SOURCES OF INFORMATION

The information required may be current or of such a nature that it is not obtainable from a reference book, and the following is a brief guide to some of the sources of information which may be used by the secretary:

Information	Source
Local Government matters	Offices of the County or District Council
Motor taxation	The Motor Taxation Offices
Income tax, PAYE, etc.	The Offices of Inland Revenue
National Insurance	Local Office of the Department of Health and Social Security
Court procedure	Clerk to the Justices
Banking and foreign currency	Bank
Travel	Travel Agency British Rail Bus Company Shipping Company Airport or Air Terminal AA or RAC Offices
Postal, telephone, etc.	Post Office
Stocks and shares	Stockbroker—the stockbroker is issued with an official list of the Stock Exchange which is published daily
Overseas trade, the home market, the business community, etc.	The local offices of the Chamber of Commerce
Employment	Youth Employment Officer and Local Offices of the Department of Employment
Books, newspapers, magazines, etc.	Local Reference Library
Interpreters, translations, etc.	Chamber of Commerce Language Schools or Colleges Travel Bureau or Embassy of country concerned Travel Agents

QUESTIONS

1. It is necessary for your employer to make frequent business trips in the United Kingdom, often at short notice, sometimes using his motor-car, sometimes travelling by railway or air.
   - (*a*) What reference books and information do you keep available?
   - (*b*) What points would you check with him before he leaves? *L.C.C. P.S.D.*

2. From where can the following information be obtained? Indicate any further data you would require before applying to the various sources of reference.
   - (*a*) The price of an insurance stamp for an office cleaner.
   - (*b*) The value of 1 000 pesetas.
   - (*c*) The price of a motor-car licence.
   - (*d*) How to dispatch a camera to Kenya.
   - (*e*) How to engage an interpreter.
   - (*f*) The name of a good hotel in the Western Highlands.
   - (*g*) The cost-of-living index figure.
   - (*h*) The value of 100 shares in a well-known public company. *L.C.C. P.S.D.*

3. In a week's time there will be a public meeting, at which Mr *X*, to whom you are private secretary, will take the chair. With him on the platform will be a number of notable persons. He is concerned about the order of precedence of these persons, and asks you to ascertain this. Place the persons on this list in the order which you consider correct, and give the names of reference books or suggest other sources, from which you could verify your opinion:

   The Archbishop of *A*.
   The Duchess of *B*.
   The Bishop of *C*.
   His Honour *D.D.*, a County Court Judge.
   Rear Admiral Sir *E.E.*, K.C.B., M.V.O.
   Air Vice Marshal Sir *F.F.*, O.B.E.
   Viscount *G*., Q.C.   *R.S.A. SD.2*

4. Where would you go to get, or to deal with, the following for your employer:
   - (*a*) a new passport,
   - (*b*) a driving licence,
   - (*c*) a broadcast receiving licence,
   - (*d*) a new cheque book,
   - (*e*) small change for a £5 note,
   - (*f*) to report the loss of a gold wrist-watch,
   - (*g*) information about the foreign country where he will be spending his holiday?
   R.S.A. SD.2

5. Where would you find the following information:
   - (i) a series of multiplication tables of sums of money;
   - (ii) the actual position in a town of a given address;
   - (iii) a list of traders carrying on the same trade in a given area;

    (iv) the position of a small town in a foreign country;
    (v) detailed information regarding the movements of shipping? *R.S.A. SD.2*

6. Where would you find the following information:
    (*a*) How to address an ambassador;
    (*b*) The name of the head of a government department;
    (*c*) Official reports of proceedings in parliament? *R.S.A. SD.2*

7. Your employer will shortly be travelling abroad. Where will you obtain:
    (*a*) Passport, (*b*) Visa, (*c*) Foreign currency?
What other arrangements might you be expected to make in order to ensure a trouble free journey for your employer? *L.C.C. P.S.C.*

8. For what type of information would you look in the following reference books:
    (*a*) *Crockford's*;
    (*b*) *Debrett*;
    (*c*) *Roget's Thesaurus*;
    (*d*) the *Law List*? *R.S.A. SD.2*

9. In what reference books would you find:
    (*a*) information about the Telex system;
    (*b*) air services between London and Scotland;
    (*c*) a list of members of Parliament;
    (*d*) an abbreviation such as "et seq."? *R.S.A. SD.2*

10. Where would you look for information about:
    (i) a qualified medical practitioner;
    (ii) a solicitor;
    (iii) a clergyman of the Church of England;
    (iv) the population of a town;
    (v) a company;
    (vi) the road mileage between two towns? *R.S.A. SD.2*

11. Your employer is travelling from London by plane to Aberdeen where he will stay for two nights, returning to London by train via Edinburgh where he will spend one night. He wishes you to:
    (*a*) book his tickets,
    (*b*) make reservations for travel and hotels,
    (*c*) arrange for him to be taken to and from the airports and the railway stations.
How will you make these arrangements? *R.S.A. SD.2*

12. (*a*) What use could you make of the following books of reference:
    (i) *The Post Office Guide*;
    (ii) *Whitaker's Almanack*;
    (iii) A Classified Telephone Directory;
    (iv) A Gazetteer;
    (v) *The Stock Exchange Official Year Book*;
    (vi) *Roget's Thesaurus of English Words and Phrases*?

(*b*) By what means can you keep yourself fully informed of the latest developments in office equipment and methods? *R.S.A. OP.2*

13. Explain what you would do to comply with the following instructions from your employer:

(*a*) "Find out for me where Mr J. L. Parsons lives and what sort of business he carries on. He is somewhere in the Cambridge area."

(*b*) "I shall be visiting our agents in Sydney next month. Let me know the times of air services there and arrange to collect £150 in travellers' cheques and also renew my passport."

(*c*) "Please let me know the name of the managing director of Cordens Engineering Limited."

(*d*) "Send for a copy of the speech made in the House of Commons last night by the Secretary of State for the Department of Trade and Industry." *R.S.A. OP.2*

14. In the past, all travel arrangements for members of your firm have been made by a travel agency. The amount of travel in Great Britain and abroad has now increased to such an extent that it has been decided to open a new department to deal with it.

(*a*) Write a report to the Office Manager suggesting what reference books should be purchased.

(*b*) The executive for whom you work wishes to travel by train to a neighbouring town in order to visit a factory which is situated three miles outside the town. He will return the same day. Write a memorandum to the travel department giving detailed instructions. *R.S.A. SD.2*

15. List four reference books which contain information about professional or well known people. *R.S.A. SD.2*

16. Re-write the following list, putting the names of the persons next to the reference books which would contain information about them:

Rev. J. M. Jones	Medical Directory
M. B. Davies, M.D.	Law List
Sir John Dunn, Q.C.	Crockford's Clerical Directory
Rt. Hon. Sir Alec Groves	Municipal Year Book
City Treasurer, Liverpool	Who's Who. *R.S.A. OP.1*

17. (*a*) If, in your work as a secretary, you need the following information, in which books would you look for it?

(i) The meaning of the phrase "pari passu".

(ii) Two or three words or phrases meaning the opposite of "inscrutable".

(iii) A list of solicitors practising in England.

(iv) The author of "All animals are equal, but some animals are more equal than others".

(v) Biographical information about a woman eminent in public life.

(vi) The poundage chargeable for an inland Telegraphic Money Order for £20.

(vii) The distance by road from Doncaster to Wetherby.

(viii) Which State of America Cincinnati is in.

(ix) The names and addresses of firms selling office equipment in Canterbury, Kent.

(x) The name of the principal of the college of further education in a neighbouring town.

(xi) Whether your local M.P. spoke in the House of Commons Debate on the Industrial Relations Act and, if he did, what it was that he said.

(xii) The total area and total population of New Zealand.

(*b*) Your employer is leaving at short notice tomorrow to make a business trip by car in France. Where could you telephone to get authoritative information on the following matters?

(i) Weather conditions likely to be encountered on the journey.

(ii) The times and costs of car ferries from Dover to Boulogne.

(iii) The address and telephone number of a French Government Department dealing with trade, which he wishes to visit on his way through Paris. *R.S.A. SD.2*

Chapter 11
Correspondence, Reports and Memos

LETTERS

The secretary must be able not only to type letters from dictation, but also to compose them from brief instructions or notes.

What is it that a business letter sets out to do? It has two primary functions:

(*a*) to provide a channel of communication between two persons, and

(*b*) to preserve a permanent record of the communication.

The purpose of the business letter is to convey information and/or to ask questions.

The following points should be observed in the construction and typing of a business letter:

1. The writer must have clear in his own mind the message he wishes to convey or the questions he wishes to ask, and know exactly how to say it both clearly and concisely.

2. The letter must be written simply and directly and with the right amount of emphasis to enable the reader to grasp the contents instantly. No room should be left for ambiguity.

3. The letter must be divided into paragraphs, each dealing with one point only and arranged as follows:

    (*a*) opening sentences;
    (*b*) the body of the letter (further subdivided into paragraphs);
    (*c*) closing sentences.

4. The points expressed in the letter must be carefully graded so that they follow in their correct sequence and each point leads systematically to the next.

5. A letter containing spelling or punctuation errors or both creates a poor impression. Whenever there is the slightest doubt over the spelling of a word,

the writer must consult a good English dictionary. Errors involving the construction of sentences are equally serious. A good vocabulary leading to the selection of the most appropriate words is also necessary to prevent ambiguity.

6. The letter must be displayed clearly and correctly. The layout given in the example in this chapter is the fully-blocked style which is now adopted by many organizations, but other forms of layout and punctuation are equally acceptable as long as consistency is maintained throughout.

7. When determining the length of a letter, the writer must ensure that courtesy of tone and exactness of meaning are not sacrificed to brevity.

Fig. 53 is a letter written by Mr Hugh Buckingham's private secretary, embodying the above principles.

Receiving Dictation

The secretary must possess an adequate shorthand speed so that she is capable of taking down bursts of dictation at high speeds.

If the employer deletes a passage which he has dictated, the secretary must be certain to cross it out completely in her notes. If a corrected passage is to be inserted, it is advisable to put a mark or number in the place where it is to go, and then, in the margin of the corrected passage, repeat the mark or number.

The secretary is justified in interrupting her employer while he is dictating to her if she has not fully understood or heard what he has said; she should never guess a word or phrase, nor be afraid to ask questions when in doubt.

The employer should not, however, be interrupted immediately the query arises, as this may cause him to lose his train of thought; instead the secretary should wait for a suitable opportunity, e.g. when he makes a brief pause. It is difficult to generalize on questions of relationship between employer and secretary, but in all matters the secretary must adapt herself to the methods preferred by her employer.

The secretary should be quite certain about all the correspondence dictated; for example, if she is doubtful about the type of salutation or subscription to use in a particular case, she should ask her employer before she leaves the office.

Audio-typing

Audio-typing is the name given to typewriting from sound, i.e. from recorded dictation. Instead of the typist's being present for dictation, the employer dictates into a recording machine, and the tape, disc, or belt is then passed on to his typist for transcription.

```
        THE WHITE HOUSE CHESSILLS ROAD BUCKINGHAM
        telephone 028 02 3296


        14 August 19--


        Mr R T Hollis
        The Firs
        14 Wansworth Road
        YORK
        YS2 3PT


        Dear Sir

        PROPOSED INTRODUCTION OF PUNCHED-CARD ACCOUNTING

        Mr Buckingham has asked me to thank you for your letter
        of 12 August, suggesting that you and he should meet on
        Thursday, 22 August for a discussion of the proposed new
        accounting system.

        I have been asked to send you the enclosed literature
        describing punched-card accounting and to refer you to
        the working instructions on pages 14 to 20.

        Mr Buckingham wishes to implement the change-over at the
        beginning of November, and in view of the relatively
        short time remaining for the preparations, he hopes that
        the date suggested for the meeting will be convenient.

        Mr Buckingham looks forward to meeting you soon.

        Yours faithfully




        Beryl N Stowe
        Private Secretary to Mr Hugh Buckingham


        enc


        your ref RTH/PT
        our ref  BNS/-
```

Fig. 53 A Displayed Business Letter

Stenotyping

Stenotyping is a form of machine shorthand in which letters of the alphabet replace shorthand symbols and are printed on a paper roll. The machine is operated with the fingers of both hands simultaneously and the depression of the keys reproduces syllables, instead of the letters found on the ordinary typewriter.

The stenotyping system is based on phonetics, and words are recorded in a contracted form according to the way in which they are spoken. The stenotyping system of recording the spoken word can be used for taking down any language with which the operator is familiar and it is equally adaptable for highly technical matter.

The paper roll containing the stenotyping is later transcribed on to an ordinary typewriter. Stenotyping machines are portable, and are almost silent in operation. Stenotypists are taught to operate the machines by touch, and different coloured ribbons are used to indicate a change of speaker.

INVITATIONS

Invitations are generally in the form of printed cards, with the guest's name handwritten. The secretary will usually be expected to know how to reply to invitations after her employer has said simply "accept" or "refuse".

The style of reply must be based on the invitation text itself, e.g. an invitation written in the third person is replied to in the same form. No salutation, subscription or signature is required.

Fig. 54 gives an example of the acceptance of an invitation.

When refusing an invitation, it is more courteous to give a reason. Note the wording for a refusal in Fig. 55.

REPORTS

The efficient secretary should be able to prepare a report of a meeting, a discussion, an interview or even on a document. She should be able to present the essential facts so that her employer can deal with his business swiftly without having to delve into a large number of unimportant details.

A report must be accurate, clear, concise and logically arranged. It should be concise to the extent that there is no "padding" or irrelevant details. The writer should "telescope" phrases wherever possible and avoid using long, involved sentences.

If the report is an individual one, i.e. from the secretary to the office manager, it should be a narrative written in the first person, but if the report is of a meeting it should be written wholly in the third person. A report of an event or a meeting should always be in the past tense.

"The Meadows"

Fulham Road

Wandsbrook

Major Terence Field thanks the Chairman

and Committee of the Boldingham Musical

Society for their kind invitation to the

Society's Tenth Annual Dinner to be held

at the Town Hall, Crockington on Tuesday,

2 September at 1945 hrs, and he has much

pleasure in accepting.

25 August 19--

Fig. 54 A Formal Acceptance of an Invitation

Planning

The preliminary preparation of a brief outline is an essential so that the matters are introduced in their correct sequence and so that each point leads naturally to the next. Here is a suggested plan:

1. The heading or title containing the following information:
   (*a*) the subject of the report, e.g. the type of meeting;
   (*b*) the date of the meeting or interview;

```
    "The Meadows"

    Fulham Road

    Wandsbrook



    Major Terence Field thanks Mr and Mrs

    Geoffrey Lloyd for their kind invitation

    to a party to be held on Tuesday,

    9 September at 2000 hrs.

    He regrets, however, that owing to a

    previous business engagement in Scotland,

    he must decline their invitation.




    25 August 19--
```

Fig. 55 A Formal Refusal of an Invitation

    (c) the place;
    (d) if a meeting, those present—specifying the chairman and officers;
    (e) file reference numbers for future identification;
    (f) the name of the person to whom the report is sent;
    (g) if the report is confidential or secret, care must be taken in marking
it accordingly.

    2. The opening paragraph, which should set out clearly the circumstances which called for the report, for example, the office Manager's memo, or changing circumstances which called for the discussion of future policy.

3. The body of the report containing the general business discussed: if it is a report of a meeting, adequate subheadings should be used; if it is an individual report, the facts of the case should be stated clearly and concisely.

4. Recommendations or conclusions.

5. The action necessary to effect the recommendations, including the following:
   (*a*) the names of the persons who should take the action;
   (*b*) the date by which the action should be taken;
   (*c*) the date of the next meeting to review the situation.

6. The name and description of the signatory.

Report Headings

1. The following is an example of an individual report heading:

```
                        25 June 19--


                        To:    Office Manager
                        Ref:   OF/1296

                        REPORT ON OFFICE FURNITURE
```

2. The following is an example of a meeting report heading:

```
THE XLNT MANUFACTURING COMPANY LTD

Report of a Discussion on
Staff Establishments at Head Office and Job Evaluation

An informal meeting was held in the General Manager's Office
on Thursday, 10 May 19-- at 1045 hrs to give preliminary
consideration to the question of staff establishments and
job evaluation.

Present:

Mr A M Willerby  - General Manager
(in the chair)
Mr T Elliot      - Staff Manager
Mr B W Sanderson - Chief Financial Accountant
Mr A Thompson    - Secretary
```

Opening Paragraphs

Individual Report

In reply to your memo dated 20 June, I have made several inquiries
of office furniture manufacturers about new furniture for the
typists' office, and the following are my suggestions.

Meeting Report

STAFF ESTABLISHMENTS

The Chairman reported that the Company's output had shown a marked
increase which had resulted in a corresponding increase in the
amount of office work being done at both the head office and the
factory. A considerable amount of overtime was being done by some
departments, whilst other departments were working practically
normal office hours. Mr Willerby called upon the meeting to consider how this unsatisfactory state of affairs could be remedied.
He reminded the meeting that not all heads of departments were
present and that it would be necessary to consider their views
as well.

The Body of the Reports

The following is an extract from an individual report:

DESKS (4 required)

I recommend the secretarial desks (Model 6550 in the attached
catalogue), which are fitted with a typewriter platform in the
right-hand pedestal. When not in use, the typewriter is housed
inside the pedestal (leaving the desk top clear). Yale locks
are fitted to both pedestals. This type of desk will enable the
machine, together with any confidential correspondence, etc, to
be locked away at night. The desk top measurement is 1524 mm x
838.2 mm, which is quite adequate for ledger work and the
preparation of financial statements.

The following is an extract from a meeting report:

PUNCHED-CARD SYSTEM

The Chief Financial Accountant suggested a changeover to the
punched-card system as the only real solution to the problem.
The machines used in this system could be adapted to a wide
variety of uses and would not require many operators.

Recommendations or Conclusions

Individual Report

MAINTENANCE ARRANGEMENTS

If three machines are purchased I consider that the existing
maintenance contract for three visits to be made in a year will
prove sufficient. Most of the work done by the mechanic in the
last few months has been on the three machines which I have
recommended for replacement.

Meeting Report

JOB EVALUATION

It was agreed that the question of job evaluation was far too
complex for adequate discussion to take place at that meeting,
and that it should be deferred until the implications of the
punched-card system had been studied.

The Delegation of Responsibility to Effect the Recommendations

The responsibility for the action recommended in the individual report
will lie with the member of staff initiating the report, and a mention of this
will not normally be required in the report.

Meeting Report

```
The Secretary was asked to make immediate inquiries of firms manu-
facturing punched-card equipment about price, etc.  He was asked to
ensure that, at this stage, the Company was not committed in any
way.  The Secretary confirmed that he would institute inquiries at
once and that he would work with heads of other departments so that
the report covered all possible requirements.

The Chairman agreed to call a further meeting after the matter had
been considered more fully and the results of the Secretary's
inquiries had been taken into account.
```

The Signature Block

The signature block will be required only for individual reports, as in the following example:

T PERKINS

Secretary

OFFICE MEMORANDUM FORMS

Memorandum forms are normally used for internal communications or for messages or reports to representatives or agents in other parts of the country

```
M E M O R A N D U M

To:     Mr L Harris
        112 Hill Street
        Bristol

From:   General Manager

8 July 19--


I enclose a copy of a letter sent to Messrs Smith & Jones, for
your information.

Will you please arrange to call on these people in about ten
days' time, unless you hear from me in the meantime?



enc              L Brown

ref B/14926
```

Fig. 56 A Memorandum

or the world. They are generally referred to briefly as "Memos". No salutation or complimentary close is used, and the heading will normally contain the name and address of the addressee and the date. The file reference is shown at the bottom of the memo.

Fig. 56 shows a memo sent from the General Manager of Messrs. White Bros. to their Bristol Agent.

QUESTIONS

1. Your Junior Assistant, who fell in the street during the luncheon interval, has been taken to hospital with a broken wrist. Your employer asks you to write a letter for his signature sympathizing with her, telling her "not to worry", and inquiring whether she has left any particular items of work unfinished or unattended to. Write this letter. *R.S.A. SD.2*

2. From the following rough notes, prepare a letter for signature by your employer:

Miss A: Just called away unexpectedly to Press Conference at same place as usual—you can get me there if you want to. Mr Jones rang. A. B. Jones, I think it is, but anyway he is Principal of Blanktown College of Arts and Crafts. He asked if I had received that letter he wrote to me over a week ago, asking me to give away the prizes at their Annual Prizegiving on 17th January. I said I would. Please write and confirm this. Ask him to let me have some literature about the work of the College, and make suitable apologies for the delay. Remember to put this date in the diary. *R.S.A. SD.2*

3. Write letters to the X and Y hotels, asking for terms for hire of a conference room on 2nd July. Find out whether the hotel can supply morning coffee, luncheon and tea for fifty sales representatives and about ten visitors. Mr A, the manager of X hotel, is a personal friend of your employer. The Y hotel is one of a group of hotels some of which have already been used by your company for similar conferences held in other parts of the country. *R.S.A. SD.2*

4. Rewrite this letter in better style:
Dear Sir,

Thank you for your communication of 10th inst., which came to hand today. The aforesaid letter is receiving our prompt attention, but we respectfully beg to point out that owing to a recent strike we are unable to deal with same within this week. Assuring you of our best attention at all times and trusting that you will continue to favour us with your esteemed orders.

                                                Yours faithfully,

R.S.A. SD.2

5. Write one of the following letters:

(*a*) From a publisher to an author who has submitted a manuscript which he rejects but which shows promise. He offers criticism of the style and subject but conveys encouragement and suggests an idea for a series of articles which might prove acceptable.

(*b*) From an industrialist to an overseas customer about to visit this country for the first time, conveying a welcome, suggesting an itinerary and outlining the Company's products and processes in which the visitor might be interested. *L.C.C. P.S.D.*

6. (*a*) What are the constituent factors in the cost of letter writing in a business?
(*b*) Explain why it is important for the business to consider the cost, and describe three ways of reducing it. *R.S.A. OP.2*

7. Reply accepting the following invitation:

The Chairman and members of The Foxford Rambling Club request the pleasure of .... at a Social Evening to be held at the Village Hall, Foxford, on Tuesday, 19th May, 19.., at 1930 hrs. R.S.V.P., the Secretary, Foxford Rambling Club, 22, Peel Road, Foxford.

8. Reply to the following invitation stating that you are unable to attend:

Major and Mrs T. R. Davis request the pleasure of .... at a luncheon to be held at The Regent Hotel, Sparkton, on Wednesday, 22nd June, 19.., at 1200 hrs.
R.S.V.P.

9. The printed notepaper of most business firms gives much useful information. What information might you expect to find? *R.S.A. SD.2*

10. Rewrite this letter in good style:
Dear Sir,

Thank you for your letter of 30th ult, which came to hand today. Your esteemed order for which we thank you, is receiving our prompt attention. The goods you require, which you desire to receive so urgently, were not all available at the time of the receipt of the order, and we have had to send away for same which we hope will soon be here and which we will send on to you as soon as received.

Again thanking you for your esteemed order and hoping to be of service to you at all times.

Yours faithfully,

R.S.A. SD.2

11. Your employer has received the following invitation:

The Blanktown Rotarians have pleasure in inviting

Mr & Mrs A. Turner
....

to their St. Swithin's Ball on Saturday, 15th July, 197–

at

The Grand Hotel, Blanktown

from 8 p.m. to midnight

RSVP   Evening Dress   Buffet

(*a*) Write a formal acceptance for him.

(*b*) Blanktown is 200 miles away from your employer's home. He asks you to make the necessary arrangements on his behalf. Describe the steps you would take. *R.S.A. SD.2*

12. Your employer is the buyer of furniture for a chain store and has asked you to attend, on his behalf, an exhibition of contemporary furniture. You are asked to write a report of the exhibition, but chiefly your employer wants to know your opinion on what the average woman wants, and what she is likely to buy in his stores. *L.C.C. P.S.D.*

13. Write a report for your Office Manager of a visit to an Office Machinery Exhibition held in your town. Make recommendations for the acquisition of suitable new items of equipment for your office.

14. Write memos from the General Manager to the Works Manager and Production Manager asking them to attend a meeting on 4th September, at 1000 hrs. in the General Manager's Office, to discuss the proposed reorganization of their departments. Tell them to discuss the matter with their deputies and bring along all factual information relevant to the subject.

15. Write a memo from the Managing Director to the Manager of the Scottish Branch. Tell him that the Managing Director will be calling on Monday, 25th August, to discuss a new contract with the firm of Messrs. Torrens Bros., 14 Lawton Road, Edinburgh. The Managing Director will be arriving at Edinburgh Station (Princes Street) at 12 noon and wishes to be met from the station.

16. You are secretary to the chairman of a company employing 500 office staff. The chairman has asked for your views on two proposals which have been made to him:

(*a*) That a staff restaurant should be opened, instead of the present system of issuing luncheon vouchers.

(*b*) That 300 junior staff at present paid weekly in cash should be paid monthly by bank transfer.

Write a report summarizing your views on either (*a*) or (*b*). *L.C.C. P.S.D.*

17. Write a report, for your Office Manager, on the condition of the typewriters in your office, some of which are getting old. Include in the report your recommendations for renewals and improvements of maintenance arrangements. *R.S.A. SD.2*

18. The Office Manager has been instructed to take steps to reduce the expenditure on telephone calls. Investigate the present position regarding the internal and external telephone calls, and prepare a report on your findings together with your recommendations. *R.S.A. OP.2*

19. (*a*) What is the difference between a memorandum and a circulation slip?

(*b*) State three other methods of passing a message between departments. *R.S.A. OP.1*

Chapter 12
Meetings

THE AGENDA

An agenda is a programme of the details of the business to be discussed at a meeting in the order in which they are to be taken.

The agenda is sent to all members of the committee or organization to give them adequate notice, and to enable them to ponder over, prior to the meeting, the items of business to be discussed. The period of notice to be given is laid down by the constitution of the organization and is normally seven to fourteen days. It is customary at committee meetings to arrange at one meeting the date of the next. The agenda usually includes the notice convening the meeting, which contains the day, date, time and place of meeting.

The agenda is prepared by the secretary in consultation with the chairman, and the items of business dealt with at the previous meeting are taken into consideration. The secretary should make a note of any matters requiring the attention of the committee, so that these may be included in the agenda for the next meeting.

Figure 57 is an example of an agenda for a committee meeting. The customary order of the business should be observed: if, for example, a chairman was to be elected, that would be the first business of the meeting, and would be carried out under the supervision of a temporary chairman.

The agenda for an annual general meeting differs slightly from the agenda for a committee meeting in two ways: copies are sent to all members of the organization and not just to the elected committee; also, there is some variation in the type of business to be discussed. The items given in the example of an agenda for an annual general meeting in Fig. 58 should be noted.

Chairman's Agenda

The chairman's agenda contains more information than the ordinary agenda, and spaces are provided on the right-hand side of the paper for the

```
THE XYZ WORKS SPORTS CLUB COMMITTEE


A meeting of the committee of the XYZ Works Sports Club will

be held at the Works Canteen on Friday, 14 February 19-- at

1530 hrs.


A G E N D A


1      Minutes of the last meeting.

2      Matters arising thereon.

3      Correspondence and apologies for absence.

4      Treasurer's financial statement.

5      Fifth Annual Dinner arrangements.

6      Purchase of cricket gear.

7      To consider suggestions for future sporting activities.

8      Date of next meeting.

9      Any other business.


J HANSON

Hon Secretary
```

Fig. 57 An Agenda for a Committee Meeting

chairman to make his own notes. The additional information gives the chairman all the relevant details which may be needed during the course of the meeting.

Staff Meeting Notice and Agenda

Staff meetings are generally quite informal. A sales manager, calling a meeting of his sales representatives, would send out a notice in the form given in Fig. 59.

```
THE XYZ WORKS SPORTS CLUB

The Annual General Meeting of the XYZ Works Sports Club will
be held at the Works Canteen on Friday, 21 February 19-- at
1900 hrs.

A G E N D A
 1      Minutes of the last meeting.
 2      Matters arising thereon.
 3      Correspondence and apologies for absence.
 4      Secretary's Annual Report.
 5      Treasurer's Annual Report and Balance Sheet.
 6      Election of:  (a)  Officers;
                      (b)  Committee;
                      (c)  Honorary Auditor.
 7      To consider the following proposed addition to
        the Club's Constitution:

        "15    All retired staff shall be installed as
               honorary members of the Sports Club."

 8      To consider the formation of a Sub-Committee to
        arrange a programme of social evenings throughout
        the year.
 9      Any other business.

 J HANSON

 Hon Secretary
```

Fig. 58 An Agenda for an Annual General Meeting

BUSINESS MEETING TERMS

The secretary will frequently meet, in the course of her duties, many technical terms connected with business meetings. A list of the most commonly used terms is given below.

Ad Hoc

This means "arranged for this purpose". An *ad hoc* subcommittee is appointed for the purpose of carrying out one particular piece of work, such as the arrangements for the visit of a very important person (V.I.P.). These committees are sometimes called special or special purpose committees.

```
THE LMN MANUFACTURING CO LTD

NOTICE OF MEETING


1 June 19--


To:    Sales Representatives

A meeting of sales representatives will be held in the Sales

Manager's Office at Head Office on Friday, 10 June 19--,

commencing at 1430 hrs, when you are specially requested to

attend.

The Agenda is set out below.



D PETTIFER
Sales Manager



A G E N D A


1     To receive apologies for absence.

2     To discuss the new selling lines which will be on the
      market in the spring.

3     To report revised prices of established products.

4     To consider suggestions for a simplified manner of
      submitting monthly returns.

5     Any other business.
```

Fig. 59 An Agenda for a Staff Meeting

Addendum

An amendment which adds words to a motion.

Addressing the Chair

A member wishing to speak on a point must rise and address the Chair in the following way:

Mr Chairman—for a gentleman.
Madam Chairman—for a lady.

All remarks must be addressed to the chairman, and members must not discuss matters between themselves at a meeting.

Adjournment

Subject to the articles, rules or constitution of an organization, the chairman, with the consent of the members of the meeting, may adjourn it in order to postpone further discussion, or because of the shortage of time. Adequate notice of an adjourned meeting must be given.

Amendment

A proposal to alter a motion by adding or deleting words. It must be proposed, seconded and put to the meeting in the customary way.

Attendance Record

The secretary, whose duty it is to record the minutes of the meeting, must also record the names of those present. If a large number of people are present it is a good idea to pass a sheet of paper round the table for signature. If it is a committee meeting, a chart showing the position of members will be very useful to the secretary who does not know the members very well. An attendance register which members sign as they enter the room, is also a satisfactory method of recording attendances.

Casting Vote

A second vote usually allowed to the chairman, except in the case of a company meeting. A casting vote is only used when there is an equal number of votes "for" and "against" a motion.

Closure

A motion submitted with the object of ending the discussion on a matter before the meeting.

Co-option

The power given to a committee to allow others to serve on the committee. A co-option must be the result of a majority vote of the existing members of the organization.

Disturbance

An obstructor causing a disturbance at a meeting may be ejected with or without the aid of the police provided that the meeting has not been announced as "public".

Dropped Motion

A motion that has to be dropped either because there is no seconder or because the meeting wish it to be abandoned.

En bloc

The voting of say a committee *en bloc*, that is electing or re-electing all members of a committee by the passing of one resolution.

Ex Officio

This means "By virtue of office". A person may be a member of a committee by reason of his office; or the tenure of one office may automatically be a qualification for the tenure of another.

Going into Committee

A motion "that the meeting go into committee" is moved if less restricted discussion is thought necessary. A motion "that the meeting be resumed" gives the meeting authority to proceed at the point where it left off.

In Camera

A meeting which is not open to the public.

Intra Vires

Within the power of the person or body concerned.

Kangaroo Closure

The Chairman of a committee is empowered to jump from one amendment to another omitting those which he considers to be less important or repetitive.

Lie on the Table

A letter or document is said to "lie on the table" when it is decided at a meeting to take no action upon the business contained in it.

Majority

The articles and rules of the organization will define the majority of votes required to carry a motion.

Memorandum and Articles of Association

These are regulations drawn up by a company setting out the objects for which the company is formed and defining the manner in which its business shall be conducted.

Motion

A motion must normally be written and handed to the chairman or secretary before the meeting. The mover of the motion speaks on it and has the right of reply at the close of the discussion. The seconder may then speak to the motion only once. If there is no seconder, a motion is dropped and cannot be introduced again. When put to a meeting, the motion becomes "the question", and when it is passed, it is called "the resolution". A motion on a matter which has not been included on the agenda can be moved only if "leave of urgency" has been agreed by the meeting or it has been included under the customary item "any other business".

Nem. Con.

This means "no one contradicting", i.e. there are no votes against the motion, but some members have not voted at all.

Next Business

A motion "that the meeting proceed with next business" is a method of delaying the decision on any matter brought before the meeting.

No Confidence

When the members of a meeting are aggrieved or at variance with the chairman they may pass a vote of "no confidence" in the chair. When this happens the chairman must vacate the chair in favour of his deputy or some other person nominated by the meeting. There must be a substantial majority of members in favour of this decision.

Point of Order

This is a question regarding the procedure at a meeting or a query relating to the standing orders or constitution raised by a member during the course of the meeting, e.g. absence of quorum

Poll

Poll is the term given for the method of voting at an election, and in a meeting this usually takes the form of a secret vote by ballot paper. The way in which a poll is to be conducted is generally laid down in the standing orders or constitution of the organization.

Postponement

The action taken to defer a meeting to a later date.

Proxy

One acting for another, or a document authorizing a person to attend a meeting and vote on behalf of another person.

Putting the Question

To conclude the discussion on a motion it is customary for the chairman to "put the question" by announcing "The question before the meeting is . . ."

Question Be now Put

When members feel that sufficient discussion has taken place on a motion, it may be moved "that the question be now put". If this is carried, only the proposer of the motion being discussed may speak and a vote is taken. If the motion "question be now put" is defeated discussion may be continued.

Quorum

This is the minimum number of persons who must be in attendance to constitute a meeting. The quorum is laid down in the constitution or rules of the organization.

Reference Back

This is an amendment referring a report or other item of business back for further consideration to the body or person submitting it. If the motion "reference back" is defeated, the discussion is continued.

Resolution

A formal decision carried at a meeting. It must be proposed, seconded and put to the meeting in the customary way. A resolution cannot be rescinded at the meeting at which it is adopted.

Rider

A rider is an additional clause or sentence added to a resolution after it has been passed and it differs from an amendment in that it adds to a resolution instead of altering it. A rider has to be proposed, seconded and put to the meeting in the same way as a motion.

Right of Reply

The proposer of a resolution has the right of reply when the resolution has been fully discussed. He is allowed to reply only once, and afterwards the motion is put to the meeting.

Scrutineer

One who counts and closely examines the votes at an election.

Seating Arrangements

It is customary for the chairman to be seated at the head of the table with the secretary on his right hand and the treasurer on his left.

Sine Die

Meaning without an appointed day, or indefinitely.

Standing Orders

These are rules compiled by the organization regulating the manner in which its business is to be conducted. It may also have the title "Constitution".

Status Quo

Used to refer to a matter in which there is to be no change.

Subcommittee

A subcommittee may be appointed by a committee to deal with some specific branch of its work. The subcommittee must carry out such functions as are delegated to it by the committee and must report to the committee periodically.

Teller

Teller is the title given to the person appointed to count the votes at a meeting.

Ultra Vires

Beyond the legal power or authority of a company or organization.

Unanimous

When all members of a meeting have voted in favour of a resolution it is said to be carried "unanimously".

MINUTES

Minutes are a record of the proceedings of a meeting and are kept to preserve a brief, accurate and clear record of the business transacted.

The secretary is responsible for attending the meeting and taking down, in note form, details of the decisions reached. She must take down in shorthand the exact wording of every resolution passed and the names of the proposers and seconders. A verbatim record is not necessary; she must ensure that all the arguments for and against the major decisions are recorded.

It is useful to keep minutes in a loose-leaf book as this enables them to be typed. If this method is used very great care must be taken in ensuring their

SECRETARIAL DUTIES FOR MEETINGS

Before the meeting	On the day of the meeting	After the meeting
1. Prepare the agenda in consultation with the Chairman and distribute it to members. 2. Prepare a Chairman's agenda. 3. Book a suitable room. 4. Obtain any necessary statements or documents from members who cannot be present but who are known to have strong views on items to be discussed. 5. Collect together the following items required for the meeting: (a) Stationery, including writing paper and shorthand note book. (b) Spare copies of the agenda. (c) Minutes of the previous meeting. (d) All relevant papers and files of correspondence, including letters of apology received from members unable to attend. (e) Attendance register or sheet. (f) Any books of reference, standing orders, etc.	1. Attend early, taking the items referred to in 5 of the previous column. 2. Arrange for direction signs to the committee room to be displayed. 3. Ensure that the seating arrangements are in order. 4. See that each member has a supply of writing paper. 5. Provide water and glasses and arrange ash-trays in convenient positions. 6. Check that members sign the attendance register. 7. Read the minutes of the last meeting; letters of apology and any other correspondence. 8. Assist the Chairman in supplying information from files as required during the meeting. 9. Record the details of the decisions reached, noting who proposed and who seconded motions as well as the results of the voting.	1. Ensure that all documents are returned to the office. 2. Prepare draft minutes for approval by the Chairman. 3. When approved type the minutes in final form for distribution to members. 4. Type any correspondence resulting from the meeting. 5. File any papers used at the meeting, as well as copies of correspondence typed in 4. 6. If the Chairman is also your employer see that the date of the next meeting is entered in his diary and yours.

safety as leaves can easily be lost or misplaced. Minutes should be kept locked away when not in use.

The safe custody of the minutes is important as they provide a permanent record of the proceedings at a meeting and they can be referred to at a later date when the business discussed is being reviewed. They can also be consulted to discover why certain decisions were taken.

Minutes should be written up as soon as possible after the meeting as it is much easier to be absolutely accurate when the discussions are fresh in the mind. They should be written wholly in the third person and in the past tense.

It is essential that minutes should be:

(*a*) **accurate** so that they present a true record of the proceedings;

(*b*) **brief** so as to provide a summary of the important matters discussed and decisions reached for reading and confirmation at the next meeting and for future reference;

(*c*) **clear** so that those absent from a meeting can be fully informed of the proceedings, and so that there is no possible doubt about previous deliberations.

When a set of minutes is typed, care should be taken to allow an adequate left-hand margin for the subheadings. Minutes should be recorded in the following order:

1. A description of the meeting which should include the type of meeting, time, date and place.

2. Names of those present with the chairman's name first and the names of the officers last.

3. Reading of the minutes of the last meeting.

4. Matters arising from the minutes.

5. Apologies for absence.

6. Correspondence.

7. General business—resolutions must contain the exact wording given at the meeting.

8. Any other business—this is recorded in the order in which it is taken at the meeting.

9. The date of the next meeting.

10. The signature block for the chairman and the date of the meeting when the minutes will be signed.

A draft is generally submitted to the chairman for his approval before the final copy is typed.

At the meeting the chairman will call upon the secretary to read the minutes of the last meeting. If the minutes had previously been circulated they may be taken as read if this is agreed by all members. If a member points out a

```
            SPORTS COMMITTEE MINUTES

            A Meeting of the Sports Committee of The Benning
            Welfare Association was held in the Sports Pavilion
            on Monday, 30 June 19-- at 1930 hrs.

            Present

            Mr J H Thomas  (in the chair)
            Miss D Ashton
            Mrs I Gardner
            Mr A Evans
            Mr J Ripley
            Mr H Spence
            Mr R T Bird (Secretary)
```

Minutes	The minutes of the last meeting were read, adopted and signed by the Chairman.
Matters Arising	Mr Evans reported that a reunion of the members of the Football Club proved very successful.
Financial Statement	A statement of the current financial position of the Committee was read and adopted. In addition, the statement for presentation to the Annual Meeting to be held on 14 July 19-- was approved.
Tennis	Miss Ashton pointed out that there was a lack of facilities for members wishing to play tennis. She stated that the one grass court belonging to the Committee was proving inadequate owing to the constant demand caused by the Club members' enthusiasm, and asked whether the Committee could see its way to secure a second court. Mr Ripley mentioned that members of the tennis section had contributed a large proportion of the funds at present in hand, and that he considered Miss Ashton's recommendation justifiable. The Chairman pointed out that the application would have to be submitted in the first place to the Board of Directors for their approval.
	RESOLVED: That the Secretary be instructed to R41 make application to the Board of Directors for the provision of a second grass court adjoining the existing grass court.
Date of Next Meeting	It was decided to hold the next meeting of the Committee on Tuesday, 23 July 19--.

```
            Chairman
            23 July 19--
```

Fig. 60 Extract from the Minutes of a Committee Meeting

mistake in the minutes the chairman or secretary, subject to the approval of the meeting, may correct the error in the minutes, before they are signed as correct. Once the minutes have been signed, they should not be altered in any way.

```
MINUTES OF MEETING          A meeting of the Conference Organization Committee of
                            the National Trade Association was held at Association
                            Headquarters on Friday, 31 May 19-- at 1430 hrs.

                            Present:

                            Mr J M Strang (in the chair)
                            Miss J T Branson
                            Mr V E Carter
                            Mr B W White (General Secretary)

Minutes                     The minutes of the last meeting, which had been circulated,
                            were taken as read and approved and were signed by the
                            Chairman.

Matters arising             There were no matters arising out of the minutes.

Apologies                   The Secretary reported that Mr Thomas had been admitted
                            to hospital. He was asked to communicate to Mr Thomas
                            the Committee's sincere wishes for a speedy recovery.

Conference                  Miss Branson and Mr Carter had visited the conference town
arrangements - venue        and looked over the two proposed venues, the Royal Pavilion
                            and the Palace Ballroom. They stated that the acoustics
                            were good in the Pavilion but there were no refreshment
                            facilities. The Ballroom had good refreshment facilities,
                            but the acoustics were poor. The Secretary recommended
                            that the Pavilion would be more practical from the point
                            of view of effective speaking.

                            The Secretary's recommendation that the Pavilion should
                            be used was agreed, provided that the conference would
                            adjourn for mid-morning and mid-afternoon breaks. It
                            was agreed that he should make the arrangements for the
                            booking.

Any other business

(a) Future conferences      Miss Branson raised the matter of future conferences and
                            asked whether the conference was held at the right time
                            of the year. She thought that Easter would be a much
                            more appropriate time than Whitsun. The Chairman said
                            that it was rather late to open a discussion on this
                            matter and suggested that it should be discussed at the
                            next meeting of the Executive Committee, to which Miss
                            Branson agreed.

(b) Report to Council       The Secretary confirmed that he would make an appropriate
                            report for submission to the Council.

Chairman

14 July 19--
```

Fig. 61 Extract from the Minutes of an Informal Meeting of an Association

Students of Secretarial Duties should note that minutes are a brief record of the proceedings of a meeting, and should not confuse them with a verbatim report or a précis. The former is one of a meeting, debate or discussion recorded and reported word for word; the latter is a summary of a literary passage, a speech, a report or of correspondence, expressing clearly and concisely all the important facts of the original.

Committee Meeting Minutes

Figure 60 is an extract from a set of minutes of a committee meeting embodying a formal resolution.

Recording Meetings

If a verbatim report of a meeting were required, it could be recorded by shorthand writers, or by a recording machine. Recording machines are not, however, so successful as shorthand writers; they cannot indicate the name of a speaker when it has not been given and several tapes would be required. Verbatim shorthand writers require speeds of 180–200 wpm, a secretary with a good speed of 120–140 wpm is normally able to record all that is required for the minutes of meetings.

Informal Meeting Minutes

Figure 61 is an extract from a set of minutes of an informal meeting of an association. In this instance, formal resolutions were not required. The arguments for and against the decisions reached and the final conclusions are all that are required in minutes of informal meetings.

QUESTIONS

1. What do you understand by "minutes"? What information would you expect to be contained in them, and why is their storage important? *R.S.A. SD.2*

2. What is the purpose of an agenda? Draft an agenda for a meeting of the Canteen Committee, giving three items to be discussed at the meeting. *R.S.A. SD.2*

3. You have been asked to check the maximum number of people who can be elected to the committee of your firm's sports club. How would you do this? Describe any means by which this number could be increased, either permanently or temporarily. *R.S.A. SD.2*

4. How are the matters for inclusion in the agenda of a meeting decided? Why is it necessary to include "any other business" as a separate item? *R.S.A. SD.2*

5. (i) What documents, books, etc., need to be gathered together for use in the meeting room on the day of the Annual General Meeting?
    (ii) What action should the Chairman of a meeting take if:
        (*a*) A member moves "that the question be now put";

(*b*) A member rises on a point of order, stating that a quorum is no longer present;

(*c*) The meeting passes a vote of "no confidence" in the Chair.

(iii) Explain the difference (when used in relation to meetings) between the following terms:

(*a*) Postponement and adjournment;

(*b*) Motion and resolution;

(*c*) Going into committee and going into division;

(*d*) Those present and those in attendance. *L.C.C. P.S.D.*

6. Your work involves the arrangement of a large number of committee meetings in regard to the various aspects and areas of operation of a large organization. Some meetings—sometimes several on the same evening—are held after office hours and are attended by members who do not necessarily work in the building. Describe an efficient system to ensure that:

(*a*) Sufficient notice is given of every meeting;

(*b*) It is immediately apparent, to the recipient of the notice, which activity of the organization is involved;

(*c*) There is immediate evidence of notice and agenda having been sent out;

(*d*) Documents, minute books, etc., required for meetings, are available for and collected after each meeting;

(*e*) It is clear to the caretaker which rooms are to be prepared and at which meetings refreshment is to be served;

(*f*) It is clear to the hall porter to which rooms people are to be routed. *L.C.C. P.S.D.*

7. You work for Mr Brown who acts as secretary to the company's Board of Directors. Make a list of those items which you think he should take with him to a meeting of the Board. *R.S.A. SD.2*

8. One of the functions of the secretary of a meeting is to assist the chairman. What would you expect the secretary to prepare for the chairman beforehand and how might she help during the meeting? *R.S.A. SD.2*

9. (*a*) What is the difference between the matters which would be dealt with at a general meeting of a club and at a meeting of one of its committees?

(*b*) What is the reason for appointing committees?

(*c*) Who may attend a general meeting of a club and who may attend committee meetings? *R.S.A. SD.2*

10. (*a*) What do you understand by an Executive Committee?

(*b*) Why does the Chairman of a meeting have a specially prepared agenda and how does it differ from the agendas provided for other members?

(*c*) What is an Annual General Meeting? What is its purpose? *R.S.A. SD.2*

11. A small society exists for experimenting with visual aids. A group is formed under the chairmanship of Miss Harris to make some educational film strips. Write, in suitable form, a minute for the committee's records on the following information. Miss Harris told the executive committee that the first meeting had been held on

January 15th in her office at Highlands School. Ten people had been present, a few of whom had had previous experience of making film strips.

They had viewed and commented on some existing film strips and had discussed what they felt was lacking in those available to schools.

There had been considerable discussion about their own future programme. One of the members, Mr Jolly, described the difficulties he had encountered when making film strips himself, but they had decided they would like to go ahead and see what they could do as a group. They felt that if they were successful, they might get help from some commercial firm who produced and sold such visual aids. *R.S.A. SD.2*

12. The following information is to be turned into an agenda for a committee meeting. Set it out as you think it should be.

A meeting of the committee of the National Association for Business Studies is to be held on Thursday, 30th June, at 2000 hrs. at the Fitzroy Hall, Reading. These are the items to be included: "We will discuss the programme for the summer. There will be a report from the Honorary Treasurer. Mr Beecham will report on a meeting which he attended on the teaching of bookkeeping. The Honorary Secretary will read her report. There should be an opportunity for members to discuss other business. The date of the next meeting is to be decided. The Fitzroy Hall will not be free next month and we must decide where to hold the next meeting." *R.S.A. SD.2*

13. Write the following in the form of a minute for inclusion in the Minutes of the Board:

"I suggest that we should allocate an appropriate sum for the purchase of an offset-litho machine which would enable us to carry out our internal printing. In the long run this would be an economy." This suggestion, made by Mr Henderson, was agreed by the Board. *R.S.A. SD.2*

14. You are responsible for arranging a committee meeting each month. You make a note in your diary two weeks before the meeting to remind yourself to prepare and send out the agenda.

Give

(*a*) two other reminders you would enter in your diary of items to be dealt with before the day of the meeting;

(*b*) two items to be dealt with on the day of the meeting. *R.S.A. SD.2*

15. (*a*) As secretary to your firm's Sports and Social Club, prepare the notice and agenda for their Annual General Meeting on 29th September.

(*b*) To whom will you send copies and when? *L.C.C. P.S.C.*

16. (*a*) What do you understand by an amendment to a motion?

(*b*) For what reason might a member of an organization be co-opted on to a committee?

(*c*) Give one reason why a meeting might be adjourned for a few days.

(*d*) What is an "ex officio" member of a committee?

(*e*) What is the purpose of a quorum? *R.S.A. SD.2*

17. In your spare time, at home, you act as secretary to the chairman of a women's organization.

The chairman sends you a list of items to be discussed at the next committee meeting. From these notes, draw up an agenda ready to send out to members of the committee. You may include any imaginary details you wish in order to make the agenda complete. The following are the notes you receive:

(*a*) We haven't decided where to have the October dinner or who should be asked to give a talk. Ask Mrs Wright to have some suggestions ready.

(*b*) Three members have complained that their change of address has not been shown on the last members' list. I enclose their letters.

(*c*) We have to deal with applications for membership. Remember to bring the application forms.

(*d*) Expenses have gone up so much recently that we ought to consider putting up membership subscriptions. We should discuss this so that we have our facts ready to present at the next Annual General Meeting. *R.S.A. SD.2*

18. In a business meeting what is the correct way for a member
    (*a*) to address the chair,
    (*b*) to present a motion to the meeting,
    (*c*) to move an amendment to a motion? *R.S.A. SD.2*

19. Your employer is Secretary to a Committee.
    (*a*) What relevant documents would you, as his personal assistant, expect to type before and after a meeting?
    (*b*) What checks would you make on his behalf prior to a meeting? *R.S.A. SD.2*

Chapter 13
Income Tax and National Insurance

A knowledge of income tax and national insurance is desirable for office staff at all levels. The shorthand-typist in the small office may, for instance, in addition to her shorthand and typewriting duties, be called upon to prepare the weekly or monthly pay packets for the staff. The private secretary should also be fully conversant with income tax as she should be capable of understanding, and if necessary compiling, her employer's personal income tax records.

Pay As You Earn (PAYE)

PAYE is the method used for deducting Income Tax from wages and salaries received from employment. The employee, under this system, pays his income tax as he earns his money. PAYE is applied to all who are employed, irrespective of age, and who receive an earned income which exceeds the allowable deductions, including personal reliefs.

The advantages of the scheme to the State are that taxes are collected regularly each week or month by employers from all their employees, thus relieving the Inland Revenue Authorities of the task of collecting the money from the individuals. The employer sends a bulk cheque to the Collector of Taxes once a month. The State is also assured of receiving all income tax due, and under this system bad debts are unlikely to occur.

The employee benefits because the amount of tax he pays is related to his actual earnings and the weekly or monthly deduction of tax is adjusted to meet any variation in such earnings; he does not have the trouble of sending his contributions along to the Collector of Taxes, as tax amounts are deducted from his weekly or monthly pay packet.

The amount of tax to be deducted by the employer each pay day depends upon:

(a) the employee's code number—listed on his tax deduction card and represents his income tax allowances;

(b) his total gross pay since the beginning of the tax year;

(c) total tax deducted on previous pay days in the current tax year.

How the Scheme is Worked

On pay day the wages clerk is required to complete a tax deduction card (form P11) for each employee as follows:

(*a*) Calculate the amount of pay due to each employee and enter it in Column 2.

(*b*) Add (*a*) to the total of all previous payments made to the employee since 6th April and enter the new total in Column 3.

(*c*) Calculate the amount of "free pay" to which the employee is entitled, in accordance with his code number, and enter this in Column 4. Reference is made to Table A (Free Pay Table) in the tax tables.

(*d*) Subtract the "free pay" in (*c*) from the total gross pay to date in (*b*) to arrive at the amount of "taxable pay", which is entered in Column 5.

(*e*) Calculate the total tax due to date by reference to the amount of "taxable pay" in Tables B to D (Taxable Pay Tables) and enter this sum in Column 6.

(*f*) Subtract the amount of tax already deducted from the total tax due to date in (*e*) arriving at the amount to be deducted from the employee's gross pay on the pay day in question and to be entered in Column 7. Sometimes—e.g. if the employee has worked a short week—the figure of total tax shown by the tax tables may be less than the tax already deducted; in that case the wages clerk must refund the difference to the employee instead of making any deduction and must enter the amount of refund in Column 7 with the initial "R".

(*g*) The amount of the National Insurance contributions should be calculated on the basis of gross pay received by reference to the Graduated Contribution Tables: the total of the employee's and employer's contributions are entered in Column 1a and the employee's contribution in Column 1b (*see also* page 232). The employer is responsible for keeping records of the figures of pay given and tax deducted at each pay day.

Tax Deduction Cards

The amount of tax on an employee's earnings is calculated on a tax deduction card (*see* Fig. 62) in accordance with the above procedure. A substitute document may, however, be used in place of the official card provided that the employer undertakes, at his own expense, to supply the

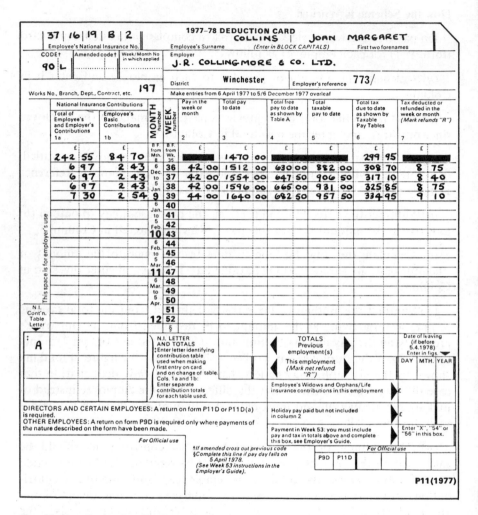

Fig. 62 Tax Deduction Card
(Crown Copyright. Reproduced by permission of the Controller, HMSO)

Collector of Taxes at the end of the year with two copies of a separate document for each employee which conforms to the official specification.

Each employee's tax deduction card must show the code number by reference to which tax is calculated. If there is an amendment to the code number, the new number, together with the week or month in which it applies, should be entered in the space provided. The blue card (form P8) explains the procedure for completing deduction cards. The completed tax deduction cards have to be returned to the Collector of Taxes at the end of the tax year.

Code Numbers

Code numbers are made up of a number and a letter. The number represents the allowances given against pay shown in the notice of coding, without the last figure, for example a person with £989 allowances is coded 98. The code number indicates the place in Table A of the tax tables to which reference must be made to find the amount of the employee's free pay to be entered on his tax deduction card. The letter "L" will usually be added to the number if the employee has been given the single person's allowance or the wife's earned income allowance. If the employee is entitled to the married man's allowance, the letter in the code will usually be "H".

If an employee's code is amended the employer will be notified by the Tax Office. Any employee who complains that his code number is wrong, or that he has appealed against it, should be referred to the Tax Office and told that the employer is obliged to act on the code number notified to him until amending instructions have been received.

The information which enables the Inland Revenue Authorities to allot the appropriate code number is obtained from the statement of total income and claim for allowances which must be completed annually by the employee. From this information are prepared and sent to the employer the necessary documents which enable him to make the appropriate deductions of tax each pay day.

Tax Tables

The Tax Tables consist of two books:

Table A: The Free Pay Tables for each week or month of the year. This shows for each code number the total free pay to date, i.e. the fixed weekly free pay multiplied by the appropriate number of weeks.

Tables B to D: The Taxable Pay Tables.

Table B shows tax due on taxable pay to date (i.e. pay to date less free pay to date) up to weekly or monthly limits.

Table C shows tax due where taxable pay exceeds the limits for Table B.

Table D comprises a set of shortened ready reckoners for each of the higher rates of tax; these will be used as directed in Table C and for codes in the "D" series.

Directions on the use of Tax Tables are provided on Card P8.

A copy of the tax tables should be made available by the employer to employees who wish to check the deductions made from their pay. Copies of the tax tables are also available for reference in public libraries, tax offices, etc.

Deduction or Refund of Tax

Tax must be deducted or refunded in accordance with the tax tables whenever any pay is paid to the employee, irrespective of the period over which the pay was earned and even if that period fell into a previous income tax year.

The tax deductions must be calculated by reference to the gross pay less any superannuation contributions but before other deductions, such as the employee's National Insurance contributions, or trade union subscriptions are made.

"Pay" for the purposes of income tax includes salaries, wages, fees, overtime, bonus, commission, pension, and holiday pay.

Income from which tax cannot be deducted, such as benefits in kind and income in the form of shares, will be taken into account in determining the taxpayer's code number, and the employer will be required to make a return of these items at the end of the year.

Employees Starting and Leaving

When an employee starts work for the first time, the employer will deduct income tax at once if the pay exceeds the PAYE threshold, i.e. the minimum amount on which tax is payable. The employee's age does not affect the amount to be paid. If the starting date is part way through the tax year, a tax refund may be given after the employee has claimed his allowances and his code number has been allocated.

When an employee for whom the employer holds a tax deduction card leaves, a certificate on form P45 "Particulars of Employee Leaving" must be prepared, as described below.

Form P45 (*see* Fig. 63)

Parts 2 and 3 of form P45 must be handed to the employee when he leaves, and Part 1 must be sent to the Tax Office immediately.

The employee should not separate the two parts. As soon as he begins his next employment he must give both parts of the form to his new employer so that the correct deductions of tax may be continued. The new employer should keep Part 2 and detach Part 3 and send it to the Tax Office.

INCOME TAX

PART 1

PARTICULARS OF EMPLOYEE LEAVING

	District number	Reference number
1. Employer's PAYE reference		

				Mr. Mrs. Miss etc.	Initials
2. Employee's National Insurance number *(copy from Deduction Card)*					

3. Employee's Surname *(Enter in BLOCK letters)*				

	Day	Month	Year
4. Date of leaving *(Enter in figures)*			19

5. Code at date of leaving *If on Week 1 (Month 1) basis also enter "X" in box marked "Wk. 1 (or Month 1)"*	Code	Wk. 1 (or Month 1)

6. Last entries on Deduction Card	Week or Month No.	Week	Month
		£	p
If Week 1 (Month 1) basis applies complete item 7 instead	Total pay to date		
	Total tax to date		
7 Week 1 (Month 1) basis applies	Total pay in this employment		
	Total tax deducted in this employment		

8. Works Number	9. Branch, Department, Contract, etc.

10. Employee's private address

11. I certify that the particulars entered at items 1 to 9 above are correct.

Employer

Address

Date

INSTRUCTIONS TO EMPLOYER

For Tax District use

1. Complete this form (including the shaded boxes) if a code is in use when an employee leaves. Take care that the carbon entries on Parts 2 and 3 are legible.
2. Enter the code (number and letter) at item 5.
3. If the employee was engaged after 6 April last include in item 6 the pay and tax notified to you in respect of previous employments.
4. **Detach PART 1 and send it to your Tax Office IMMEDIATELY.**
5. **Hand PARTS 2 AND 3 (unseparated) to the employee WHEN HE LEAVES.**
6. If the employee has died, please enter "D" in this box ▶ and send **ALL THREE PARTS** of this form (unseparated) immediately to your Tax Office.

For Centre use		
Amended	M/E	P

P45   Ff. Ltd. CON: 1124 3/73

Fig. 63 Income Tax Form P45

If a new employee does not produce form P45 or a code card, it may be because he has lost it, or because he has not been in any previous employment, or because he objects to disclosing the figures to his new employer. In any such case, if the period of employment is for more than one week the employer should send form P46 at once to the Tax Office and prepare a deduction card. Tax should then be deducted in accordance with the code specified for emergency use until further directions are received from the Tax Office. If an employee's pay does not exceed the PAYE threshold, form P46 should be completed but the deduction card is not required. A record of the employee's name, address and amount of pay should, however, be kept.

Refunds when Employee is away from Work

If the employee is absent from work, e.g. through sickness, he is entitled to receive any refund of income tax which is due to him on the normal pay day, provided that he makes the necessary arrangements for collecting the refund. If he does not collect it, the tax liability is adjusted up to date on the first pay day after return to work.

If an employee is unemployed for a short time, the tax tables will normally ensure that when his new employer first pays him he will receive the benefit of his allowances for the period of unemployment. He will either have less tax to pay or a refund of tax which will be added to his pay.

Certificate of Pay and Tax Deductions

After the 5th April each year the employer is required to give a certificate of pay and tax deductions (form P60) to each employee who is in his employment on that date and from whose pay tax has been deducted. The certificate should show the total amount paid to the employee during the year ending on that date and the total tax (less refunds) deducted.

Errors in Deducting or Refunding Tax

It is very important that the entries on the tax deduction cards are made correctly, and a check of the additions and subtractions on the cards is desirable. If the employer finds, during the course of the year, that an error has been made in deducting tax in an earlier week or month of the year, the matter should be put right in the week or month in which the error is discovered.

When the payment made in a week was wrongly recorded, a line should be drawn through the original figure of pay in the week (but so that it can still be read) and the correct figure inserted. All other original entries should not be altered or erased but a mark should be made against them to indicate that the error has been discovered and put right in the later week.

Return of Cards

The income-tax year runs from 6th April to 5th April. The employer is required to make returns to the Collector of Taxes, not later than 19th April in each year, of the pay, tax deductions and National Insurance contributions of all the employees for whom he has used a tax deduction card during the year ended on the previous 5th April. This is done by sending all the cards to the Tax Office with a covering certificate.

Claim for Allowances

The following procedure is adopted in calculating the employee's code number:

1. The Claim for Allowances and Statement of Income is completed by the employee and sent to the Tax Office.
2. Notice of Coding for the next tax year is sent by the Collector of Taxes to the employee and to the employer.
3. The employer notes on the new tax deduction card for the next tax year any revision in the employee's code number.
4. The employee should check the Notice of Coding. If he objects to the coding he should give further particulars of the allowances claimed to the Inspector of Taxes.
5. Changes in allowances should be notified to the Tax Office immediately they occur.

The most general allowances are personal allowance for single or married persons, housekeeper, children, dependent relatives and life assurance.

These allowances must be claimed at the time the income tax return is completed.

Employer's Guide

A comprehensive *Employer's Guide* is prepared by the Board of Inland Revenue and should be referred to when queries arise in connexion with PAYE procedure.

The secretary and wages clerk should note all changes brought about by the Chancellor of the Exchequer's Budget Speech proposals each year. Circulars are sent out advising taxpayers of the changes as they are made.

Students Employed during Vacations

Deduction Cards should normally be used for all employees receiving more than the amount on which tax is payable.

The Tax Office may, however, notify an employer that tax need not be deducted from payments to students employed during vacation periods, provided a statement is signed by the student at the commencement of employment and a declaration is made by the employer. Where these conditions are satisfied, the employer should prepare a deduction card for recording National Insurance contributions if the student's earnings are not less than the National Insurance Lower Earnings Limit. The cards and completed forms should accompany other employees' cards sent to the Collector at the end of the tax year.

NATIONAL INSURANCE

The National Insurance Scheme provides cash benefits for unemployment, sickness, injury at work, maternity, widowhood, retirement and death in return for regular weekly or monthly contributions. It is quite separate from the National Health Service, which provides medical attention and treatment for everybody, whether they are insured or not and only a small proportion of the contribution goes towards this service.

National insurance contributions for employees are related to their earnings and are collected along with income tax under the PAYE procedure. They consist of:

(a) primary Class 1 contributions from employed earners; and
(b) secondary Class 1 contributions from employers.

Employee's contributions are either:

(a) standard rate payable by most employees; or
(b) reduced rate payable by certain married women and most widows entitled to national insurance widow's benefit.

Employer's contributions are at the same rate regardless of whether the employee is liable to pay at the standard or reduced rate.

Liability for the contributions of both employers and employees is limited by upper and lower earnings limits. Where earnings do not reach the lower limit there is no liability for contributions from either employee or employer, although the employee is covered for industrial injuries benefits. The contribution rates and the upper and lower earnings limits are reviewed each year and the figures applicable to the next year are fixed by legislation. There is liability for contributions on any payment of earnings made to an employee from the date on which he reaches the minimum school-leaving age, even though he may be still at school, and irrespective of whether the pay was earned before or after that date.

National insurance contributions are always calculated on gross pay. Normally this will be the same as the amount of pay entered on the deduction card for income tax purposes. If, however, the employee contributes to a superannuation scheme and he is entitled to relief from tax, the employer must calculate the national insurance contributions on the pay before deductions of superannuation and must keep a separate record of the superannuation contributions. Liability for contributions begins with the first payment to an employee and is calculated independently of any pay he receives during the same earnings period from a job with a different employer. The employer is responsible for payment of both the employee's and the employer's contributions, but he is entitled to deduct the employee's contribution from the payment of earnings on which that contribution has been calculated.

National Insurance Numbers

The Department of Health and Social Security allocates national insurance numbers to all contributors to enable contributions to be correctly recorded on their accounts. Generally, young people will have a national insurance number allocated to them shortly before they reach school leaving age and will be given a national insurance number card. Any person who has not been given a number must, when he first becomes liable for national insurance contributions, or wishes to pay contributions voluntarily even though he is not liable, e.g. because he is non-employed but wishes to pay for pension purposes, apply to the Department of Health and Social Security. A person starting work for the first time should be asked to produce evidence of his national insurance number. If he is unable to do so he should be told to apply to his local Social Security office and to produce for inspection the national insurance number card subsequently issued to him. A new employee who is changing jobs will normally produce a form P45 on which his national insurance number should have been entered by his previous employer.

Calculating National Insurance Contributions

An employer will normally calculate contributions by reference to contribution tables supplied by the Department of Health and Social Security.

The tables show both the weekly and monthly rates. In the case of weekly contributions the tables are banded in steps of 50p of earnings, each contribution being calculated on the mid-point of the band. For example, the contribution shown against the earnings of £30 is calculated on earnings of £30.25 and is the contribution payable on earnings from £30 to £30.49.

The following contribution tables are issued:

Table A	— Standard-rate contributions for employees over age 16 and under pension age (65 men, 60 women) or under age 70 men and 65 women who have not retired.
Table B	— Reduced-rate contributions for those married women and widows authorized to pay contributions at the reduced rate.
Table C	— Employer-only contributions for those who are not liable for primary (employee) contributions.

The table letter should be entered in the first "NI Contribution Table Letter" space provided at the bottom of the deduction card.

The contributions deducted during an income tax month, together with the employer's contributions and any income tax deducted under the PAYE procedure, must be paid to the Collector of Taxes within 14 days of the end of that month. If it is found that an incorrect contribution has been recorded on the deduction card a line should be drawn through the original figure (but so that it can still be read) and the correct figure inserted. The amount is recovered or, in the case of an excess charge, refunded, during the current year.

Absence from Employment through Illness

If you are absent from your employment through illness you should:

1. Ask your doctor for a medical statement, fill in both sides, and send it without delay to the local Social Security Office.

2. If your doctor gives you a form or note other than the statement, send it to your local Social Security Office with a letter to say you are claiming national insurance benefit. Give your full name, address, date of birth and, if you can, your national insurance number.

3. Notify your employer and send a doctor's certificate if this is the procedure laid down by your employer.

4. Your doctor may give you a "closed" statement, i.e. one on which he advises you to stay off work until a specified date. If you are not fit to return to work on the day your doctor has recommended, you must ask for another statement from him and send it to the Social Security Office.

5. If your doctor gives you an "open" statement you will need a further one when it ends. The first "open" statement will cover a period, during which, in your doctor's opinion, you should not work. If at the end of the period your doctor thinks you should still be away from work, he will issue a further statement. If your doctor has given you an "open" statement you must, before returning to work, ask him for a "closed" statement.

An employee who is absent from work through sickness does not have to pay National Insurance contributions. A contribution is normally credited when the Department of Health and Social Security has satisfactory evidence of the employee's incapacity.

Where an employee receives sick pay, the amount of which is fixed on condition that he hands over to his employer any national insurance sickness benefit he receives, contributions are payable on the sick pay less the amount of the benefit. The net pay, i.e. sick pay less benefit, should be entered on the deduction card.

General Advice

The local Health and Social Security Office will give advice on all matters connected with the National Insurance scheme, and full details can be found in the *Employer's Guide to National Insurance Contributions*, a copy of which should be available in all wages offices.

SAVE AS YOU EARN

The Save as you Earn Scheme (SAYE) is a savings contract in which the investor agrees to make sixty regular monthly payments over a period of five years. Each of the sixty contributions are index-linked, i.e. they are adjusted in line with any change in prices that has occurred between the time of making the contribution and completion of the agreement. Any sum (in whole £s) from £4 a month to £20 a month can be saved. The amount of the monthly contribution remains the same throughout the five years of a contract. If the investor decides to withdraw his savings at the end of five years, the sixty revalued contributions will be added together to arrive at the total repayment value of the contract. On completion of a five year contract the investor may opt to leave the money invested for a further two years. No further contributions are made during this period. If the investor chooses to do this, his contributions will be adjusted in line with the retail price index on the seventh anniversary of the starting date of the contract. In addition, he will receive a tax free bonus equal to two monthly contributions. Any person of 16 years of age or over may enter into a SAYE contract. A person wishing to open a contract must complete a SAYE proposal form. Payment may be made through the Post Office or bank or by an employer deducting it from pay.

CONTRACTS OF EMPLOYMENT

Some of the major provisions relating to contracts of employment in the Employment Protection Act, 1975 and the Contracts of Employment Act, 1972 are as follows:

1. Minimum Periods of Notice to Terminate Employment   The employee must give at least one week's notice if he has been with his employer continuously for 13 weeks or more, but this does not increase with length of service.

The employer must give at least one week's notice after 4 weeks' service, and thereafter one week for each completed year of service up to 12 weeks after 12 years.

2. Written Contracts of Employment   Employers must give their employees written particulars of their main terms of employment not later than 13 weeks after commencement of employment. These should include: job title; date when employment began and whether any previous employment is to be counted; rate of remuneration; intervals at which remuneration is paid; hours of work; holidays; sick pay entitlement; pension schemes; length of notice by both parties; grievance procedure and any disciplinary rules applicable.

3. Medical Suspension   An employee who would normally be able and willing to work but who has been suspended from work on medical grounds, e.g. under certain specific health regulations, will be entitled to receive a week's pay from his employer while he is suspended, for a maximum of 26 weeks.

4. Maternity Provisions   It is unfair to dismiss an employee merely because she is pregnant. Also, a woman who has worked for her employer for two years and who remains at work until 11 weeks before the baby is expected, is entitled to return to work on terms and conditions not less favourable than those on which she was formerly employed. This right is dependent on the employee having told her employer, in writing if requested, at least three weeks before leaving that it is her intention to return to work and it may be exercised up to 29 weeks after the baby is born, and submission of a doctor's certificate.

5. Written Statement of Reasons for Dismissal Any employee with at least 26 weeks' service who is dismissed by his employer is entitled to ask his employer for a written statement of the reasons for the dismissal, and if he does so request, the employer must give him one within 14 days of the request being made. New remedies for unfair dismissal are contained in the Employment Protection Act, 1975.

DEDUCTIONS FROM PAY

Statutory Deductions

The employer is required by law to make these deductions from the pay of all employees, where applicable:

(1) Income Tax
(2) National Insurance } — variable deductions

Voluntary Deductions

These deductions are not compulsory and are made only with the consent of the employee. They are fixed deductions and may include contributions to a social fund; National savings; holiday savings and a benevolent fund.

A variable deduction is one which must be calculated separately on each pay day and may vary according to the amount of gross pay received, whereas the fixed deductions remain the same and in a mechanized wages system can be printed in advance on the pay documents, i.e. the pay roll, the employee's pay record and the pay slip.

ITEMIZED PAY STATEMENTS

The Employment Protection Act, 1975, gives employees the right to be given itemized pay statements by their employers. The pay statements must specify the following:

The gross amount of pay; the amounts of any fixed deductions and the purposes for which they are made; the amounts of any variable deductions and the purposes for which they are made; the net amount of pay, and where different amounts of the net amount are paid in different ways; the amount and method of payment of each part-payment.

QUESTIONS

1. What is P.A.Y.E.? Does it apply to everybody, and what are its advantages:
(*a*) to the State, and
(*b*) to the individual? *R.S.A. SD.2*

2. What is the purpose of P.A.Y.E., and to whom does it apply? *R.S.A. SD.2*

3. Under the P.A.Y.E. system, on what does the amount of tax to be deducted depend? *R.S.A. SD.2*

4. Describe the action necessary in connexion with P.A.Y.E. when an employee changes his employment. *R.S.A. SD2*

5. A new junior employee arrives without a National Insurance number, saying she has never had one, but that she has worked on Saturdays during her last year at school. What should be done? *R.S.A. SD2*

6. If an employee is absent through sickness, is he:
(*a*) entitled to any refund of Income Tax and
(*b*) obliged to pay National Insurance Contributions?
What action should be taken, and by whom, in both these circumstances? *R.S.A. SD.2*

7. (*a*) What documents should a man produce when he changes his employment?
(*b*) What information about him should his new employer record at that time and during his employment:
(i) for the purpose of preparing wages, and
(ii) for inclusion in general personnel records? *R.S.A. OP.2*

8. What action in relation to sickness benefit is necessary if you are away from your employment through illness? *R.S.A. SD.2*

9. It is your duty each week to inform the accountant of the overtime worked by shorthand-typists and typists. Your own overtime rate is £1 an hour, and you have worked 3½ hours. The other shorthand-typist has worked 4 hours and her rate is 80p an hour. The typist receives 75p an hour and has worked 1½ hours. Set out a clear statement for the accountant. *R.S.A. SD.2*

10. What is meant by (*a*) P.A.Y.E. code numbers, and (*b*) tax deduction tables? *R.S.A. SD.2*

11. What deductions must be made, by law, from an employee's pay? *R.S.A. SD.2*

12. When should a new employee bring a P45 with him and why is it necessary? *R.S.A. SD.2*

13. What is the difference between P.A.Y.E. and National Insurance? Explain briefly why such deductions are made from your salary. *R.S.A. SD.2*

14. A typist in your firm enquires about the Save As You Earn scheme. What are the main features of the scheme which should be explained to her? *R.S.A. SD.2*

15. State briefly the advantages and/or the disadvantages of the P.A.Y.E. system of collecting income tax (a) to the state, (b) to the employer, (c) to the employee. *R.S.A. SD.2*

16. You deal with the wages of the staff in your office. Two new employees start work. One has not been employed before, the other has come from another firm. What documents would you expect them to bring with them and what action would you take with these documents? *R.S.A. SD.2*

17. You started work four years ago when you were seventeen years old. During this time your employer has made the necessary statutory deductions for National Insurance, Superannuation Contributions, and Income Tax from your wages. What benefits could you expect to receive in each of the following circumstances?

(a) You are away from work for three weeks, suffering from tonsilitis.

(b) The firm for which you work closes down, and you do not obtain other employment for two weeks. *R.S.A. SD.2*

18. What does an employer do with the money he collects from his employees for the following:

(a) P.A.Y.E.;

(b) National Insurance contributions? *R.S.A. SD.2*

19. Anne, a typist, and Joan, a shorthand typist, are both 19 years of age. Anne earns £26 and Joan £34 a week. Do they pay the same amounts for the following:

(a) P.A.Y.E.;

(b) National Insurance Contributions? *R.S.A. SD.2*

Chapter 14
Petty Cash

The secretary will be expected to keep her employer's personal cash transactions recorded in an efficient and businesslike manner.

A Petty Cash Book is used for recording small items of business expenditure or the private expenditure of the employer. An agreed sum of money is allocated to the secretary out of which her incidental cash payments are made. At the end of a month or other period of time, the amount spent is refunded to her, thus restoring her allocation to the original amount. The original

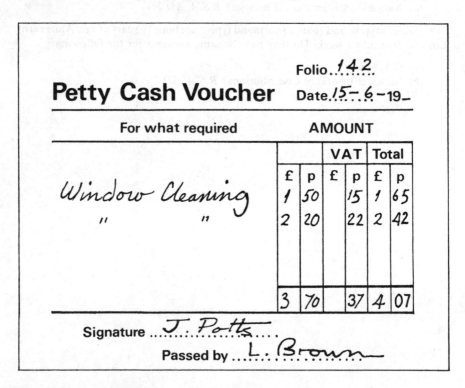

Fig. 64 Petty Cash Voucher

amount is called an "imprest" or "float". This method of keeping the petty cash is known as the "imprest system".

The three stages in the procedure of the imprest system are:

1. A sum of money estimated to be sufficient to cover the month's disbursements is allocated to the petty cashier.

2. During the course of the month the petty cashier uses this money for paying for small purchases.

3. At the end of the period the petty cashier receives a sum of money to cover the expenditure, thus bringing the total cash back up to the original amount.

Whenever cash is paid out a voucher or receipt should be obtained, which means that at all times the total of the cash plus the current month's vouchers should equal the amount of the imprest. In the case of postage stamps there will usually be no receipt, but reference can be made to the postage book where an up-to-date record is available of all stamps purchased and used. The vouchers should be numbered as they are received and filed in numerical order. A specimen petty cash voucher is given in Fig. 64.

In a business the petty cash book is a subsidiary of the cash book and it relieves the cash book of the many small items of cash expenditure which are so necessary for day-to-day organization.

The following procedure is adopted in connexion with petty cash:

1. When cash is paid from the cashier to the petty cashier:

Cr. Cash Book
Dr. Petty Cash Book

2. When a petty cash payment is made:

Cr. Petty Cash Book

3. At the end of the period:

Dr. Ledger Accounts with the totals of the petty cash book columns.

4. When a trial balance is taken out the petty cash balance must be debited.

An example of a Petty Cash Book is given in Fig. 65 in answer to the following question set by The Royal Society of Arts:

Question

Enter the following transactions in the Petty Cash Book of Roberts & Co. Ltd., showing the analysis under the headings of Postage, Stationery,

Carriage, Travelling Expenses, and Office Expenses:

    19..

Feb. 1. Received £15 for petty cash float.
            Bought postage stamps for £1·63
     5. Paid fares £0·69
     6. Paid £0·55 for cleaning office windows (5p VAT included)
   10. Paid £0·23 for tea.
   11. Paid for carriage £0·74
   15. Bought postage stamps for £1·98
   18. Paid £0·37 for fares.
   20. Paid £1·71 for stationery. (15p VAT included)
   23. Paid £0·89 for carriage.
   27. Bought postage stamps for £1·92
   28. Paid office milk bill £0·37
Mar. 1. Received total amount of expenditure for February.

The arrangement of the columns in the petty cash book is important and the columns, numbered for reference purposes, in Fig. 65 represent:

    1. the date of cash received or balances brought down;
    2. details of cash received;
    3. Folio column, i.e. the reference number of the double entry. In this instance the item of £15 cash paid to the petty cashier, can be seen on cash book, page 1;
    4. total amounts of cash received;
    5. the date payment is made;
    6. details of the payment made;
    7. the receipt or voucher number entered;
    8. the total cash paid out;
    9. various analysis columns. (Each column represents an account in the ledger.)

The analysis columns can be varied to suit individual requirements. Each column represents an account in the ledger, and at the end of a month or other period the total in the column is transferred to the ledger account. The total of the analysis columns should equal the main total (No. 8). The following points should be noted in connexion with the example given:

(*a*) The £15 received on 1st February was debited "To cash". The items on the debit side are always preceded by the word "To" and the items on the credit side by the word "By".

(*b*) When postage stamps were bought on 1st February, the amount of cash was taken out of the petty cash box and an entry made on the credit

Dr. | | | | | | | | | | | | | Cr.

(1) Date	(2) Details	(3) Fo	(4) Total £	(5) Date	(6) Details	(7) V N	(8) Total	Postage	Stationery	(9) Carriage	Trav. Exp.	Office Exp.	VAT
			£				£	£ 1·63	£	£	£	£	£
19.. Feb. 1	To Cash	CB1	15·00	19.. Feb. 1	By Stamps	1	1·63	1·63					
				,, 5	,, Fares	2	0·69				0·69		
				,, 6	,, Cleaning	3	0·55					0·50	0·05
				,, 10	,, Tea	4	0·23					0·23	
				,, 11	,, Carriage	5	0·74			0·74			
				,, 15	,, Stamps	6	1·98	1·98					
				,, 18	,, Fares	7	0·37				0·37		
				,, 20	,, Stationery	8	1·71		1·56				0·15
				,, 23	,, Carriage	9	0·89			0·89			
				,, 27	,, Stamps	10	1·92	1·92					
				,, 29	,, Milk	11	0·37					0·37	
							11·08	5·53	1·56	1·63	1·06	1·10	0·20
								L·1	L·2	L·3	L·4	L·5	L·6
			15·00	,, 28	,, Balance c/d		3·92						
March 1	To Balance b/d	b/d	3·92				15·00						
,, 1	,, Cash	CB2	11·08										

Fig. 65 Petty Cash Book

side of the book, first of all in the total column and then in the analysis column "Postage". Every item of expenditure is entered twice, once in the total column and once in the respective analysis column.

(*c*) On 28th February all the money columns were totalled up; the analysis columns were underlined and the ledger account numbers written under the double underline, e.g. L.2. The amount of the total column was deducted from the debit side (cash received) and the difference (known as the balance) entered below the total spent, namely £11·08. The debit and credit side totals were added up and entered on the same line. The balance of cash in hand, £3·92, was carried down to the debit side below the total.

(*d*) On 1st March the amount spent, namely £11·08, was received to restore the "imprest" to £15.

QUESTIONS

1. On the 1st of the month, £50 was handed to you by the cashier to open a petty cash account. Using the imprest system, and in analysis form, enter the following transactions. Balance the petty cash account on the last day of the month, and carry down the balance.

			£	VAT included £
March	1	Postage stamps .	5·00	
	2	Laundry of towels	0·78	0·07
	3	Date stamp and pad .	0·75	0·07
	4	Telegram .	0·40	
		Blotting paper .	0·55	0·05
	5	Office cleaning .	0·53	
	8	Air mail letter forms .	0·25	
	9	Shorthand notebooks .	1·10	0·10
	10	Adhesive tape .	0·29	0·03
	16	Refills for ballpoint pens .	0·22	0·02
	19	Office cleaning .	1·05	
	24	Mr Brown's expenses in Manchester	2·24	
	26	Office cleaning .	0·53	
	29	Dusters .	0·35	0·03
	31	Milk account .	0·46	
		Window cleaning	1·10	0·10

R.S.A. SD.2

2. You are in charge of the petty cash account which is kept under a monthly imprest system. Decide upon the amount of the "float", set out a suitable ruling and enter the following items which constitute a month's transactions; include an appropriate amount in each case:

flowers for reception desk;

106 stamps for circular;
taxi fare;
electric bulb;
fee charged on understamped packet;
gratuity to messenger;
pad of petty cash slips;
Biro refill;
coffee;
milk;
sugar for "elevenses";
sealing wax;
magazines for waiting room;
6 pencils;
charlady's wages;
office boy's fare to collect parcel;
postage on air mail packet to U.S.A.;
carbon paper;
window cleaning;
blotting paper;
cleaning materials for charlady. *L.C.C. P.S.D.*

3. What do you understand by an imprest system of keeping petty cash? Making suitable rulings and not more than five headings, enter the following petty cash transactions, indicate expenditure on the items shown, and show the balance carried forward.

Cash in hand £0·99, cash received £19·01. Expenditure: typewriter ribbon; gratuity to delivery man; magazines for waiting room; wreath; drawing pins; messenger's bus fares to deliver packet; bandages for first-aid box; postage on under-stamped letter; weekly wage of afternoon tea-lady; sticks of chalk; seven air letter forms; flowers for foyer; tube of poster paint; registered envelopes; taxi fare. *L.C.C. P.S.D.*

4. Your employer grows roses as a hobby and is the secretary of the local Rose Growers' Association. He spends cash from day to day on stamps and other small items. From time to time he draws £5 from the Association as petty cash. He keeps this money with his own and gives you a note each time he spends anything. You enter this in a special petty cash book. Frequently, he asks you if he has used up his £5. Draw up a suitable ruling for this book which will enable you to give him the information quickly whenever he asks for it. Make four or five specimen entries. *R.S.A. SD.2*

5. What books and equipment would you need to control the petty cash float in your department? Explain briefly the purpose of each item on your list. *R.S.A. SD.2*

6. You work for a firm where you are in charge of petty cash. The firm has three departments and expenses are allocated accordingly. These departments are Sales, Purchases, and Publicity. You are allowed to pay out petty cash up to £1, provided that the voucher is correctly completed.

(*a*) What would you look for before paying money out against a voucher?

(*b*) Draw up a voucher showing the necessary entries. *R.S.A. SD.2*

7. You are responsible for the petty cash account which is kept on the Imprest System.

(*a*) Enter the following transactions in an account using appropriate analysis columns:

			£	VAT included £
19				
June	1	Cash in hand	8·31	
	1	Cash received	11·69	
	2	Postage stamps	2·00	
	3	Magazines for waiting room . . .	0·50	
	6	Telegram	0·40	
	7	Air letter forms	0·15	
	10	Taxi fare	0·37	0·03
	13	Tea, milk and sugar	2·28	
	14	Refills for ball-point pens . . .	0·22	0·02
	15	Window cleaning	1·65	0·15
	20	Paper clips	0·22	0·02
	24	Flowers for foyer	0·55	0·05
	30	Draw and cash a cheque for the expenditure to date to restore the float.		

Balance the account and carry down the balance to 1st July.

(*b*) What do you understand by the Imprest System?

(*c*) How would you file the petty cash vouchers? *R.S.A. OP.2*

8. From the information in the following Petty Cash Book (which is kept on the Imprest System) answer the questions given below.

Dr.							Cr.
Cash received £	Date 19	Details	Totals £	Postages and Telegrams £	Carriage £	Stationery £	VAT £
4·07½	Jan. 1	Balance					
15·92½		Cash					
	3	Postage	1·50	1·50			
	5	Stationery	3·56			3·24	0·32
		Carriage	0·53		0·53		
	6	Postage	1·25	1·25			
	7	Telegrams	0·57	0·57			
		Carriage	1·29		1·29		
	8	Stationery	5·43			4·94	0·49

(*a*) What is the amount of the petty cash float?

(*b*) What was the balance of Petty Cash at the end of the period?

(*c*) How much was spent in Postage and Telegrams during the period?

(*d*) How much was spent in Stationery during the period?

(*e*) What was the total amount spent during the period?

(*f*) How much must the Petty Cashier receive at the end of the period to make up the float? *R.S.A. OP.1*

9. You are responsible for writing up the Petty Cash Book in your office. The three analysis columns are headed Office Expenses, Postage and Stationery, Cleaning.

(*a*) State under which heading you would enter the following payments: refills for ball point pens; laundering of towels; erasers; tea, milk and sugar; stamps; tip for van driver; roll of self adhesive tape; magazines for waiting-room; dish-cloths; air mail letter forms.

(*b*) What do you understand by analysis columns?

(*c*) Explain fully the *uses* of the Petty Cash Book. *R.S.A. OP.1*

10. Why would you expect to find two signatures on a completed petty cash voucher? *R.S.A. SD.2*

11. In a petty cash book, why are payments entered twice, once in the total column and again under an appropriate heading? *R.S.A. SD.2*

12. You have recently started a new job and among your duties is that of responsibility for the Petty Cash. This has previously been kept in a somewhat haphazard fashion, payment being made on production of odd pieces of paper, and your new employer has asked you to devise an acceptable system. Explain fully how you will do this and draw up six specimen entries. The firm is a small one consisting of 12 employees, two of whom make several calls in the London area. *L.C.C. P.S.C.*

13. The total of petty cash vouchers together with the money remaining in the petty cash box should always equal the petty cash float. Explain this. *R.S.A. SD.2*

Chapter 15
Business Documents

Business transactions and communications are normally conveyed in written form in order to provide a record for both recipient and sender. The principal documents used in buying and selling transactions are given in this Chapter in order to outline the information which must pass between the buyer and the seller; the purpose of the forms used and the uses made of these forms within the firm.

The transactions are started in the Design Office at Office Products Ltd., manufacturers of office furniture, when a requisition is sent to the Buying Department for six drawing boards and tee squares (*see* Fig. 66).

A Requisition is an internal request for goods to be purchased or drawn from stock.

Distribution

1 copy to Buying Department.

On receipt of the requisition the Buying Department write letters of inquiry to two or three firms who are known to supply drawing boards (*see* Fig. 67).

A letter of inquiry is sent by the buyer to a likely supplier requesting details of goods offered for sale.

Distribution

1 copy in Buyer's file.

In reply to the letter of inquiry J. K. Brown & Co. Ltd. send a quotation to Office Products Ltd. supplying the information requested (*see* Fig. 68).

A quotation gives full particulars of goods offered for sale and the conditions of sale. Similar information may be supplied in catalogues, price lists and estimates.

Distribution

1 copy to Buyer of the enquiring firm.
1 copy in Sales Department's file.

REQUISITION			
Department	*Engineering (Design)*		
Supplier's name (if known)	—		
Address	—		
Estimate Reference No. *AB 123*			
Capital/~~Revenue~~			

Quantity	Details	Cat. No.	Price each
6	*Drawing Boards and tee squares*	—	£
Signature of Head of Department	*G. Smith*		**Date** *3/1/7-*

Fig. 66 A Requisition

Trade Discount

is an allowance from the invoice or list price of goods; it is deducted on the invoice and it does not depend on the time of payment. It is given as an allowance for a large order, an agent's profit, trade allowance or as a correction of the list price.

Cash Discount

is an allowance made as a consideration for the prompt settlement of an account within a stated period; it is deducted when payment is made.

OFFICE PRODUCTS LTD

79 Bradford Street
MANCHESTER M1O 7EY
Registered Company No.
109091 England

Telephone: 061–205 5123

Telex: OPLCLA 24819

4 January 197–

J K Brown & Co Ltd
9 Angel Road
BURY ST EDMUNDS
Suffolk
BS2 90P

Dear Sirs

With reference to your advertisement for drawing office
supplies in "Office Equipment News" I shall be glad if
you will kindly send me your quotation for supplying six
blockboard drawing boards (size 470 x 650 mm) and tee
squares. Will you please include your most favourable
terms and earliest date of delivery.

Yours faithfully

J Browning

J Browning
Chief Buyer

Our Ref: JB/JMH

Your Ref:

Fig. 67 Letter of Inquiry

QUOTATION

J K BROWN & CO LTD

9 Angel Road   Bury St Edmunds   Suffolk BS2 9OP

Telephone: 0284-2342

VAT No.   159 6423 72

Telex: JKBN 19873
Company No.
243816 England

BANKERS   Midland Bank Ltd   Bury St Edmunds
Account No. 819236

National Giro Account No. 2/416/8488

Quotation Ref: PR. 1962

Dated: 6 January 197–

To:

Office Products Ltd
79 Bradford Street
Manchester M10 7EY

For the attention of Mr J Browning

In reply to your inquiry dated 4 January 197–
we have pleasure in quoting you for the following —

6 blockboard drawing boards (size 470 x 650 mm)
and opaque plastic blade tee squares (650 mm) @
£3. (as illustrated in the enclosed Catalogue –
item P.148.)

Prices include delivery by our van.

Delivery: 2 weeks on receipt of order
Trade discount: 15%
Cash discount: 2½% for payment within one month
VAT at the standard rate

We look forward to receiving your instructions which
will receive our prompt attention.

Fig. 68 Quotation

ORDER   **OPL**   No. 1234

Date: 8 January 197–

From:

OFFICE PRODUCTS LTD
79 Bradford Street
MANCHESTER M10 7EY

To:

J K Brown & Co Ltd
9 Angel Road
Bury St Edmunds
Suffolk BS2 90P

Telephone: 061-205 5123

Telex: OPLCLA 24819

Please supply —

Quantity	Description	Cat. No.	Price
			£
6	Blockboard Drawing Boards and plastic tee squares (as per your quotation No. PR.1962 dated 6.1.197–)	P.148	3.00

Deliver to: the above address

J · Browning
J   Browning
BUYER

Fig. 69 Order

The quotations received from the various suppliers are compared and an order is placed by Office Products Limited with the most favourable one (*see* Fig. 69).

The Order form is used as an official request for goods to be supplied.

Distribution

1. Supplier.

2. Goods Received Section (notification of goods to be received).

3. Stores (stock control).

4. Accounts Department (checking invoice).

5. Buyer (file).

J. K. Brown & Co. Ltd. send an advice note if the goods are despatched by post or rail, and a delivery note for the van driver if the goods are delivered by road transport (*see* Fig. 70).

The driver is given two copies of the delivery note: one copy is given to the Goods Received Section and the other one is signed by the recipient of the goods and returned by the driver to J. K. Brown & Co. Ltd.

The advice note is similar to the delivery note.

When the goods are delivered to the Stores of Office Products Ltd. a Goods Received Note is issued internally (*see* Fig. 71).

Distribution

1. Buyer (as notification that goods have arrived).
2. Accounts Department (for checking the invoice).

The invoice is usually prepared at the same time as the delivery/advice notes, the prices being added on the right-hand side (*see* Fig. 72).

An invoice is a document sent by the seller to the buyer giving details and prices of goods sold.

Distribution

1. Top copy to Office Products Ltd. (Accounts Department) for checking against order, goods received note and for entering in accounts. Other copies at J. K. Brown & Co. Ltd. to:

2. Accounts Department (entering in accounts).

3. Stores (stock control).

4. Despatch (delivery note).

5. Sales Department (file).

DELIVERY NOTE   No. 483

from

J K BROWN & CO LTD
9 Angel Road   Date: 22 January 197–
Bury St Edmunds
Suffolk BS2 90P   Your Order no. 1234

Telephone: 0284-2342

Telex: JKBN 19873

To:

    Office Products Ltd
    79 Bradford Street
    Manchester M10 7EY

Please receive

SIX	Blockboard Drawing Boards (470 x 650 mm) and plastic blade tee squares (650 mm)	one crate

Received by: *T. Cox*

Fig. 70 Delivery Note

Value Added Tax

This is a tax, replacing selective employment tax and purchase tax, on goods and services by way of business. A standard rate of tax is payable on any goods and services which fall within the scope of the tax.

GOODS RECEIVED NOTE No. 148

Supplier: J K BROWN & CO LTD

Date Received: 22/1/7–

Delivery/Advice Note No. 483

Received per: firm's van

Order No.	Description	Quantity Received
1234	Drawing Boards and Tee Squares	6

Received by	Date	Entered in Stock by	Date
T. Cox	22/1/7–	R. Clarke	23/1/7

Inspected by	S. Shawman	Date	22/1/7–

Shortages/
Damage recorded: 1 tee square cracked

Fig. 71 Goods Received Note

Whenever a trader buys goods or services to which VAT applies, he receives from the supplier a tax invoice indicating the cost of the goods and the VAT charged on them. When, in turn, the trader supplies taxable goods and services to his customers he charges them tax at the same rate. At regular intervals, normally every quarter, the trader makes a tax return to Customs and Excise, showing the tax charged to him (input tax) and the tax he has charged to his customers (output tax) and will pay the difference.

INVOICE

J K BROWN & CO LTD

No. 1384

9 Angel Road   Bury St Edmunds   Suffolk BS2 9OP

VAT No. 159 6423 72

Telephone: 0284-2342

Telex: JKBN 19873

To: Office Products Ltd
      79 Bradford Street
      Manchester M10 7EY

Date: 22 January 197–

Your Order No.	Delivery Note No.	Tax Point	Terms: 2½% payment within one month
1234	483	22.1.7–	

Quantity	Description	Cat. No.	Price each	Cost	VAT Rate	VAT Amount
			£	£		£
6	Blockboard Drawing Boards (470 x 650 mm) and plastic blade tee squares (650 mm)	P148	3.00	18.00		
	DEDUCT: 15% trade discount			2.70		
	Net goods value			15.30	10%	1.49*
	ADD: VAT			1.49		
	Invoice Value			16.79		
	Carriage: By our van					

Fig. 72 Invoice   * Based on 10% of £14·92, i.e. £15·30 – Cash discount £0·38.

If his input tax is greater than his output tax he is entitled to claim a refund of the difference.

VAT is a tax on the consumer, since a taxable trader is able to take credit for the tax charged to him and to collect from his customers tax charged by him.

Small traders whose business turnover in taxable supplies of goods or services is not more than £5 000 a year may not be registered for VAT purposes.

VAT is administered by H.M. Customs and Excise who issue guides for traders and other employers.

CREDIT NOTE

No. C183

J K BROWN & CO LTD

9 Angel Road Bury St Edmunds' Suffolk BS2 9OP

VAT No. 159 6423 72

Telephone: 0284-2342

Telex;   JKBN 19873

To: Office Products Ltd
79 Bradford Street
Manchester M10 7EY

Date: 25 January 197–

Invoice No. 1384	Dated 22.1.7–	Tax Point 22.1.7–

Quantity Returned	Description	Cat. No.	Cost £	VAT Rate	VAT Amount
1	Tee square returned as defective	P148	1.00		£
	Less 15% trade discount		0.15		
			0.85	10%	0.08
	Add VAT		0.08		
	Credit Value		0.93		

Fig. 73 Credit Note

NOTE: Tax Point is the time when VAT becomes chargeable and is usually the date when goods or services are delivered or invoiced.

One of the tee-squares was received in a damaged condition (see the goods received note Fig. 71 in which reference was made to it) and J. K. Brown & Co. Ltd. agreed to credit Office Products Ltd. with its cost and a credit note was issued (*see* Fig. 73).

A credit note is a statement of an allowance made by a seller of goods returned, overcharges, packing cases returned, short weight and price reductions.

STATEMENT
JK BROWN & CO LTD

9 Angel Road   Bury St Edmunds   Suffolk BS2 90P

Telex: JKBN 19873

Telephone: 0284-2342

VAT No.   159 6423 72

To: Office Products Ltd
    79 Bradford Street
    Manchester M10 7EY

31 January 197–

Terms: 2½% payment within one month

Date	Ref. No.	Details	Debits	Credits	Balance
197–			£	£	£
Jan 22	1384	To Goods	16. 79		16. 79
" 25	C183	By Returns		0.93	15. 86

The last amount in the balance column
is the amount owing.

Fig. 74 Statement of Account

Distribution

1. Top copy (printed in red) to Office Products Ltd. (Accounts Dept.) for entering in accounts. Other copies at J. K. Brown & Co. Ltd. to:

2. Accounts Dept. (entering in accounts).

3. Goods Received Section (for receiving goods).

4. Sales Dept. (file).

In credit transactions, such as this, the buyer is not expected to pay each invoice as it arrives but waits to receive a statement of account listing all of the transactions which have taken place since the last statement was received (*see* Fig. 74).

A Statement is an account setting out the amount due by the purchaser to the seller and containing a record of all the transactions since the last account was issued. It is a copy of the debtor's account in the sales ledger.

Distribution

1. Top Copy to Office Products Ltd. (Accounts Dept.) requesting payment.

2. Copy in Sales Ledger (Accounts Dept.) of J. K. Brown & Co. Ltd.

If Office Products Ltd. pay within one month they will be entitled to deduct $2\frac{1}{2}\%$ cash discount from the amount payable.

QUESTIONS

1. It has been decided to purchase a new spirit duplicator for your office, and the model has been chosen after a demonstration by a salesman.

(*a*) State the names of the documents which will pass between your firm and the supplier, from the placing of the order to the payment for the machine.

(*b*) Make a list of the supplies which will have to be obtained before the machine can be put into operation.

(*c*) For what types of work will the machine be most suitable? *R.S.A. SD.2*

2. (*a*) (i) To whom is a Quotation sent?
(ii) How is a Delivery Note dispatched?
(iii) What is the purpose of an Advice Note?
(iv) What is a Credit Note?

(*b*) A.B.C. Decorators of 12 Romford Road, Ilford, Essex, sent the following Order to Glossy Paint Co. Ltd., of 50 London Road, Brentwood, Essex:

Details of Order: Order No. 1234. Date 1st June 197–.

Please supply:

100 gal. of White undercoat paint @ £3 per gal.

100 gal. of White gloss paint @ £3·75 per gal.
Trade Discount 25%. Add VAT at the standard rate
Delivery—immediate—to the above address.
Terms of Settlement 5% monthly.

From the above information complete an Invoice on the understanding that the goods ordered were in fact supplied on the 4th June 197–. *R.S.A. COS.*

3. Give six essential items of information which should be shown on an invoice. *R.S.A. SD.2*

4. On 1st May 197– your company (Wilton, Watkins and Irvine Ltd.) sells 20 tables to J. Berry Ltd., 10 Lower Street, Sornborough, at £15 each. You allow a trade discount of 15% and 4% cash discount within one month.

(*a*) Complete an invoice for this sale. VAT is charged at the standard rate

(*b*) Distinguish between Trade Discount and Cash Discount.

(*c*) What sum would J. Berry Ltd. pay if the account were settled on 15th May, 197–?

(*d*) What would have to be paid if the account were settled on 15th June 197–? *R.S.A. OP.2*

5. The purchasing department of a firm wishes to order a large quantity of a new item which it has not obtained previously. Describe the office procedures which will be followed and the documents which will be involved up to the stage when the firm pays for the items obtained. *R.S.A. OP.2*

6. What is the importance of a cash discount in a business transaction? *R.S.A. OP.1*

7. (*a*) Complete a Goods Received Note using the following information:
Barry Fabrications Limited ordered

24 rms A4 Typing Paper white   code 726
36 rms A4 Duplic Paper white   code 747
10 boxes (100 sheets) carbon paper code 761

against their purchase order number 27486274 from Office Equipment Limited, Townlea, Berks. The buyer's name was J. Coles, and the cost code 72/224. Office Equipment Limited despatched the goods per B.R.S. in 3 boxes this morning under their Advice Note number 11345.

On checking the goods it was found that the delivery was short by 2 rms of A4 Typing paper, and 2 rms of A4 Typing paper were badly damaged and were thus recected.

(*b*) Give reasons for the use of a Goods Received Note in a company.

(*c*) Name two other Departments to which copies of the Goods Received Note would be sent. *R.S.A. OP.1*

8. (*a*) On an Order form enter the following particulars:

DATE: Today's date
Order No.: 0351/7
CUSTOMER'S ACCOUNT NO.: 75223
OUR STOCK REF.: AB2361

To: Wells Wholesale Office Supplies Ltd., Swan Street, Worlea   M16 3RS

6	Typists' Chairs with Adjustable Back-rests. Cat. No. XL6049	£9 each
3	Filing Cabinets 496 mm. wide, with two drawers. Cat. No. T499	£18·50 each
2	Single Pedestal Desks. Cat. No. 6321	£22·75 each
1	Stencil Cabinet. Cat. No. E243	£39·40 each
1	Coin Sorter. Cat. No. SPD96	£20·25 each

(*b*) Name some ways in which a prospective buyer might obtain all the information he requires from the seller before he decides to place his order.

(*c*) In what way does the purpose of an order differ from that of an invoice?

(*d*) If the seller undercharges the buyer how will he correct this error? Please answer in detail. *R.S.A. OP.1*

9. Complete an invoice form using the following data:

Customer's name   Mr T. Barratt
                384 Thornton Road
                GLOUCESTER

      ,,   order number 50732

20 reams A4 bond paper	@	£0·60
20 reams A4 ink duplic. paper	@	£0·80
2 bottles Snopake	@	£1·25
1 box offset paper plates	@	£2·50

Add VAT at standard rate

Delivery one month by road; invoice no. 2766362. *R.S.A. OP.1*

10. Following the visit of a sales representative, your firm is about to purchase a new photo-copier. Write a short paragraph on each of the business documents involved in this transaction. (The usual procedure in your office is monthly settlement of all accounts.) *R.S.A. OP.1*

11. Distinguish between a delivery note and an invoice. Part *R.S.A. OP.1*

12. (*a*) On a Credit Note Form enter the following details:

On the 24th June Browning & Co., 13 Lake Street, Grasmere, Cumbria, returned to Burke & Co., 14 High Street, Dublin, the following, by B. & C. Steamship Co. vessel "Brigand":

6 crates at 15p each;
120 bottles at 2p each;
6 bottles of Whisky (damaged) at £3 each;
3 small bottles of Whisky (sent in error) at 70p each.

(*b*) How does this Credit Note affect the account of Browning & Co. with Burke and Co.?

(*c*) Give THREE reasons for which a Credit Note might be sent out. *R.S.A. OP.1*

Chapter 16
Correction and Preparation
of Printed Matter

The secretary must be familiar with the methods of preparing printed matter and with the signs used for correcting printed proofs.

When submitting manuscript for printing, the author is normally expected to prepare it as follows:

1. Manuscripts should be typed on one side of the paper only, with double spacing and with a two-inch margin at the left-hand side of each sheet.

2. The sheets of typescript should be consecutively numbered.

3. Footnotes should be typed immediately following the line containing the reference.

4. Headings are often used within chapters to break up the text into convenient sections. Where more than one type of heading is employed, their relative importance should be clearly indicated, e.g. section heading, subheading, sub-subheading, etc., so that these variations may be interpreted typographically with the correct emphasis.

When sending "copy" to a printer for printing the secretary must state her requirements, such as the type sizes to be employed, quality of paper on which the document is to be printed, colour, size and the quantity required, etc.

The printer will usually supply two "pulls" or sets of proofs before he carries out the actual printing. No major alterations should be carried out on the proof, otherwise this will involve the printer in a considerable amount of work and consequently the cost will be increased.

No.	Correction	Sign in margin	Sign in text
1	Insert full stop	⊙	⋏
2	Insert colon	⊙	⋏
3	Insert comma	,/	⋏
4	Insert semi-colon	;/	⋏
5	Insert question mark	?/	⋏
6	Insert exclamation mark	!/	⋏
7	Insert apostrophe	⁷	⋏
8	Insert quotation marks	⁷ ⁷	⋏ ⋏
9	Insert hyphen	I-I	⋏
10	Insert dash	I-/	⋏
11	Insert brackets	(/)/	⋏ ⋏
12	Insert square brackets	[/]/	⋏ ⋏
13	Use capital letters	Caps	▬▬▬
14	Use small capital letters	S.C.	▬▬▬
15	Underline word(s)	Underline	▬▬▬
16	Insert word(s)	Words to be inserted /	⋏
17	Use italics	ital	▬▬▬
18	Use Roman type	Rom	encircle word(s)
19	Use bold type	Bold	∼∼∼∼∼
20	Use lower case letters	l.c.	encircle letter(s)
21	Transpose words or letters	trs	⎵⎴
22	Delete	⌀/	Word(s) or letter(s) crossed out
23	To remain as it was before correction	Stet	·········· under word(s) to remain
24	Space required	#	⋏
25	Equalise the spacing	eq.#	⋏
26	Close up the space	◠	◠
27	Start a new paragraph	N.P.	⌐
28	Continue without a new paragraph	Run on	⌐___⌐
29	Improve damaged character	✕	encircle character
30	Wrong fount	w.f.	encircle character
31	Letter upside down	⑨	encircle character
32	Move to the left	⌐	⌐
33	Move to the right	⌐	⌐
34	Place in the centre	Centre	⌐⌐ indicating position
35	Raise line	Raise	▭
36	Lower line	Lower	▭
37	Straighten margin	‖	‖
38	Passage omitted	Out see copy	⋏
39	Remove printer's space	⊥	encircle space
40	Abbreviation or figure to be printed in full	Spell out	encircle words or figures

Fig. 75 Usual Printers' Correction Signs

When the first proof is received it should be examined and checked very carefully with the "copy" and the secretary should take note of the following matters at this stage:

1. Mark the proof clearly with the correct signs—a table setting out the usual printers' correction signs is given in Fig. 75.

2. Every error must be marked in the margin and in the text itself.

3. See that the matter is displayed clearly.

4. On a second copy repeat all the correction marks made on the proof. This copy should be retained for reference purposes.

5. (*a*) If a second proof is required mark the corrected proof "Revise".

(*b*) If the first proof is quite satisfactory and no further proofs are required mark the proof "Press" or "Press after correction" (where minor corrections have been made).

Centre

(13) *Caps*
(40) *Spell out*

(11) ⸮/   ⸝/
(2) ⦿
(1) ⊙   *Caps*
        (13)

(24) #

(7) ⸜⸝

(33) ⸜

(28) *Run on*
(3) ⸝/
(50) *lower*

(58) *Out see copy*

(16) *development*
of /

(39) *l.c.*

┌
Fulbridge Manufacturing Company Limited

    The (10th Ord. Gen.) Meeting of Fulbridge Manufacturing
Company Limited was held recently in Bristol. [Mr. Hugh
Watkins/ the Chairman/ presided and, in the course of his
speech, said/ It is pleasing for the (D)irectors to be able once
again to report record trading profits/these, I may say/have
been achieved under the most difficult circumstances when
prices of raw materials have shown marked change from
time to time, and when the prices of some metals which we
have to buy in very large quantities have increased considerably.   This striving after the highest possible production
has been the company/s regular policy since 1950.   At the
present time we are proud to say we have not passed on
any increases to our customers since the last general increase
took place nearly four years ago.
    I am sorry to say that the prices of ~~all our~~ new commodities
are still rising, the demands of all branches of (l)abour for
(h)igher wages are increasing, and if these movements continue we shall, of course, sooner or later be compelled to
pass on some part of these increased costs.
    The financial position of the company is/I think you will
agree/very strong.   Adequate stocks of materials are available and we are making steady progress towards improving
the position of our deliveries.
    Perhaps our greatest difficulty has been to obtain sufficient
labour for our requirements, and to meet this position we
have spent large sums on the provision of mechanized new
equipment and also on the/improved ~~production~~ methods
in each of our factories, and we are now benefiting from
these changes.
    You will also be pleased to know that your New Zealand
(B)ranch has shown (r)emarkable progress during this year.
                                                                                    ┐

N.P. (27)

l.c. (20)
⸝/ (3)
⊥ (49)

⊂ (26)

⸝/ (22)
✕ (29)

⸝/ (3)

trs (21)
stet (23)

⸝ (31)

Fig. 76 A Printer's Proof with Corrections Marked

Figure 76 is a printer's proof with a selection of the correction signs given in the chart overleaf; Fig. 77 shows the same passage after the printer has made the corrections. The numbers refer to the signs given in Fig. 75. A full list of printers' correction signs is given in *Proof Correction and Copy Preparation* (BS 1219:1958).

FULBRIDGE MANUFACTURING COMPANY LIMITED

The Tenth Ordinary General Meeting of Fulbridge Manufacturing Company Limited was held recently in Bristol.

Mr. Hugh Watkins (the Chairman) presided and, in the course of his speech, said: It is pleasing for the directors to be able once again to report record trading profits. These, I may say, have been achieved under the most difficult circumstances when prices of raw materials have shown marked changes from time to time, and when the prices of some metals which we have to buy in very large quantities have increased considerably. This striving after the highest possible production has been the company's regular policy since 1950. At the present time we are proud to say we have not passed on any increases to our customers since the last general increase took place nearly four years ago.

I am sorry to say that the prices of new commodities are still rising, the demands of all branches of labour for higher wages are increasing, and if these movements continue we shall, of course, sooner or later be compelled to pass on some part of these increased costs. The financial position of the company is, I think you will agree, very strong. Adequate stocks of materials are available and we are making steady progress towards improving the position of our deliveries.

As our output has expanded so has the volume of our export sales. Particular attention has been given to the expansion of sales to dollar countries.

Perhaps our greatest difficulty has been to obtain sufficient labour for our requirements, and to meet this position we have spent large sums on the provision of new mechanized equipment and also on the development of improved production methods in each of our factories, and we are now benefiting from these changes.

You will also be pleased to know that your New Zealand branch has shown remarkable progress during this year.

Fig. 77 The Corrected Version of Fig. 76

Printing Terms

The secretary should be familiar with common printing terms and a selection of these is given here. A complete list of terms is given in the *Authors' and Printers' Dictionary*, which those who frequently prepare printed material should have available.

Copy

MS. (manuscript) or typescript submitted by the author which is set up by the printer.

Dummy

A specimen plan or layout of a proposed document, prepared by the printer, to give the author an indication of the finished product.

Fount

A complete set of type of a specific face and size.

Galley

A flat tray for holding composed type before paging.

Galley or Slip Proof

A proof taken before the pages are made up. Each sheet is about eighteen inches long. Alterations on a galley proof can be effected more easily and cheaply.

Half-tone Block

A printing block which reproduces light and shade reproductions from photographs, paintings, etc.

Italics

A style of type in which the letters slope upwards to the right.

Justifying a Margin

The term "justifying a margin" is used by printers to refer to the equal spacing of words and lines to a given measure to facilitate equal and perfectly straight left- and right-hand margins.

Line Block

A printing block in which the originals must consist of lines and solid portions in black on a white background, generally taken from drawings, diagrams, etc.

Overrun

To rearrange type from one line to the next, e.g. as a result of the insertion of additional matter.

Author's Proof

A proof returned and corrected by the author.

First Proof

The proof, as corrected by the compositor, which the author first receives.

Proof

A trial impression of the printed matter taken for correction.

Proof Reader

The name given to the person who reads and corrects printers' proofs.

Roman Type

Ordinary type as distinct from italics or fancy type.

Set Up

To compose the type face.

Space

A blank for placing between letters, words or lines.

Type Face

The printing surface of type.

QUESTIONS

1. The following is a printer's proof. Correct this proof by means of the conventional signs used for this purpose.

The conditions experienced throughout the yera under review ere more difficult than we had expected.

They fall quite clearly into two groups the first coinciding with a period free from control, and the second one in which the effects of Government restriction on hire purchase were definitely felt. During the first period trading continued in the very promising manner on which we reported to you last year. Indeed, sales during this period far exceeded those of last year, and the risk taken in the introduction of many entirely new designs was amdly rewarded But af ter the were unable to offer to our customers those credit facilities which result in increased first first quarter of the year the controls imposedon hire-purchase meant that we sales, and we suffered a set-back in company with our competitors.

Below is a correct copy of the passage.

The conditions experienced throughout the year under review were more difficult than we had expected. They fall quite clearly into two groups, the first coinciding with a period free from control, and the second one in which the effects of government restriction on hire-purchase were definitely felt.

During the first period trading continued in the very promising manner on which we reported to you last year. Indeed, sales during this period far exceeded those of the corresponding period last year, and the risk taken in the introduction of many entirely new designs was amply rewarded. But after the first quarter of the year the controls imposed on hire-purchase meant that we were unable to offer to our customers those credit facilities which result in increased sales, and we suffered a "set-back" in company with our competitors. *R.S.A. SD.2*

2. The following is a printer's proof. Correct this proof by means of the conventional signs used for this purpose.

In the Course of his statement, circulated to shareholder in advance the Chairman said: Our business continues to expand, and the number of holders has greatly increased. Our policy of branch extension has made satisfactory progress during nineteen hundred and seventy-four, nad we have opened twenty-one new offices. In spite of this increase there has been a slight reduction in the total staff employed.

the accounts show a net profit of one million four hundred and seventy-five thousand pounds, which is thirty-eight thousand pounds more than last year, and have we been able to maintain the dividend at eighteen per Cent per annum; this dividend is a disappointment to some of our shareholders, since several of our COMPETITORS have been able to declare increased dividends: but for many years this bank has paid a higher dividend than almost all its competitors, and we are still in that very proud position.

Below is a correct copy of the passage:

In the course of his statement, circulated to shareholders in advance, the Chairman said:

Our business continues to expand, and the number of account holders has greatly increased. Our policy of branch extension has made satisfactory progress during nineteen hundred and seventy-four, and we have opened twenty-one new offices. In spite of this increase there has been a slight reduction in the total staff employed.

The accounts show a net profit of £1 475 000, which is £38 000 more than last year, and we have been able to maintain the dividend at eighteen per cent per annum. This dividend is a disappointment to some of our shareholders, since several of our competitors have been able to declare increased dividends; but for many years this bank has paid a higher dividend than almost all its competitors, and we are still in that proud position.

3. List the points to which the secretary should pay attention when preparing and checking a printer's proof.

4. Your employer has written an article for a professional journal. Describe in detail the various steps to be taken between the original manuscript being handed to you and the final proof as returned to the printer. *L.C.C. P.S.C.*

5. (*a*) What signs are used, in margin and in text, to indicate the corrections needed in a printer's proof for:

    (i) insert full stop,

    (ii) transpose,

    (iii) make spacing equal,

    (iv) move to the left,

    (v) close up,

    (vi) change to small capitals?

    (*b*) Why are standard proof correction signs essential? *R.S.A. SD.2*

Chapter 17
Visual Aids in the Office

Statistical information is much more clearly grasped when illustrated on a graph, chart or planboard than when it is given in typewritten or printed form. Visual control systems enable progress and situations to be observed and controlled systematically and efficiently, and they are even capable of indicating current trends and future requirements. The information is clearly displayed so that the observer can digest facts and figures at a quick glance.

Line Graphs

Line graphs can be used to show almost any kind of statistical information concerning, for instance, sales, purchases, gross profits, net profits, imports and exports, average prices, temperatures, lighting-up times, birth, marriage and death rates, populations, cost of living, wage fluctuations, and crime rates. The graph should be drawn on as large a scale as the paper will allow, and the divisions should usually represent units of multiples of five.

Figure 78 is an example of a line graph chart which answers the following question:

A chart is required to show the weekly home and export sales over a period of three months. Plot the following data on line graphs, using scales of 1 in (25·400 mm) = £200.

Week ended	Home Sales £	Export Sales £
5th Oct.	18 500	4 000
12th ,,	17 000	4 250
19th ,,	19 000	4 500
26th ,,	17 025	5 000
2nd Nov.	17 025	5 250
9th ,,	17 500	4 750
16th ,,	17 750	4 500
23rd ,,	17 800	4 750
30th ,,	17 000	4 750

7th Dec.	18 000	4 500
14th ,,	18 025	5 000
21st ,,	18 000	5 250
28th ,,	17 500	4 750

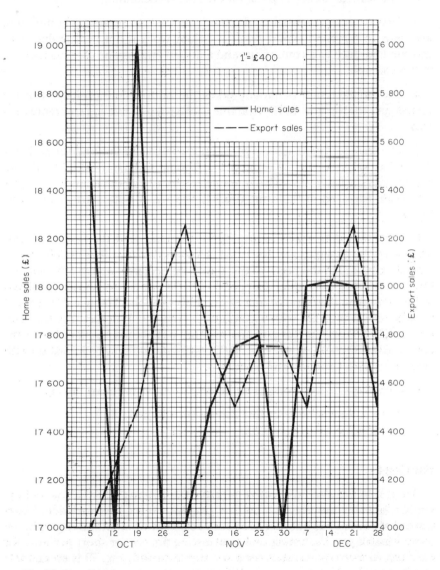

Fig. 78 Line Graph

The following points should be noted in connexion with the question and answer given:

1. The weeks are set out on the bottom horizontal line (or axis), each week occupying five squares.

2. The scale of money is given on the side vertical lines.

3. Two or three colours may be used, e.g. red, to represent home sales, and blue, to represent export sales. If colour work is not permissible, contrasting lines such as a continuous and a dotted line may be used, as they are in this example.

4. The smallest sum of money takes the bottom line position and the largest sum the top line. In the example each group of five squares represents £100.

5. The scale for home sales is given on the left-hand line and the scale for the export sales on the right-hand line; home sales start at £17 000 and export sales start at £4 000. This is not necessary when both items for analysis are being displayed in the same price range, i.e. if both start at the same figure.

6. Care should be taken in joining up the lines, and the first few transactions of the example are described. Home sales start at £18 500. A dot should be placed at the point of this figure immediately above 5th October. On 12th October home sales dropped to £17 000, and a dot should be placed in line with the £17 000 point and above 12th October. The two dots should now be joined together with a continuous line. On 19th October the sales rose to £19 000 and at this position another dot should be placed over the correct date. The line ending on 12th October should now be joined up with the dot for 19th October, and so on.

7. Clear keys or foot notes must be displayed on the chart, giving:

(*a*) the colour scheme or line formation adopted;
(*b*) the scale, i.e. 1 in = £200.

Bar Graphs

Bar graphs are also an effective means of displaying information and are similar in many respects to the line graphs, except that individual bars instead of continuous lines are used for each week or month. Bar graphs are more suitable for illustrating and contrasting figures for short periods; for example, in monthly statistics for a six-month period. Fig. 79 is an example of a bar graph which answers the following question:

A chart is required to show the monthly sales of typewriters, filing cabinets and duplicating machines over a period of six months.

Display the following data on bar graphs, using scales of 25·400 mm (1 in) = £1 000.

19..	*Typewriters*	*Filing Cabinets*	*Duplicating Machines*
	£	£	£
January	4 000	3 400	4 100
February	2 900	2 000	5 000
March	3 100	3 100	5 000
April	3 900	2 200	4 900
May	1 200	2 900	4 800
June	2 000	3 500	4 500

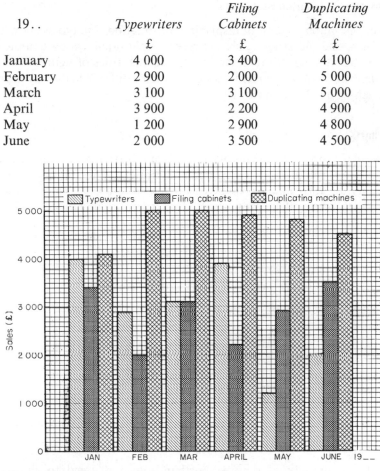

Fig. 79 Bar Graph

The following points should be noted concerning this example:

1. The left-hand vertical line shows the sums of money ranging from £0 to £5 000.

2. The bottom horizontal line gives the months; each bar occupies three squares.

3. Coloured bars are most effective, but contrasting black designs can be used.

4. As with line graphs, the keys or foot notes must be clearly displayed.

Typewritten Tabulation Statements

A very common method of displaying information is in typewritten tabulated form, and the secretary should receive a thorough training in the preparation of all kinds of tabular work. Large quantities of figures involving several products or departments, which would be difficult to display in graph form, can be displayed in this way.

Pie Charts

A pie chart formed by means of a circle is another method sometimes used to display information in magazines and posters. The full circle usually represents the total amount involved and the sections making up the full amount are ruled off in proportion. The pie chart illustrated in Fig. 80

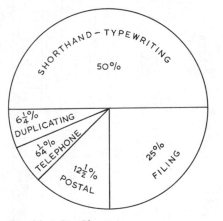

Fig. 80 A Pie Chart

analyses the amount of time a shorthand-typist devoted to shorthand-typewriting and other secretarial duties in the course of a week.

Visual Control Boards

Situations, progress, and current trends can be watched and thus controlled by visual control boards which are versatile and readily adaptable to show changes as they occur. A board requiring adjustment once a month

Fig. 81 A Visual Control Board
(Reproduced by permission of Movitex Signs Limited)

need not be an elaborate one, and to display on it the graphs and charts described earlier in this chapter may be all that is required; but if the board requires altering from hour to hour a much quicker and more highly mechanized arrangement would be needed. As with graphs and charts, different colours are used in most visual control boards to distinguish and contrast the situations.

Visual control boards are not only employed in controlling production, sales, progress, stores, parts available for assembly, stock control, shop loading, dispatch work and statistics but they can also be used to indicate trends in expenditure, the allocation of personnel, and for many other purposes.

Several kinds of visual control board are manufactured (an example is shown in Fig. 81) and a brief description of the principal ones are given:

1. The channel type plan board consists of cards, work tickets, job cards or plastic strips which are fitted into channels. This is simple to operate and

economical to maintain because pieces of plain card on which the details are hand- or type-written are normally all that is necessary.

2. Perforated panels and pegboards consist of a flat panel perforated to give a regular pattern or grid of slots or holes. Signalling devices in the form of studs, clips, plugs, pegs or flat discs are fitted into the slots or holes to indicate the pattern of the situation depicted in the chart.

3. The card rack type consists of a framework of channels or racks into which cards are fitted and displayed. Each rack is provided with a description column on the left of the board, and along the top of the frame, or within each rack, a time scale is given for the purposes of shop loading, or dispatch work, etc.

4. Revolving disc charts and figure registers contain a series of revolving discs mounted on spindles, which are rotated manually to display one of ten colours or digits. This method is particularly good where rapid changes in the information on the chart are necessary and for all forms of analysis involving figures.

5. The ball type column chart employs steel balls which are released from a hopper to build up columns in transparent tubes; a similar principle is used in a thermometer. The height of the balls in each tube is controlled by a press button. This type of chart is more suitable where the control work is of a statistical nature, as in stocks, sales, and purchases. It is similar to the bar graph, with the additional advantage of mechanical operation.

6. In the overlapping leaf type an arrangement of flat square tabs, which are made in a variety of colours, is used. The tabs are suspended on rings in miniature pigeon holes. The board consists of a grid of pigeon holes and the coloured tabs are fitted over the holes to indicate its present state. The tabs are changed by simply flicking them over to bring the desired colours on top.

7. A magnetic system employs individual name strips which are magnetically fitted to a board. The strips can be moved easily and the magnetic system is particularly good whenever rapid re-allocation of information has to be made. This system can be used for allocation of personnel in departments, reservation of hospital beds, hotel bookings, etc.

8. Plastic self-adhesive boards contain a smooth transparent skin of plastic. The markers are pieces of plastic made in various shapes, sizes and colours which contain a small quantity of static electricity. They are lightly pressed on to the board and fixed securely. Information can be written on the markers which renders them suitable for a wide range of applications

including machine loading, flight reservations, stock control, sales records, etc.

Only a few of the many types of visual control board available have been mentioned here, but they should be sufficient to impress on the reader the important part played by charts and control boards in the organization of offices and factories in these days of ever-increasing mechanization.

QUESTIONS

1. A chart is required to show the weekly sales of Mr X and Mr Y over a period of three months. Plot the following data on line graphs using scales of 1 in = £400.

Week ending	Mr X £	Mr Y £
2nd August	2 500	2 900
9th ,,	3 400	2 800
16th ,,	5 000	3 000
23rd ,,	4 500	4 000
30th ,,	5 800	5 100
6th September	3 000	6 000
13th ,,	2 900	4 400
20th ,,	4 000	3 500
27th ,,	6 000	5 500
4th October	4 800	3 400
11th ,,	2 200	4 200
18th ,,	5 600	3 800
25th ,,	4 500	4 100

R.S.A. SD.2

2. Your employer, calling on a long-distance telephone, asks you to read from a bar graph (*see* page 278), the following information:

(i) Mr X and Mr Y's sales figures for January, 1973;

(ii) at what period the sales of Mr Z exceeded the combined figures of both the others;

(iii) how all three salesmen stood at the end of March, 1973, in relation to the average sales figures for the corresponding period last year (September, 1971 to March, 1972). *R.S.A. SD.2*

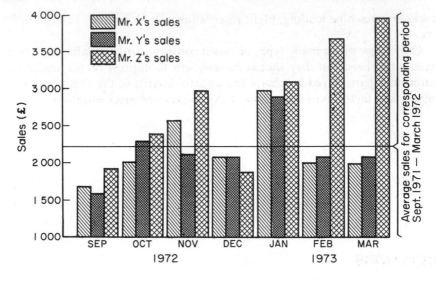

3. From the chart printed below, state:
   (*a*) in which years home sales exceeded £10 000;
   (*b*) in which years home sales exceeded 50 per cent of total sales;
   (*c*) in which years total sales exceeded £35 000. *R.S.A. SD.2*

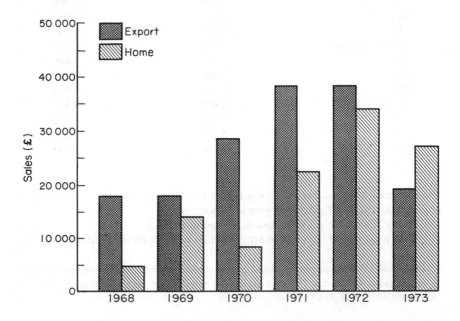

4. On the accompanying graph paper, construct a line graph from the following information to show the comparative sales of a London branch and a provincial branch of a trading concern:

	London £	Provincial £
1966	5 000	20 000
1967	10 000	17 000
1968	12 000	15 000
1969	15 000	10 000
1970	17 000	8 000
1971	12 000	12 000
1972	10 000	20 000
1973	4 000	23 000

R.S.A. SD.2

5. A chart is required to show the monthly sales of fruit, vegetables and flowers in a shop over a period of six months. Display the following information by using bar graphs with scales of 1 in = £100.

19—	Fruit £	Vegetables £	Flowers £
July	340	400	420
Aug.	480	620	740
Sept.	500	400	660
Oct.	640	740	800
Nov.	300	420	680
Dec.	460	660	720

6. From the bar graph (shown on page 280) give the following information:

(a) In which year was the greatest net dividend paid?

(b) In which year were no profits retained?

(c) In what years were the retained profits approximately equal to net dividends paid?

(d) In what year was there a marked rise in the cost of administration? *R.S.A. SD.2*

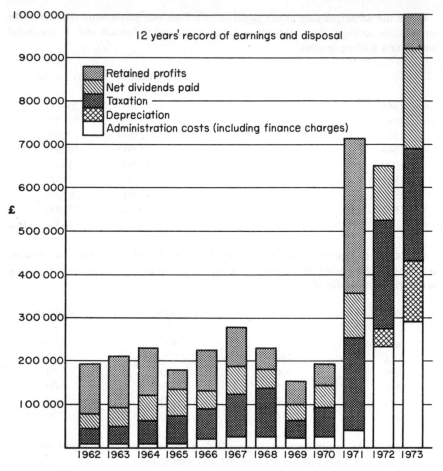

7. Describe the various methods which can be used to display facts and figures in the office.

8. (i) What are the advantages of recording statistical data in graphic form?

(ii) Explain the difference between a line chart and a bar chart and give an example to show when each might be used. *L.C.C. P.S.C.*

9. What is the purpose of using graphs? Suggest an occasion when a graph might be of value in:

(a) your college or school;

(b) an office. *R.S.A. SD.2*

10. Your employer runs a poultry farm. He has been experimenting by feeding one group of birds with food into which special chemicals are mixed, and the other with their normal rations. He wishes you to construct two graphs on the same axis in 4-week periods to compare the average number of eggs per bird laid by each group.

The figures are:

4-weekly periods	Group A (*fed with special chemicals*)	Group B (*fed on normal rations*)
1	14	12
2	18	15
3	22	19
4	20	18
5	17	15
6	15	13
7	15	13
8	12	12
9	15	15
10	4	5
11	6	7
12	11	12
13	11	9

R.S.A. SD.2

11. (*a*) Twenty commercial apprentices are employed by your firm and during their apprenticeship they spend three months in each department. Design a visual control board or display chart, to be kept in the Personnel Manager's Office, to show clearly the location of apprentices during the current three-monthly period.

(*b*) Describe briefly other visual aids which can be used in the office to display facts and figures. *R.S.A. OP.2*

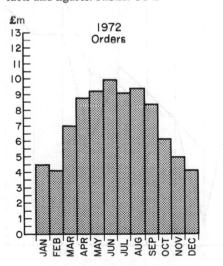

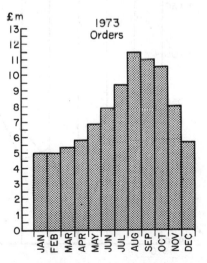

12. The two graphs on page 281 show the orders that a company received each month in the years 1972 and 1973.

(*a*) Find the percentage increase of the peak month orders in 1973 over the peak month orders in 1972.

(*b*) Convert the two block graphs into line graphs on one axis. *R.S.A. SD.2*

13. The diagram given below shows in £m. the value of imports and exports for a period of three and a half years, each year being divided into its four quarters. Answer the following questions:

(i) What kind of graph is this?

(ii) What are the names given to the lines along which the £m. and the years are shown?

(iii) At what period did imports exceed exports by the greatest amount?

(iv) In what periods did exports exceed imports?

(v) How large was the greatest gap between imports and exports?

(vi) What was the difference between the gap at the beginning of 1970 and the gap at the end of the second quarter of 1973?   *R.S.A. SD.2*

Table of imports and exports

14. Draw a pie chart showing the information given below.
    The turnover of a garage consists of:
        Sales of cars—50 per cent
        Sales of accessories—25 per cent
        Sales of petrol and oil—25 per cent

R.S.A. SD.2

Chapter 18
Office Furniture and Supplies

Carefully selected furniture can make an important contribution to the morale of staff and can also be the means of increasing business efficiency and making the most effective use of space. Unsuitable furniture may have serious repercussions on the health and welfare of staff which may ultimately result in a high level of absenteeism and staff turnover.

The secretary's office will normally contain the following items of furniture and equipment:

Desk with accommodation for holding a typewriter;
Typist's chair and additional chairs for callers;
Typewriter with pad and cover;
Filing cabinets with appropriate folders and files;
Stationery cupboard or container;
Wastepaper basket;
Bookcase with appropriate reference books;
Telephones—external and internal;
Clock;
Wallboard for charts and plans;
Safe with cash box and books;
Fire extinguisher;
Dictating machine, adding/listing machine, and duplicator, as required.

Desks

The following types of secretarial desks are available:

(*a*) Flat-topped desk;

(*b*) Desk with a fixed sunken well to hold a typewriter;

(*c*) Desk with a collapsible well containing a typewriter, and when the typewriter is not required the desk is converted into a flat-topped desk;

(*d*) Desk with a fold-away mechanism which enables the typewriter to be housed in the pedestal cupboard when not required.

The measurements for typists' desks recommended by the British Standards Institution are as follows:

284

(*a*) Height of surface on which typewriter stands   635·0 to 647·7 mm
(25 to 25½ in)
(*b*) Knee hole space height   .   .   .   .   609·6 mm (24 in)
(*c*) Minimum horizontal clearance (front to back) immediately below surface on which typewriter stands   .   .   .   .   .   .   304·8 mm (12 in)
(*d*) Minimum horizontal clearance (front to back) at ground level .   .   .   .   .   457·2 mm (18 in)
(*e*) Minimum knee hole width .   .   .   .   584·2 mm (23 in)

Chairs

Correctly-designed chairs are of the utmost importance for typists, and when choosing her chair the secretary should take into account the following characteristics:

1. A typist's chair should be fully adjustable and should have a swivel seat which is adjustable for height.

2. There should be a pivoted back-rest which is adjustable both horizontally and vertically.

3. The back-rest should be padded and should give firm support to the typist.

4. The adjustment should be arranged in such a manner that there is no danger of the lubricant getting on to clothing.

5. The British Standards Specification gives the following measurements for typists' chairs:

(*a*) Height of seat from ground .   .   .   393·7 mm (15½ in) adjustable to 495·3 mm (19½ in)
(*b*) Back to front of seat   .   .   .   not less than 330·2 mm (13 in)
(*c*) Width of the seat   .   .   .   406·4 to 431·8 mm (16 to 17 in)
(*d*) Back-rest height from seat level   .   .   adjustable between 203·2 and 304·8 mm (8 and 12 in)
(*e*) Depth of back-rest   .   .   .   127·0 to 152·4 mm (5 to 6 in)
(*f*) Width of back-rest   .   .   .   not greater than 304·8 mm (12 in)

These characteristics are designed to ensure that the typist sits comfortably on the chair, with the small of the back supported by the backrest and with the feet resting firmly on the floor.

PHYSICAL CONDITIONS IN OFFICES

Offices, Shops and Railway Premises Act, 1963

Legislation for the protection of factory workers was introduced as long ago as 1802, but none of the successive statutes for the safety, health and welfare of industrial employees applied to the office worker until the Offices, Shops and Railway Premises Act, 1963, was passed. All offices in which persons are employed are covered by this act and an office is included even if it is only part of a building used for other purposes, such as an office in a farm house, hospital, factory or club. A room which is not itself an office, but which is used in conjunction with office purposes is included. "Office purposes" include administration, clerical work, handling money and telephone and telegraph operating. Clerical work consists of writing, book-keeping, sorting papers, filing, typewriting, duplicating, calculating, etc. The act does not apply to premises occupied by the employer's relatives or where less than 21 hours weekly are normally worked.

The performance of clerical work suffers if the physical conditions are below standard and the regulations contained in this act are, therefore, very important for efficient office administration.

After providing that all premises must be kept clean, with floors cleaned at least once weekly, the act deals with overcrowding. There must be not less than 3·715 square metres (40 sq ft) of floor space for each worker—this is inclusive of furniture and equipment. A reasonable temperature must be provided and maintained in all rooms in which employees work otherwise than for short periods. A temperature will not be regarded as reasonable if it falls below 16°C. (60·8°F.) after the first hour of work.

Suitable and sufficient lighting must be provided. No specific standard is stated regarding the intensity of the light, but later regulations may do this (20–30 lumens are normally regarded as satisfactory). Adequate supplies of either fresh air or artificially purified air must be circulated to secure the ventilation of offices.

Premises must have suitable conveniences and washing facilities at places conveniently accessible to all employees. Running hot and cold water must be supplied, together with soap and clean towels. Drinking water must be available and also suitable places to hang up clothing and facilities for drying them. First aid boxes must be provided in all premises so as to be readily accessible. Safety measures and fire precautions are also included in the act.

Seats provided for workers who normally perform their work sitting must be suitable in design, construction and dimensions for the worker and for the kind of work done.

Generally speaking the occupier of premises is responsible for complying with the provisions of the act, but some responsibilities are transferred to the owner in cases where the premises are held on lease and do not take up a whole building; or where the premises are contained in a building of which different parts are owned by different persons. The responsibility of enforcing the act rests with inspectors appointed by local authorities. All premises must be registered with the local authority.

The local authority must be notified immediately of any accident which causes the death of a person employed in the premises or which disables a person for more than three days from doing his usual work.

An abstract of the Act and Regulations prescribed by the Department of Employment should be displayed in a prominent position for the information of employees.

Stationery

Office stationery (or consumable office supplies) are the materials which are used in the administration of office work. They include typewriting paper, writing paper, shorthand notebooks, envelopes, labels, postcards, carbon paper, ink, typewriter ribbons, paper clips and fasteners, duplicator supplies, files and folders, string, sealing wax, adhesive tape, pencils, erasers, compliment slips, memo forms, petty cash vouchers, telephone message pads, blotting paper, and supplies of various office forms, etc.

The standard measurements for typewriting and duplicating paper are as follows:

A3	297 mm by 420 mm	$11\frac{3}{4}$ in $\times$	$16\frac{1}{2}$ in
A4	210 mm by 297 mm	$8\frac{1}{4}$ in $\times$	$11\frac{3}{4}$ in
A5	148 mm by 210 mm	$5\frac{7}{8}$ in $\times$	$8\frac{1}{4}$ in

Paper is supplied in either quires or reams; a quire contains 24 sheets and a ream has 480 sheets.

CARBON COPYING

Several copies can be made of one document with the aid of carbon paper. Special typewriter carbon papers are manufactured in a number of grades, colours and sizes.

To avoid mistakes in using carbon paper, the typist should carry out her preparation systematically. The following system is one which is to be recommended:

1. place the paper on a flat surface face downwards;

2. lay a sheet of carbon paper of the same size over the paper, with the carbonized surface facing upwards;

3. add another sheet of paper of the kind used in the office for carbon copies;

4. if more than one copy is to be made, add further sheets of carbon paper and copy paper in the same way;

5. collect the prepared paper and carbon paper and place it in the machine with the carbonized surface facing the operator;

6. If a large number of carbon copies is being taken, it may be necessary to use the paper release lever to insert the paper into the typewriter.

A soft platen will not produce as many carbon copies as a hard one, because it yields to the blow of the type instead of resisting it. A medium to hard platen, which is the best for general correspondence work, should produce up to four good copies, but if more than four copies are regularly needed, a hard platen should be used. A hard platen is not, however, very suitable for single copies, as there is a tendency for the type to be indistinct, and the ribbon will soon wear out because of the steel type bars hitting against the hard platen.

The paper used for the original and duplicates must be consistent with the number of copies required, for example thinner paper must be used for six copies than for two. It is necessary to strike the keys a little more sharply when carbon copies are made, in particular "m", "w", "g", the upper-case characters, figures and fractions. The punctuation marks should, however, be typed with a lighter touch.

Care should be taken not to crease the carbon paper as the crease will mark the paper. The following precautions should be taken in the care of carbon paper:

(*a*) keep the carbon in a flat box;

(*b*) keep the carbon box away from a hot fire or radiator, or from the sun;

(*c*) be careful when fitting the carbon paper into the machine as, at this stage, careless handling will cause the carbon paper to crease;

(*d*) if the paper and carbon paper feed unevenly, find out whether the feed roll mechanism on the typewriter requires adjustment.

When choosing the particular kind of carbon paper to use, several considerations should be taken into account:

1. the number of copies usually taken, and the quality and thickness of the typewriting paper;

2. the purpose for which the carbon copies are to be taken and their importance;

3. the capabilities of the typewriters used for carbon copying, i.e. whether they are electrically or manually operated;

4. colours required.

Some carbon papers are supplied with a special plastic coating on the back which prevents it from curling and is easier to handle. Another development is the use of plastic film instead of paper which does not smudge and is cleaner to handle. The plastic film gives more copies than conventional carbon paper.

Correction of Errors on Carbon Copies

1. Place a small piece of paper between each sheet of carbon and of paper, in the position where the erasure is to be made.

2. Erase the top copy.

3. Lift the first sheet of carbon, erase the error on the copy and remove the piece of paper.

4. Proceed as before for the additional copies.

5. Before typing in the correct word or letter, make sure that all the pieces of paper have been removed.

A two-sided carbon paper is manufactured and is useful when a large number of copies is required. The paper, as the name implies, is coated on the back and on the front and only half the normal number of sheets of carbon paper is needed. Provided that very thin copying paper is used, the reverse image printed on the back of the sheet can be read without difficulty. Alterations are difficult to make.

Bi-chrome carbon paper contains two colours, usually black and red, and it is useful for copying financial documents. The red part of the paper, in the form of two vertical columns, allows for the reproduction of red credit items.

Sets of forms such as those used for invoices or orders may be interleaved with sheets of "one time" carbon paper. This carbon paper is of an inexpensive type and is intended for use once only. It is supplied and fixed in position by the manufacturer and is quick and easy to use.

Forms are sometimes supplied with a carbon backing which takes the place of separate carbon paper. When the top copy of the form is completed one or two copies are automatically produced below it.

NCR (no carbon required) paper may also be used for forms as an alternative to using carbon paper or carbon backed paper. The reverse side of the top copy and the top sides of the sheets below are specially treated with chemicals to allow copies to be made without carbon paper. When an impression is made on the top copy it causes the chemically treated surfaces of the paper to reproduce the impressions on the copies beneath.

Stock Control

It is important to maintain a satisfactory stock-control system as the stationery must always be available when it is required, and it must be kept in good condition in the storeroom. A room is usually set aside for the storage of stationery and a member of the staff is appointed to take charge of the work involved in buying and issuing it. The different items of stationery should be carefully labelled on the shelves or in cupboards in the storeroom.

The stationery clerk should issue stationery only on receipt of a requisition signed by the head of the department or office concerned. A stock card should be kept for each item of stationery (*see* Fig. 82). The stock card gives the maximum and minimum stock figures and when the balance in stock has

STATIONERY STOCK CARD

ITEM: A4 White Duplicating Paper....   MAXIMUM STOCK: 50 reams...

MINIMUM STOCK: 20 reams...

DATE	RECEIPTS			ISSUES			BALANCE IN STOCK
	Quantity Received	Invoice No.	Supplier	Quantity Issued	Reqn. No.	Dept.	
1.1.19..							25
14.1.19..				5	x14	Accounts	20
20.1.19..	30	19263	Elite Paper Co.				50
27.1.19..				3	x 29	Sales	47

Fig. 82 Stationery Stock Card

been reduced to the amount of the minimum stock the stationery clerk knows that he must order a further quantity of the item. He is guided in the amount of his order, as the total of the balance in stock and the new order must not exceed the maximum stock figure (stated on the card). A record is kept of the receipt of stationery from the suppliers and the issues to departments.

Stock records may be kept on ordinary index cards, or on one of the visible card systems described on pages 101 to 104, and coloured plastic or metal signalling devices may be used on the edge of the cards to indicate the level of stock. Visual control boards, referred to on pages 275 to 277 may also be employed to keep stationery stocks and requirements constantly under review.

Effective systems for controlling stationery are very important, as the efficiency of an office depends very largely upon the availability of suitable materials as and when they are required by members of the staff.

Every piece of paper or envelope used unnecessarily adds to the cost of running the business, and the utmost care must be taken by all staff to ensure that stationery is used economically.

QUESTIONS

1. A great deal of research has recently been carried out on suitable seating for clerical workers. What points would you consider when choosing a typist's chair? *R.S.A. SD.2*

2. It is required to secure greater economy in the use of stationery in your office. You are asked to investigate the present position and submit a report of your findings together with suggestions. *L.C.C. P.S.D.*

3. The desks, tables, and chairs in your typists' office are being replaced by new ones. You are asked to make a report for the Office Manager as to suitable modern equipment. What would you recommend him to buy? He has asked you to set out your reasons clearly. *R.S.A. SD.2*

4. Design a stock-record card suitable for office stationery and materials, and outline a system for ordering, receiving and issuing the stock. *R.S.A. OP.2*

5. Much stationery has been wasted, owing to departments ordering too much at one time. It has been decided to have a weekly issue, and each department has been instructed to complete a requisition form showing the estimated needs for the coming week.
A simple standard form must be drawn up and duplicated.
Design a form to include ten items of stationery. *R.S.A. SD.2*

6. You have been promoted from the typing pool to become secretary to the Manager, who has never before had his own secretary. An additional small room has been acquired for you. It is newly decorated but is empty. Make a list of the furniture and equipment you will need. *R.S.A. SD.2*

7. (*a*) What is continuous stationery and for which purposes is it most suitable?

(*b*) Explain briefly the difference between "bank" and "bond" quality paper. Give examples to show when you would use either paper. Give reasons for your answer. *L.C.C. P.S.C.*

8. Memorandum—To: *Company Secretary*

From: *Managing Director* via *Personal Secretary*

I am disturbed at the state of affairs existing in relation to our stationery stocks. I find that no one person is responsible for ordering and dispensing stationery; instead, when any item cannot immediately be found, any of the senior staff telephone further orders. Tables, shelves and floor in the stock room are piled high with mixed stationery; many packets have their wrappers torn open allowing contents to become soiled and creased. I would recommend that we institute a control system right away and I submit the following ideas for your consideration:

Complete this memorandum. *L.C.C. P.S.D.*

9. What do you understand by "stock-taking"? Why must it be carried out at least once a year? *R.S.A. SD.2*

10. You are responsible for the ordering and issuing of stationery in your department. What precautions would you take to ensure (*a*) that you do not keep too large a stock, and (*b*) that the stock does not run out? Give a sample of a ruling for the Stationery Stock Book. *R.S.A. OP.1*

11. (*a*) Rule up a stationery stock-record card for A4 typewriting paper and make the following entries:

Maximum stock: 50 reams   Minimum stock: 20 reams

1.3.	Balance in stock: 45 reams.
8.3.	Issued 10 reams to Sales Department.
10.3.	Issued 12 reams to Typing Pool.
22.3.	Bought 25 reams from L. P. Stevens & Co. Ltd.
1.4.	Issued 8 reams to Purchases Department.
12.4.	Issued 10 reams to Typing Pool.
23.4.	Issued 10 reams to Works Department.

When re-stocking this item on 30th April, what quantity would you order?

(*b*) Explain the importance of the maximum and minimum figures in connexion with stock-taking.

(*c*) What do you understand by (i) a ream, (ii) A4? *R.S.A. OP.2*

12. A new employee in the Stores Department tells you that he cannot see why the firm goes to the trouble to take stock—it only wastes the time of people busy enough already. State how you would explain, (*a*) the reasons for taking stock and, (*b*) the way in which stock is valued for stock-taking purposes.

Suggest any means of making the stock-taking burden easier. *R.S.A. COS.*

13. Most office workers keep in their desks such small items of equipment as pencils, rubbers and pins. List six others. *R.S.A. SD.2*

14. (*a*) Your Office Junior frequently asks for fresh supplies of carbon paper. What advice would you give her on the use and care of carbon paper.

(*b*) What is N.C.R. paper? *R.S.A. OP.1*

Chapter 19
Personal Qualities and Training

The various personal qualities, duties and training necessary for staff occupying the positions of clerks, shorthand typists and private secretaries are treated separately, as they each need special consideration.

QUALITIES

Clerical Staff

The qualities a clerk should possess are:

1. A sound general education.
2. A pleasant disposition.
3. An ability to express herself fluently.
4. Initiative.
5. Good general appearance, i.e. she should be neatly and suitably dressed.
6. An aptitude for clerical work.
7. Good health.
8. An ability to answer questions at an interview with alertness, precision and interest.
9. Ambition.
10. A willingness to continue her education.

Shorthand Typist

The shorthand typist should possess all of the qualities mentioned above and, in addition, the following technical qualities:

1. A thorough training in Shorthand and Typewriting. Her qualification should be *at least* at the level of the RSA Stage II, i.e. Shorthand 80/100 wpm and Typewriting 35/40 wpm.

2. Evidence that she has studied some other subjects, e.g. English, Business Calculations, Accounts, Secretarial Duties or Commerce.

294

Private Secretary

The qualities of a private secretary can be divided into two categories: business attributes and personal attributes.

Business Attributes

1. A good basic training in shorthand and typewriting and secretarial duties.
2. Initiative.
3. Punctuality.
4. Conscientiousness and willingness.
5. Discretion, tact and diplomacy. This is especially important in the handling of inquiries, telephone calls and visitors.
6. Loyalty to her employer.
7. Responsibility. The secretary is usually responsible for a certain amount of her employer's routine work, which she should carry out cheerfully and efficiently.

Personal Attributes

1. A good general appearance. She should always be neatly and suitably dressed for the office.

2. A pleasant manner, both on the telephone and in greeting visitors.

3. Willingness to help her employer at all times by staying late at night or coming in early in the morning to clear outstanding work.

4. A desire to add to her general knowledge by reading good books and newspapers, and a reasonable knowledge of all the new developments in the particular line of her employer's business.

Personal Standards in the Office

The following general remarks concerning personal standards in the office are applicable to all who are engaged in office work. The office employee should:

1. Be punctual and always available when needed by her employer;

2. Be pleasant at all times, even when there are difficult situations to handle;

3. Possess a good sense of humour;

4. Always listen attentively to instructions given to her by her employer so that she need be told only once;

5. Be silent in matters such as her own personal troubles, office gossip and her employer's affairs and business;

6. Carry out the essential routine tasks regularly, such as keeping her employer's calendars up to date, his blotting paper and ink supply replenished, his engagement cards or diary constantly reviewed and up to date, charts examined, etc.;

7. Keep her own office and desk meticulously tidy. All personal belongings must be kept to the minimum and out of sight in a drawer or cupboard. An adequate stock of stationery and materials should be held and very great care taken in maintaining typewriters and other equipment;

8. Be quiet, which means that doors must be closed softly and conversations carried on quietly;

9. Have a good selection of reference books available, including a dictionary. She should always check any doubtful spelling, the correct form of address, etc.

TRAINING AND QUALIFICATIONS

Training for secretarial work may be carried out by:

(*a*) full-time attendance at a secretarial college or technical college;
(*b*) part-time day release classes, i.e. the student is allowed a day or half a day from her employment to attend a technical college;
(*c*) evening classes;
(*d*) "on the job" training.

Clerical Staff

The subjects studied by a clerk should be of a general commercial character, such as Accounts, Commerce, Office Practice, Business Communication and Business Calculations. A course of typewriting is also a very useful attribute for a clerk.

The Certificate in Office Studies is a good qualification for junior clerical staff. Courses leading to the certificate examination are of one or two years' duration and students are normally required to attend day-release classes at technical colleges or colleges of further education. The subjects consist of

Clerical Duties and Communication, which are compulsory, and two other subjects selected from Calculations, Book-keeping, Typewriting and Office Machinery, Commerce, Social Studies, Law and the Individual, etc.

The Royal Society of Arts Use of Office Machinery examination is also a very useful examination for clerical staff, especially those concerned with the operation of machines.

Shorthand Typist

In addition to the subjects studied by the clerk, the shorthand typist should specialize in Shorthand and Typewriting. Very good qualifications for the shorthand typist are the Stages II and III Shorthand Typewriting Certificates of the Royal Society of Arts. The Stage II Examination consists of the accurate typewritten transcription of matter dictated, a portion of printed material, and a letter to be composed by the candidate.

The Stage III Shorthand Typewriting Examination is similar to Stage II but at a higher level. The passages, which may consist of any of the items in Stage II and specifications, minutes of meetings or legal documents, vary in length but together total 1 200 words.

Another good qualification for the shorthand typist is the London Chamber of Commerce Junior Secretary's Certificate. The examination for this certificate consists of Shorthand-Typewriting Duties, English, Background to Business and Office Practice. The Shorthand-Typewriting Duties section is primarily the dictation of correspondence and other matter through the medium of long-playing gramophone records. The candidates are expected to produce mailable copy for signature, and carry out efficiently any instructions which may be given in the course of the recording.

Private Secretary

The London Chamber of Commerce Private Secretary's Certificate and Private Secretary's Diploma are sound qualifications for the private secretary, and a training which leads up to these examinations should be sought. The London Chamber of Commerce consider, quite rightly, that examinations should be made as practical as possible. In their examinations the dictating is done under normal conditions, and provides for bursts at relatively high speeds in order to ensure that the holder of the certificate or diploma would be able to take dictation from an employer who is normally a fast dictator.

Private Secretary's Certificate

The Private Secretary's Certificate examination is intended for Junior secretaries and those who seek employment as private secretaries to middle-management. The examination consists of Communications; Private Secretarial Duties; Office Organization, Equipment and Services; Structure of Business; Shorthand-Typewriting Duties (Record) and an Interview.

Private Secretary's Diploma

The Private Secretary's Diploma examination is set at a higher level than the certificate examination and it is appropriate for senior private secretaries wishing to be employed by top-level management.

The examination consists of six sections, namely: Communications; Private Secretarial Duties; Management Appreciation; Meetings (film); Shorthand-Typewriting Duties (record); and an Interview.

The examiners set out to assess skill in shorthand and typewriting, common sense, tact, poise, experience and efficiency—all indispensable for success as a private secretary. Today there is a big demand for the well-trained secretary possessing the Private Secretary's Certificate and Diploma, and these examinations are designed to establish recognized national standards.

Diploma for Personal Assistants

This scheme, offered by the Royal Society of Arts, is intended mainly for students following post GCE "A" level secretarial courses. It is intended to represent a high standard of ability in the secretarial field and to meet the needs of girls aiming at such positions as personal assistants or personal secretaries to senior management. The subjects in the scheme are Communications; Office Administration (including Techniques of the Office and Office Management); Practical correspondence (tape-recordings); together with either Economic Aspects of Business or Law and Procedure of Meetings.

Personal Secretarial Practice RSA Stage III

This examination covers the responsibilities of, and the background knowledge required by, a senior private secretary, an executive assistant or anyone, however designated, who acts as a personal assistant to a senior executive.

Institute of Qualified Private Secretaries

Holders of the LCC Private Secretary's Diploma are entitled to apply for membership of the Institute of Qualified Private Secretaries and to use the designatory letters PS Dip. Successful candidates of the LCC Private Secretary's Certificate may apply for associate membership. Further details may be obtained from the Institute of Qualified Private Secretaries Ltd., c/o 126 Farnham Road, Slough, Bucks, SL1 4XA.

APPLYING FOR A VACANCY

Very great care should be taken in preparing the letter of application for a post so that the prospective employer will be favourably impressed. The following points should be observed:

1. The letter should be written in ink in the applicant's best handwriting, unless the prospective employer has requested a typed letter.

2. There should be no errors of grammar or punctuation.

3. The letter should be worded in a businesslike manner, with no commercialisms.

4. The letter should be planned carefully, covering all the essential points asked for in the advertisement.

5. The salutation should normally be "Dear Sir" or "Dear Madam" and the subscription "Yours faithfully".

6. If the applicant is asked to state her qualifications and experience, she would be well advised to display the details in a schedule enclosed with the letter.

7. The prospective employer will require the applicant's:
   (*a*) full name and address;
   (*b*) date of birth;
   (*c*) education;
   (*d*) examination successes;
   (*e*) additional training and qualifications for the post;
   (*f*) present employment and previous experience in the work;
   (*g*) the names and addresses of persons to whom reference may be made;
   (*h*) the earliest date when the applicant could take up the appointment.

8. If testimonials are enclosed with the letter of application, these should be copies of the originals, and should be typed accurately with the word "**Copy**" typed at the top.

9. The source of the advertisement should be referred to in the letter of application, e.g. if the advertisement was read in the *Birmingham Mail* say "In reply to your advertisement in yesterday's 'Birmingham Mail' . . ."

10. If a letter is received inviting the applicant to attend for interview, she should reply by return of post confirming that she will attend at the time stated.

On Being Interviewed

During the course of our lifetime we are faced with all kinds of interviews with headmasters, employers, police, lawyers, clergymen and so on, and it is important to approach the interviews in a positive, calm and efficient manner. The following words of advice should be noted:

1. The person being interviewed should discover all she can about the person who is to interview her before the day of the interview. A reference book such as *Who's Who* may be useful here.

2. The applicant should verify all the essential details about herself, such as dates of previous posts held, education and training.

3. The applicant's dress and general appearance should be smart and tidy, particular attention being paid to hands and hair.

4. She should be punctual. If there is any doubt about the location of the place of interview, she should look it up on a town guide or street map beforehand.

5. The applicant may be tested at the interview and the necessary materials should be taken, such as a notebook and pen.

6. When the applicant is answering questions at the interview, she should be perfectly natural and speak clearly and deliberately.

7. She should not be afraid to look at the questioner.

8. She should keep to the point when answering questions and make the most of the topics of which she has a good knowledge.

9. She should be perfectly honest about her capabilities and always speak the truth.

10. She should let the questioner know that she is anxious to obtain the post offered; that, if appointed, she would work very hard; and that she is ambitious.

These are a selection of questions which may be asked of a private secretary at an interview:

(*a*) What are the essential qualities a private secretary should possess?
(*b*) Define the type of responsibility a secretary should be able to take.
(*c*) What is your ambition?
(*d*) What is your present job?
(*e*) What are your interests?
(*f*) What are your qualifications and where were they attained?
(*g*) Are you taking any further courses of study at present?
(*h*) Why do you wish to apply for this post?
(*i*) Why did you choose a secretarial career?
(*j*) Have you any questions you would like to ask?

Personal questions about schools attended, best subjects, present employment and salary may also be asked.

Before going to an interview, the applicant is advised to think over the answers to these questions, and others, and generally prepare herself.

PREPARATION FOR A POST

Adequate and thorough preparation for a new post is essential. A newly-appointed private secretary to an eminent man would need to take the following preparatory steps:

1. Acquire a good all-round knowledge of the business of her new employer by:

(*a*) familiarizing herself with the history of the organization as a whole and of her future employer. (The reference book *Who's Who* may be found useful.) It is possible that the new secretary would be able to spend at least two weeks with the previous secretary, during which time she should find out her employer's personal likes and dislikes.

(*b*) obtaining copies of trade magazines and journals, together with any applicable reference books, to give her a general picture of the business or profession.

2. Discover the firm's methods of displaying correspondence, minutes of meetings and tabulation work, etc., and obtain a good dictionary giving the terms of the trade. She should compile an alphabetical list of business terms

and phrases in shorthand, with suitable intersections for quick and easy reference.

3. Rent a flat or acquire accommodation as near to the office as possible, so as to be readily available.

4. Ensure that she has adequate clothes, a good suitcase, a briefcase equipped with stationery, pencils, etc., and spare toilet requisites in case of urgent business trips at short notice.

5. Take a short holiday, if possible, to ensure perfect health and fitness.

THE NEW EMPLOYEE AND HER DUTIES

When a new employee begins work she may be asked to produce the following documents:

(*a*) **A National Insurance Card.** This card should contain the correct value of stamps for the previous employment.

(*b*) **Income Tax Form—P45 (in duplicate).** One section of the form is sent by the new employer to the Income Tax Office and the remaining section is retained by the employer.

(*c*) **Birth Certificate.** To verify her age.

(*d*) **Medical Certificate.** This is necessary to indicate the state of health of the employee for the purposes of pension or superannuation schemes.

Clerical Staff

The clerk should expect to undertake some of the following duties:

1. General postal work, including opening the mail in the morning and dispatching the mail in the evening.

2. The efficient operation of the telephone—most likely a switchboard.

3. Filing and indexing.

4. Reception duties, such as the receiving of visitors.

5. Typing envelopes and operating addressing machines.

6. Duplicating.

7. Collating and stapling documents.

8. Routine accounts.

9. Delivery of local letters, including errands to the post office, bank, etc.

10. Making the office tea.

Shorthand Typist

The duties of a shorthand typist may include any of those enumerated for a clerk and also:

1. Receiving dictation and transcribing on the typewriter letters, business documents, reports, etc.

2. The typing of tabular statements, including specialized forms and financial records.

3. The preparation of stencils.

Private Secretary

The following is a selection of the duties of a private secretary:

1. Receiving dictation and transcribing on the typewriter the personal and business correspondence of her employer.

2. Taking care of her employer's petty cash and bank transactions.

3. Reception duties, including the receiving and entertaining of visitors and the handling of telephone calls.

4. Keeping the employer's diary and arranging his appointments and engagements.

5. Making her employer's travel arrangements, booking of hotels, etc.

6. Filing her employer's personal and business correspondence.

7. Attending meetings and recording the minutes.

8. Keeping her employer's wall charts up to date and ensuring that his office is well provided with stationery, etc.

9. Generally relieving the employer of many of his routine business and private matters.

10. Keeping records of investments and income tax matters.

11. Supervision of junior secretarial staff.

THE SECRETARY'S RELATIONSHIP WITH HER EMPLOYER

The qualities which go to make the ideal relationship between employer and secretary are:

1. The secretary must ensure that all the work that leaves her office is accurate, so that her employer is relieved of the duty of examining every document, and she must show her employer that she is capable of doing work on her own initiative.

2. The secretary must be able to deal diplomatically with any telephone inquiries, and the employer must be able to trust the secretary to treat all matters handled in the office as confidential.

3. The secretary must be able to convey to her employer the essential facts contained in reports and magazines, so that he does not have to study them himself in detail.

4. She should understand that she must stay late if there is an urgent job to be done; but, nevertheless, an employer should not always expect his secretary to be in the office after hours at times when the work is not of an urgent nature.

5. There must be a clear understanding about the scope of the work the secretary should undertake in her employer's absence and the employer in his turn should be perfectly satisfied that his secretary can cope with the work which may arise when he is not there.

6. The employer, for his part, should keep the secretary fully informed of all that he is doing so that she can be of most use to him.

7. He should appreciate that some errors are caused by him and apologize if he is in the wrong.

8. The employer must be able to rely on the secretary's punctuality, but she should be prepared for her employer's lack of punctuality on occasions.

9. There should be a sense of humour on both sides.

10. The secretary should set a high standard of behaviour and efficiency for the rest of the office staff. She must always be neat and tidy in appearance, as this enhances her employer's and her own reputation.

11. The secretary should ask about private matters as they occur, e.g. flowers for special occasions, greetings cards, etc.

BACKGROUND OF THE OFFICE WORKER

This book is concerned primarily with the methods and machinery for carrying out the various secretarial duties, but if the secretary is to be competent in carrying out these tasks and relieve her immediate employer of a great deal of routine work and enquiry, she must possess a good background knowledge of the structure of business. This entails understanding the differences between the various types of business organization (e.g. single proprietor, partnership, limited liability company, nationalized enterprises, etc.) within the public and private sectors.

The secretary, and indeed any office employee, must also know the structure of the organization of her firm so that she is familiar with the functions and relationships of the various levels of management (e.g. board of directors, managing director, general manager, departmental managers, sectional heads and supervisors) and the departments (e.g. company secretary, accountant, sales, purchases, works, personnel, etc.).

It should be realized that neither individual executives nor the office or department for which they are responsible, work in isolation one from the other, but operate as essential links within the organization of the business.

QUESTIONS

1. Assume that you have just obtained an appointment as private secretary to a man of some eminence. Apart from the care you will give to the actual work you will be required to perform, what immediate steps will you take to ensure your ability to fill this position satisfactorily? *L.C.C. P.S.D.*

2. Because of the increased volume of work in your office, it is proposed to appoint a junior shorthand-typist to work under you. Draft the advertisement to appear in the press, and give your employer a short note on what you consider to be the necessary qualifications and personal attributes of the person to be appointed, together with some questions which he can put to candidates at an interview. *R.S.A. SD.2*

3. Discuss the statement that a private secretary is more than a good shorthand typist.

4. The following ten people are all employed in one department:

An Office Manager, a Chief Clerk (Deputy Office Manager), the Personal Secretary to the Office Manager, two Ledger Clerks, two Shorthand Typists, a Filing Clerk, a Telephonist, and an Office Boy.

They are each entitled to a fortnight's holiday in either July or August. The filing clerk deputizes for the telephonist, and one of the shorthand typists for the personal secretary. The other shorthand typist deputizes for the filing clerk.

Make a holiday roster. *R.S.A. SD.2*

5. Write a letter of application to the following advertisement:

Private Secretary required by Sales Manager of large engineering concern. Applicants should be between 21 to 30 years of age and single. Must be competent shorthand typist, capable of typewriting at 50 wpm from dictation. Good education, smart appearance and personality are essential. Write to Box MTY, Daily Herald and Gazette, 14 Sandon Street, Blanktown.

6. Your young sister is leaving school and wants to "go into an office". From your own experience, list the duties you consider she should expect to undertake as a junior clerical worker, and suggest any specialized training which might equip her for her work. *R.S.A. SD.2*

7. In your firm, secretaries are appointed from among the shorthand typists in the pool in which you work. The Sales Manager's secretary is leaving, and you are among those invited to apply for the post. Write this letter of application, addressed to the Personnel Manager. *R.S.A. SD.2*

8. (*a*) Discuss the qualities which go to make up the ideal relationship between employer and secretary. In taking up a new appointment what steps do you take to establish and maintain such a relationship?

or

(*b*) Your office employs five male executives and twenty-five female staff. Reply to the following memorandum:

From: *Managing Director*   To: *Personal Secretary*

I have been looking through our records and am concerned at the considerable turnover rate of female staff over the past two years. From your own contact with the staff you will undoubtedly have opinions on this score and possibly ideas as to how the staff situation can remain more stable. Please let me have your comments, in writing, in time for me to discuss this matter with my executives at the Friday meeting. *L.C.C. P.S.D.*

9. You have been appointed to replace a secretary who has given many years of service to her employer and who is now forced to resign in order to nurse a sick relative. The secretary has written to you, suggesting that you call at the office before she leaves, so that you may have an opportunity of asking her for any additional information about the job (apart from conditions of service). Set out, with brief reasons where necessary, those matters which you would raise. *L.C.C. P.S.C.*

10. Owing to the introduction of new equipment and methods in office work, the duties of office staff are changing. Apart from shorthand typing, what jobs might a junior be asked to do? *R.S.A. SD.2*

11. (*a*) Design an application form suitable for persons seeking employment in your office.

(*b*) List the personal qualities you would look for when selecting office staff. *R.S.A. OP.2*

12. Name the major departments which you would expect to find in a large business firm. *R.S.A. SD.2*

13. Since you finished your training, you have worked successively for:
(*a*) Mr Andrew Hancock—an author;
(*b*) Mr J. Lovell—junior partner in Brown, Green and Lovell, accountants;
(*c*) Mr G. Partridge—General Manager of The South Wessex Co-operative Society;
(*d*) Mr W. Cotton—Departmental Head of the Central Purchasing Department of the Redhill Departmental Stores Ltd.
Who was your employer in each case? What are the basic differences between the business units mentioned in (*b*) and (*d*)? *R.S.A. SD.2*

14. Your brother has been working as a mechanic in a small, privately owned garage. He is now joining one of the large motor manufacturers which is a public limited company.
He asks you what differences he will find. You point out that, obviously, there will be a far greater number of employees. Give three other differences which will, in some way, affect your brother. *R.S.A. SD.2*

15. Discuss the ways in which an organization may provide for the safety, health and welfare of its office employees. *R.S.A. OP.2*

16. You work for one of your firm's buyers, Mr Lawrence. As his work causes him to travel, you are often left to look after the work in the office although you can, of course, always refer to another executive.
Your work consists of taking dictation when Mr Lawrence is in the office, transcribing tapes which he sends when he is away, making his travel arrangements, and taking clear and adequate messages in his absence.
You have been told that you are to be promoted to a senior post in another department and that you are to train another girl to take over your present job.
Which of the following would you suggest should take over from you? Give your reasons.

Anne (19): Good shorthand-typist, well-mannered and attractive. Casual. Began to train as a hairdresser when she left school and has worked in an office for only one year.
Joan (20): Slow shorthand. Slow, but very careful and accurate typist. Conscientious. Neat appearance. Very quiet and shy.
Sandra (22): Shorthand fair. Typing uneven, with poor corrections. Mature. Considerable common sense. Good telephone manner. Has previously worked in a travel agency. *R.S.A. SD.2*

17. "A high salary is not always the means of producing the best effort." Expand this statement. *L.C.C. P.S.C.*

18. "A secretarial post calls for much initiative because it is possible for a good private secretary to save her employer a great deal of time by the quick anticipation of his requirements and possible future action." Justify this statement. *L.C.C. P.S.C.*

19. How would you expect the nature of your work to differ if you were:
(*a*) secretary to the owner of a retail business selling photographic equipment to the public

(*b*) secretary to the sales manager of a limited company manufacturing photographic equipment? *R.S.A. SD.2*

20. Describe the working function of:
   (*a*) a personal assistant to the managing director of a company,
   (*b*) a shorthand typist working for several junior executives. *R.S.A. SD.2*

21. (*a*) A firm is arranging to interview a number of candidates for some vacancies
in its office. Before the interviews take place, what information should be prepared
for (i) the candidates and (ii) the people in the firm who are responsible for the
recruitment of staff?
   (*b*) What are the purposes of interviewing candidates? *R.S.A. OP.2*

Chapter 20
Private Secretarial Practice

In Chapter 19 the qualities, duties and training which are essential to the private secretary were outlined; in this chapter these theories are put into practice by examining a number of hypothetical secretarial situations. Several aspects of private secretarial practice and office organization are described in other chapters of this book, such as keeping the diary, preparing travel itineraries, writing minutes and using the telephone. It is, of course, impossible to deal with every one of the diverse duties which the private secretary may be called upon to perform. These include the handling of situations which call for tact, integrity and efficiency, and an ability to organize meetings, conferences, cocktail parties, dinner-dances, outings, works visits, etc.

SOME VARIED SITUATIONS

While the private secretary must learn how to handle an enormous variety of situations from her own practical experience, there is no doubt that much can be learnt from the experience of others and a few situations, which have been set in recent Secretarial Duties and Private Secretarial Practice examinations, are dealt with in this chapter. The opinions given are those expressed not only by the author, but by students of his Private Secretary's Diploma Classes, where meetings have been held to discuss the questions. The answers are given briefly and categorically to enable the student to grasp and memorize the salient points. It should be remembered that there are likely to be several quite correct solutions or approaches to these situations, and the reader must appreciate this fact and examine them in the light of her own experience.

Question

Mr X, for whom you work, has driven to the local airport to meet an important oversea client, Mr Y, due to arrive from Brussels at 1500 hrs. While Mr X is on his way to the airport, you receive a cable stating that Mr Y has been obliged to change his plans, and will arrive by train at 1800 hrs. He also assumes that hotel reservations have been made for him. As far as you know, this has not been done. State how you will deal with the situation. *R.S.A. SD.2*

Answer

The secretary should take the following action:

1. Telephone the airport and ask the reception clerk to contact Mr X and give him the message that Mr Y will not be arriving at 1500 hrs. and that he should be asked to telephone his secretary immediately.

2. Telephone the railway station to make certain that there is a train arriving at 1800 hrs.

3. Refer to Mr X's diary to see whether he has any other appointments in the evening.

4. When Mr X telephones, mention the following matters:

(*a*) Mr Y has been obliged to change his plans and will arrive by train at 1800 hrs. Mention that the time of the train has been confirmed.

(*b*) Ask if it will be convenient for Mr X to meet Mr Y at the railway station at 1800 hrs.

(*c*) Inquire whether a hotel reservation has been made for Mr Y. If not, ask whether Mr X has a preference in this connexion, and whether he knows how long Mr Y will need accommodation.

(*d*) Check the dinner arrangements and, if necessary, confirm these with Mrs X.

(*e*) Mention any further engagements, as referred to in 3 above, which Mr X has for the evening, and ask whether he wishes any action to be taken on these.

5. Telephone the hotel to book accommodation for Mr Y (if required in (*c*) above) and write a letter of confirmation.

Question

Your company has seventy branches distributed over the southern counties of England, from Penzance in the west to Leatherhead in the east. Make a list of the points you would consider and arrangements you would make if asked to organize a dinner-dance to which branch managers, and Head Office staff, numbering twenty-five, together with their ladies, are to be invited. The company defrays all reasonable expenses and is liberal in its translation of "reasonable". *L.C.C. P.S.D.*

Answer

1. The employer should be consulted about the date and time of the function, form of dress, menu, wines, etc.

2. Bournemouth would seem to be the most central town, with a good choice of hotels and an efficient rail service. The secretary should visit the town and make the following arrangements:

(*a*) View several large hotels, taking particular note of whether they are licensed, possess ballrooms, have adequate car-park facilities and are able to accommodate most of the guests. If necessary, alternative sleeping arrangements could be found in other nearby hotels.

(*b*) Reserve an additional room for a reception and cocktails.

(*c*) Discuss with the manager of the selected hotel: terms, menu (including wines for dinner), orchestra, photographer, floral decorations, late-night buffet, etc.

3. On returning to Head Office the secretary should take the following action:

(*a*) Type a list for the employer of all the arrangements made in Bournemouth, and, after obtaining his approval, confirm the arrangements, in writing, with the Hotel Manager.

(*b*) Have one hundred and twenty invitation cards printed giving relevant details, viz. time, date, place, orchestra, form of dress, RSVP, etc.

(*c*) Invitations should be sent out three weeks beforehand, together with a circular letter requesting the return of a perforated slip, giving details of accommodation required, not later than one week before the dinner-dance.

4. Arrange for the menu card to be printed. Before this could be done, however, the employer would have to decide on the speeches and toasts he may wish included in the proceedings.

5. Prepare the table "place names" and send a complete guest list to the Hotel Manager so that he can arrange the necessary accommodation and seating for the dinner.

6. Warn the hotel manager that some of the guests may be arriving in the afternoon and will probably require afternoon tea.

Question

You receive a cable advising you that your employer, returning by sea from America, has been taken ill on board. What action do you take? *L.C.C. P.S.D.*

Answer

As an Atlantic crossing takes only a few days, everything possible for the welfare of the employer must be done by the time the ship docks; the private secretary should take the following lines of action:

1. Contact the employer's wife (or immediate family) and offer her services. After consultation, she should inform the employer's own doctor, who will attend him when he returns to his home. It is possible that the doctor may wish to be present when the ship docks and accompany his patient to hospital.

2. Telephone the Dock Authority to discover the time the ship docks and the number or name of the bay, and arrange, if possible, for priority in the employer's passage through customs.

3. Arrange for an ambulance to collect the employer from the ship and take him to the hospital nearest to the port, where a private ward should be booked. The employer's doctor should be consulted about these arrangements.

4. Inform the employer's deputy, consult him over business correspondence other than routine letters, and ask him to take on urgent matters and appointments.

5. Look through the employer's office diary, make a note of appointments which are not of an urgent nature and write letters postponing or cancelling them.

6. In consultation with the employer's wife, take the appropriate action over private engagements. This involves writing letters of apology for any invitations which have been accepted.

Question

You happen to hear that your employer is scheming to take certain action which will harm the company. Where does your loyalty lie—to your company or to your employer?

Answer

(*a*) When the secretary hears that her employer is contemplating action harmful to the company, she should talk to him and warn him of the rumour. (This is the secretary's loyalty to her employer.)

(*b*) If the employer admits dishonest behaviour and does nothing about putting right the wrong he is doing, the secretary should show her disapproval by resigning as his secretary.

(*c*) The secretary should then warn the appropriate officer of the company of what is being done without mentioning any names. (This is the secretary's loyalty to her company.)

THE PERSONAL ASPECT OF PRIVATE SECRETARIAL WORK

An important element of the private secretary's success and of her value to her employer lies in her skill in dealing with people, and in creating an impression which will enhance her employer's reputation. She must identify herself with the life and work of her employer and be intensely interested and ambitious in all that he does. Her responsibilities are enormous, for she is his personal organizer, generally deciding whom he sees and to whom he speaks, what matters receive his urgent personal attention, and what can be redirected to others. It is this opportunity of personal service which makes the private secretary's job so different from that of the ordinary shorthand typist, and indeed so much more rewarding.

QUESTIONS

1. Describe the action you would take if the firm's duplicator broke down at 1730 hrs, and an important job had to be duplicated ready for the morning?

2. You work for an architect who is an official of his professional association. He has been asked to represent his association at an international conference in Paris. He decided to combine the conference with a holiday in France and, therefore, is travelling in his own car.

The day before the conference, he telephones from a small French village to say that he has crashed his car and, although not seriously hurt, he is feeling very shaken and quite unable to continue his journey to Paris. He asks you to take whatever action you consider appropriate with regard to the conference. What action would you take in the circumstances? *R.S.A. SD.2*

3. Your employer is the conference secretary of a national organization which is to hold a conference at a seaside resort in the summer. List the points to which you

would give attention in making the arrangements for the conference. It should be noted that the delegates will be accompanied by their wives.

4. If there was a grammatical error in some work which your employer had dictated would you tell him you had altered it?

5. There has been a fire in your office during the night. The firemen have laid out for your inspection everything that they have salvaged. Your employer is very anxious that business should continue without a break.

(a) What would be the first things you would look for when examining the salvage?

(b) Describe the emergency steps you would take to deal with the essential work. In answering this question, assume and state the extent of the damage. *R.S.A. SD.2*

6. You are secretary to the works manager of a factory employing two hundred and fifty workers of both sexes. Your employer is considering organizing a summer outing. He asks you to assist him by making suitable recommendations and drawing up a list of points which will require consideration. *L.C.C. P.S.D.*

7. Three junior members of staff in your firm are consistently late in the mornings, extend their lunch hour beyond the permitted time and all rush away at night, leaving work unfinished. The Office Manager, to whom you are secretary has asked you to bring about some improvement, adding that unless this can be effected they will have to find other posts. Their work, in the main, is not good. How will you go about this? *L.C.C. P.S.C.*

8. You are in charge of a number of junior staff. Your immediate superior often criticizes individual juniors in full hearing of other employees. How would you try to overcome such unpleasant episodes? *R.S.A. SD.2*

9. Owing to an epidemic of influenza, a large number of clerical staff is absent from your office. Correspondence and copy typing are falling behind schedule. What suggestions would you make to your employer to ease the situation? *R.S.A. SD.2*

10. On 13th June your employer started two weeks' leave, intending to tour the north coast of Devon and Cornwall in his private car. No specific arrangements have been made for him to keep in touch with the office. On 16th June you receive a cable indicating the need for your employer to be in New York by 24th June for a meeting of extreme importance to your company. What action do you take? *L.C.C. P.S.D.*

11. You have been employed for the past five years as secretary to the managing director of a medium-sized company. Following the sudden decease of your employer a new managing director has been appointed from outside the organization. Discuss briefly what will be your attitude to the changed circumstances and in what ways you can be of particular assistance to your new employer. *L.C.C. P.S.D.*

12. For the last seven years you have been employed as secretary to the Managing Director of a large industrial company. Owing to increasing pressure of business in your department your employer has engaged a second (junior) secretary. After a short time it becomes apparent that she is in appearance smarter than you, in general

knowledge better informed and in secretarial practice more efficient. Explain in detail how you are going to cope with this situation. *L.C.C. P.S.D.*

13. You work for a personnel officer. While she is on holiday you are left to deal with emergencies, although you are, of course, able to ask the advice of executive members of the staff.

A telephone operator does not turn up for work for two days and neither telephones nor writes. Decide what you would do in these circumstances and write a memorandum describing your actions so that the personnel officer will be fully informed on her return. *R.S.A. SD.2*

14. Your employer and his wife are touring by car and you can contact them only every few days.

You go each day to their house to collect mail and to see that everything is all right.

One day you find a cable from their adult son to say that he is arriving from Kenya the next day and will be staying with them for a few days. He gives his flight number and time of arrival.

What would you do? *R.S.A. SD.2*

15. The firm for which you work owns a small house which it has converted into offices.

One evening, having agreed to work till 1830 hrs to finish some letters, you are the last to leave. You decide to go across the road to the letter-box to post the letters and to come back for your things. When you get back you find that the latch on the front door has dropped (there is no back door) and your handbag, keys, meat for dinner and the work which you had promised to deliver on the way home are inside.

What would you do? *R.S.A. SD.2*

16. Initiative is a quality in a secretary valued by employers. Suggest five examples showing the use of initiative in secretarial work. *R.S.A. SD.2*

Index